OVERCOMER

A Journey Back to the Biblical Basics of Thorough Victory Over Life's STRONGHOLDS

D. L. Springfield

Table of Contents

ACKNOWLEDGMENTS   III

INTRODUCTION   IV

CHAPTER 1: THE RISE AND FALL OF A STRONGHOLD: MY STORY   1

CHAPTER 2: ASSURANCE   15

CHAPTER 3: SANCTIFICATION   31
- One Way for Salvation; One Way for Sanctification!   40
- Getting To the Root of Our Problems   52
- No More Halfhearted Efforts   60

CHAPTER 4: "DENY YOURSELF"   65
- An Overview of the Self-Nature   70
- Denying Self Must Be Done Intentionally and Patiently   78

CHAPTER 5: "TAKE UP YOUR CROSS"   81
- The Things of the World   90
- The People of the World   96
- The Philosophies of the World   99
- How To Overcome the World — Wake Up!   105

CHAPTER 6: "FOLLOW ME" IN THE SPIRIT   112
- God's Model for the CHRISTian   115
- Faith and Love: The Two Pillars of Spiritual Fruitfulness and Power   125

CHAPTER 7: "FOLLOW ME" BY FAITH   135

- Biblical Faith is Single-Minded and Wholehearted ... 135
- Biblical Faith Must Be Grounded In and Established By the Word of God ... 139
- Biblical Faith is Authenticated by Trusting Surrender ... 154

CHAPTER 8: "FOLLOW ME" IN LOVE ... 168
- Faith Must Function Through Love ... 169
- How Walking in Love Enables Us to Overcome Sin ... 176
- What is the Evidence That We're "Walking in the Spirit" Through Love, and Not Simply Straining in the Flesh? ... 183
- Decisively Resolve to Follow Christ ... 185

CHAPTER 9: BRINGING IT ALL TOGETHER ... 188
- "That I May Know Him" — Pressing Forward ... 191
- Bringing It All Together Into Some Final Reminders and Insights ... 196

Acknowledgments

"Brethren, if a man is overtaken in any trespass, you who are spiritual restore such a one in a spirit of gentleness, considering yourself lest you also be tempted. ² Bear one another's burdens, and so fulfill the law of Christ" (Galatians 6: 1-2)

The South African preacher, evangelist, and man of God, Keith Daniels, captured the essence of this scripture in a sermon titled, *"When the Godly Fall."* In it, he described an accident that occurred at a Christian gathering. A young lady was walking across the floor of a large assembly room. Suddenly, she lost her footing and violently fell to the floor, smashing her face on the hard surface. In a moment of time, Keith Daniels surveyed all of the reactions in the room. Some looked on in indifference. Some were too stunned to act. Some whispered. Some laughed.

Keith ran to the young lady and helped her to her feet. Deep pain and embarrassment filled her face. He told her these words; *"I'm going to stand right here with you until you can tell me that you're ok."* According to Keith, no one else in that room had the privilege of seeing the gratitude in her eyes. He then spoke words that could very well fit among the proverbs of Solomon. *"You can tell who the spiritual saints are by what they do when someone falls."*

The Lord sent a number of these *"spiritual saints"* to bear me up when I suffered the severe spiritual trauma of a fall. I'd like to take a moment to acknowledge them.

My pastor, Ken Hampton, though a stern, no-nonsense preacher, proved to be one of the most gracious and compassionate men that I know. He held me up, encouraged me, and vigilantly sought to restore me according to the scriptures. He helped to bear my burden, and in doing so, fulfilled *"the law of Christ."* Craig Massey, my elder and friend, exemplified the model of the *"spiritual"* Christian. He walked close beside me through my *"dark night of the soul"*, and wisely and patiently helped me back on my feet. The late Elder Blanding and his gracious wife, Mother Blanding, were unparalleled examples of the lovingkindness of the Lord.

My spiritual brother and fellow servant, Jeremiah Christian, was a great help and encouragement to me. I had lost touch with him for several years, and he knew little about my situation. In 2012 I reached a point of deep discouragement, and was too despondent to write another word. A few days after I'd quit writing, Jeremiah was led of the Holy Spirit to call me. Without having any knowledge that I was writing a book *(for I told no one but my best friend, who'd never met Jeremiah)*, he asked me if I was writing a book. Then he told me that the Lord put it on his heart to do a cover for my book, if I was indeed writing one. This call revived my spirit to write, and I never looked back since.

My friend and missionary to *"broken people"*, Kris Cain, was a kindred spirit in the things of Christ, genuine friend, and fishing partner. My sister, Lisa, was a consistent comfort and encourager — a true sister through thick and thin. Finally, my best friend, Louis Lockett, proved to be an all-weather friend indeed. He was a close confidant for my transparent thoughts, a sounding board for my rants, and a silent ear for my expressions of deep grief. I am immensely grateful to the Lord for all the godly people He has put into my life.

There are many others that I could name who stood with me and played pivotal roles in restoring me, but space doesn't allow me to do so. However, before I finish my acknowledgments, allow me to add my late father, Minister Clarence Springfield. When the bottom fell out for me, he gave me a scripture — the only scripture that he ever spoke over me. It was the same scripture that his mother gave to him in a time when he was discouraged. This scripture has become precious to me — it is one of my life verses now.

"Fear not, for I am with you;
Be not dismayed, for I am your God.
I will strengthen you,
Yes, I will help you,
I will uphold you with My righteous right hand" (Isaiah 41: 10).

The Lord has made good on His promises.

Introduction

When it comes to epic fight scenes, The Matrix set a standard that many filmmakers soon followed. Some of us are familiar with how the lead character, Neo, trained and matured as a fighter. It wasn't long until he grew to be a match for one of the "Agents"; Agents were impossible to defeat in hand-to-hand combat. But in spite of Neo's advanced fighting skills and determination, he still was no match for the endless onslaughts from the enemy. But then it happened. In one of the final scenes he opened a door, and an Agent shot him multiple times at point-blank range. He died.

As the Agents walked away, assured that Neo was dead, something happened. Life returned to Neo's body and he rose up. The Agents turned in disbelief and opened fire with their guns. Then Neo did something that no one expected; he looked toward his assailants, raised his hand, and calmly said "No." The bullets stopped in thin air. Neo picked one of the bullets out of the air and looked at it. He then looked forward and all the other bullets fell to the ground. The lead Agent tried to attack him, but Neo, without even looking, effortlessly blocked every blow. After he made quick work of the lead Agent, the other two Agents ran for their lives. The battle was over. No longer was Neo a fighter; he was an **Overcomer**.

After many years of fighting with my fierce enemy—pornographic bondage—I finally reached a defining point of transformation like Neo did. I'd been on a roller coaster of victory and defeat, desperately trying every "remedy" available, until one day I was delivered…and I knew it. I remember sitting at my desk and being struck with a realization that I'd never grasped before. I thought within myself, "It all makes sense now. I finally understand." Immediately, I determined that I no longer needed to pay for my internet filter. I called and cancelled it. I didn't even wait to make sure that I was delivered before cancelling it; I simply knew. Like Neo, I was done fighting. The battle was over. From then on whenever the Enemy fired his bullets of temptation at me, I calmly said "no", and his allurements fell limp to the ground.

How did I reach this point of effortless victory? For many years I'd heard the testimonies of people who had been miraculously delivered from different forms of bondage. But I also knew many more who had not been delivered. It didn't make sense to me. Why would God deliver some but not others? But now, for the first time, I myself experienced what this amazing

~ VII ~

deliverance felt like. But my story is not like most of the testimonies that I've heard before. Most people will testify that they *"can't explain it; the Lord just took the desire away!"* Although they knew that they were delivered, they didn't know how to explain *from the Bible* how someone else could be delivered. This frustrated me!

I tried virtually every one of man's solutions to overcome my struggle, and they were all useless. The church proved to be an empty well; it was completely ill-equipped to *biblically* explain how to overcome a stronghold. All the church offered were religious clichés, empty unbiblical advice, and pre-packaged, over misused scriptures. After many years of warring with cheap weapons, I finally determined to get back to the basics of the Bible. I spent years in ceaseless prayer and earnest study of the scripture to find the answers. When all the pieces came together, everything made sense, and I simply knew the battle was over — and it was.

This book is devoted to explaining to you, in the simplest manner possible, how to overcome any sinful stronghold — not just porn — *any sinful stronghold* in your life according to the Word of God. After you've learned and applied what the scripture says, your stronghold will be no match for you. But I forewarn you, following the Truth of scripture will cost you. Like Neo, there will be sacrifice. Some of you will turn away discouraged, like the "rich young ruler" of Matthew 19, when you learn the cost of victory.

You may still think there's an easy, Christianized, quick-fix solution out there. Like many dieters, most struggling Christians are searching for the next *"8 minute Abs"* answer to their issue. There's not — I've been there and done that, and man's psycho-religious solutions are insufficient. Nor have I heard a single, solitary testimony from anyone else who's tried man's methods, where the person has experienced the Spirit-filled liberation that scripture promises. To be frank, it is impossible for man's methods to give the freedom that Christ gives.

Decisive, sustained, thorough deliverance only comes through what God teaches in His Word. Sin, at its core, is not a psychological problem, a behavioral issue, or a chemical imbalance; it is a catastrophic disaster that has so ruined the human race that God Himself had to die in order to destroy it! Therefore, only God can completely free a human being from the accursed bondage of sin in their life. Do you believe that?

"Then Jesus said to those Jews **who believed Him***, "If you abide in My word, you are My disciples indeed.* [32] **And you shall know the truth, and the truth shall**

*make you free.*³³ They answered Him, "We are Abraham's descendants, and have never been in bondage to anyone. How can You say, 'You will be made free'?"³⁴ Jesus answered them, "Most assuredly, I say to you, **whoever commits sin is a slave of sin**. ³⁵ And a slave does not abide in the house forever, but a son abides forever. ³⁶ **Therefore if the Son makes you free, you shall be free indeed."**

Not partially free. Not free from some sins yet still in bondage to others. Not the roller coaster of victory and defeat. Not freedom sustained by your willpower and strict self-discipline. Not freedom where the person has mastered their sin, but *"it's still a daily struggle."* Not freedom where an accountability partner is the basis of your motivation to abstain from the sin. Man's solutions may offer you a sense of partial victory through behavior modification and religious programs, but none of them offer complete liberation of heart, mind, soul, and body. The Lord makes us *"free indeed"* from bondage to all sin! *"The Battle is the Lord's!"* When you learn how to submit yourself to the power of His Spirit, you'll experience an amazing freedom that you never thought possible.

Let me take you down this road to biblical victory; and if you follow closely, you will discover the greatest joy, peace, fruitfulness, and spiritual vibrancy a human being can experience. But before we go down that road, I want you to learn a little more about my story.

*"It is only when God has altered our disposition and we have entered into the experience of sanctification that the fight begins. **The warfare is not against sin; we can never fight against sin**: Jesus Christ deals with sin in Redemption. **The conflict is along the line of turning our natural life into a spiritual life**, and this is never done easily, nor does God intend it to be done easily."*

—Oswald Chambers

CHAPTER 1

THE RISE AND FALL OF A STRONGHOLD: MY STORY

What Is A Stronghold?

According to Merriam-Webster, a stronghold is "a fortified place"; "a place of security or survival" — a fortress. It is a military structure designed for defense and combat. Its walls are typically broad and tall. Heavily-armed combatants fiercely defend it against invading forces. At stake is a valuable stretch of land, a strategic post, a city, a kingdom. A stronghold is not only a crucial mainstay for the survival of its inhabitants, but it's also a formidable obstacle for the progress of its invaders.

All Christians have strongholds built into their lives. These bulwarks typically are constructed by the old sinful nature before a person becomes a Christian. Its bricks were formed by ungodly decisions unwittingly laid day by day. Its mortar is the consistency of these decisions over the course of time — the longer a person entertained a sin, the more that sin "settled" like concrete in their lives. When a stronghold is built, it is fiercely defended by three mighty forces: the allurements and ideologies of the *world*, the urges and rationale of the *flesh*, and the deceptions and temptations of the *Devil*. The following scripture gives us a glimpse into how these three evil influences work together.

"*And you He made alive, who were dead in trespasses and sins, ² in which you once walked* **according to the course of this <u>world</u>**, *according to* **the <u>prince of the power of the air</u>** [Satan], *the spirit who now works in the sons of disobedience,* ³ *among whom also we all once conducted ourselves in* **the lusts of our <u>flesh</u>**, *fulfilling the* *desires of the flesh and of the mind, and were by nature children of wrath, just as the others"* (Ephesians 2: 1-3).

Our struggle is not against the world, *or* the Devil, *or* the flesh—it's against all of them. **Satan** continuously dangles the deceptions and allurements of this *world* in front of us, and we are aroused or enticed within our own *flesh* to take the bait. These three enemies, together, are the greatest obstacles that stand between the Christian and a life of spiritual vibrancy, fruitfulness, and unmitigated freedom.

When a person becomes a Christian, they obtain a new, spiritual nature in Christ through work of the Holy Spirit. This new nature immediately finds itself in heated combat with the stronghold and its defenders—the flesh, the world, and Satan. Strongholds can come in many forms: covetousness, idolatry, lying, anger, pride, fear, unforgiveness, gossip, gluttony, carnality, laziness, bitterness, etc. But some strongholds are more infamous and *visibly* destructive than others: alcoholism, drugs, gambling, theft (kleptomaniac), homosexuality, and other various sexual sins.

Many of these sins may not feel like, or fit the concept of a stronghold. However, it's typically when we attempt to overcome a sin that we realize how deeply entrenched it is in our flesh. Multitudes of Christians find the struggle too difficult and give up the fight, settling for a spiritually fruitless, defeated Christian life. Many others fail to take their sin seriously, choosing rather to redefine it as a harmless, minor indiscretion, character flaw, or shortcoming. But there are many Christians who take their sin deathly seriously, and they're not ready to give up the fight. The quickened spirit within them is desperate for victory, and it will not rest until it obtains it. Any soul who has resolutely settled within its heart that it will not rest until decisive victory is obtained will find all the powers of God Almighty dispatched on its behalf.

I learned of this overcoming power after a long, arduous battle with my personal stronghold: pornography and lust. This is the muffled struggle of untold millions of *Christian* men—and even Christian women. I sparingly use the term "addiction", and choose rather to use terms like "stronghold" or "bondage". Addiction implies that a person is simply sick and needs treatment or a program. I'm not talking about sickness; I'm talking about sin. The Bible clearly teaches that bondage to sin is a very real calamity within the human race.

The statistics concerning sexual bondage are heart wrenching, but what's more deplorable is the fact that the church largely ignores this very common issue. Because church leadership tiptoes around this issue, most people within the church are ignorant of how pervasive an issue this really is. Most statistical studies show approximately 60% of *Christian* men struggle with pornographic bondage. Approximately 20% of *Christian* women struggle with this same issue. And worst of all, a staggering percentage of pastors struggle with pornographic bondage in varying degrees!

"Fifty-one percent of pastors say pornography is a possible temptation. Nearly 20% of the calls received on Focus on the Family's Pastoral Care Line are for help with issues such as pornography and compulsive sexual behavior. And of the 1,351 pastors that Rick Warren's website, Pastors.com, surveyed on porn use, 54% said they had viewed internet pornography within the last year and 30% of those had visited within the last 30 days.

Patrick Means, author of, <u>Men's Secret Wars</u>, reveals that 63% of pastors surveyed confirm that they are struggling with sexual addiction or sexual compulsion including, but not limited to, the use of pornography, compulsive masturbation, or other secret sexual activity"[1]

I became one of these statistics. However, although my personal issue was sexual sin, *whatever your sin may be, God's solution is the same.* **It's important for me to stress that this book is not written merely for those who struggle with sexual bondage, but for Christians who struggle with any form of bondage.** Man creates para-church ministries and programs that nitpick individual issues; God's biblical way to victory makes a clean sweep of every issue. In spite of how deeply entrenched and multifaceted your issue may be, God can and will decisively deliver you. I invite you to completely change your paradigm on how to overcome sin; sin is not the issue, it's a symptom. Christ liberates us by getting at the core issue, and when the core issue is addressed, all of the symptoms lose their power over you.

Pulled From a Pit, yet Snagged By a Thorn

The bricks of my stronghold were laid when I was a young teenager. I think it's appropriate that I spare you the details of all the events surrounding my struggle for two reasons. For one, when person is already struggling with a habitual issue, often when they hear someone else giving TMI (too much information) about their own issue, it often serves to rouse the temptation of the person who's already struggling—it rarely helps. Some of the alluringly debauched ideas that wedged themselves within *my mind* came from hearing the TMI of others—others who ironically were attempting to help! It's irresponsible for a former alcoholic to spell out the dirty details of their addiction with a struggling alcoholic; a former gambler with a struggling gambler; a former drug addict with a struggling drug addict, etc. I will not impose such information on some struggling soldier of Christ who is desperately seeking help within these pages.

Secondly, there have already been a thousand such stories where the writer felt the need to air the details of his dirty laundry. There is no need for me to add to the putrid stench. This book is about overcoming sin, not glamorizing it!

However, I will give a general idea of the extent and depth of my stronghold so that the reader can realize that I do indeed understand your struggle. During my teenage years I committed this sin just as carelessly as any other lost sinner commits any sin. But around the age of 20, I was led to saving faith in the Lord Jesus Christ. My life took an immediate U-turn. The Lord began to steer me away from my ungodly thinking and ways. An insatiable hunger and thirst for Christ and His Word awoke within me, and I began diligently seeking the Lord. Unfortunately, it wasn't long after my conversion that I learned that one particular sin was like a thorn barbed in my flesh--porn. What followed was a fierce battle that would leave in its wake many casualties.

Like many Christians who struggle with a form of bondage, the battle was a roller coaster. I was a new creature in Christ to be sure; unfortunately, being a new creature does not automatically propel someone into sinless perfection. Every Christian experiences a struggle with one sin or another, and I was no exception to the rule. I went back and forth between blissful periods of victory, interrupted by grievous setbacks of defeat. But, in spite of my many triumphant periods, I wasn't progressing—my setbacks were getting worse! Once my sinful flesh became bored with one variant of this sin, it yearned for deeper means of fulfillment. And no matter what I tried, I had no power within me to *decisively* overcome this snowballing stronghold.

For several years I desperately tried every solution that I could find under the sun. I read books, memorized scriptures, saw counselors, attended seminars, saw a psychologist (albeit, after one visit I'd heard enough), got accountability partners, confided in mature Christians, pastors, and elders, tried to *"give it to the Lord"*, dabbled with "Celebrate Recovery", asked the Lord to "take it away from me," fasted, pleaded with God, tried the "Bondage Breaker", positive thinking, reckoned myself dead to sin, tried to hide the word in my heart, will-power, claimed victory, repented with deep resolution and determination, filled my time with positive activities, internet filters, and I'm sure I've missed a few others not listed here. I tried them all, and nothing worked!

On one occasion I attended a men's conference. A friend of mine was the keynote speaker. He was also a pastor of a Brethren Church in Detroit, Michigan. In his message, he graphically explained his years of struggling with porn. He gave the invitation to an auditorium filled with hundreds of men to come down and seek help—I was the only man who was honest enough to stand up. Afterward, the brother who sat with me, an elder in the church, whispered that he should have got up as well.

Although multitudes are too deeply ashamed to open up about this sin, I've always been very honest and forthcoming—I've consulted many Christian men over the years. I desperately longed victory, and the deep grief of struggling with this sin was far worse than the deep shame of coming clean with it. Unfortunately, no one had a clear, biblical explanation for how to obtain victory.

Few things grieved my heart more than reading the hundreds of emails I received from fellow struggling Christians through the ministry of *"Every Man's Battle."* The heart-wrenching grief and hopeless despair that these men expressed was painful and discouraging to read. I recall listening to a popular Christian psychologist on the radio. He said that many Christian men will struggle with this sin for the rest of their lives. He spoke in a defeatist tone, giving no concrete, resolute answers of hope and certainty to the listener. It was a glaring testament to the impotency of the Christianized psychology that he practiced.

I began to lose hope. Even those who claimed to have gained victory were not set free. *Every one of them* that I heard or read (without exception) would say something like, *"I'm winning the battle, but it's still a daily struggle."*

Even the leaders of these porn-addiction ministries still had to keep close tabs with their accountability partner in order to keep from sinning. This isn't victory! This isn't freedom! This is not the Power of Christ; it's the impotency of man!

Many times I wished that my struggle was with alcohol, drugs, or some other *well-known* addiction — anything but sexual sin. Then I could've had one of those riveting testimonies of deliverance, and everyone would sympathetically understand that my struggle was indeed real, and I wasn't just some perverted, dishonest scoundrel. Unfortunately, it's typically only those in the world of psychology and church leadership who recognize that sexual addiction is just as severe as, if not more severe, than any other "addiction" *(Side note: Man is often capable of diagnosing sin, but he is utterly incapable of overcoming sin. The law could identify sin, but it could not conquer sin. On the contrary, it aroused sin!).*

An article written on Psychcentral.com stated the following: *"It is well known among people in the 12-step programs that of all the addictions, sex is the most difficult to master. Far from the notion that sex addiction is the 'fun' one, the suffering of people dealing with this affliction is enormous."*[2] I can speak from experience of the enormity of the suffering — not of the consequences — but of the sin.

*"I find **more bitter than death** the woman whose heart is **snares and nets, whose hands are fetters** (shackles). He who pleases God shall escape from her, but the sinner shall be trapped by her"* (Ecclesiastes 7: 26).

"More bitter than death!" No other form of bondage is even remotely described like this within the scripture. These words could not have been spoken more truly. And no one would have known the reality of these words more than Solomon, the man who penned them. God knows how many times I preferred (and even prayed for) death instead of another fall. I was *"trapped by her"*, and I didn't know how to escape — not yet.

Advancing In the Faith, yet Losing In the Fight

In spite of my battle with this sin, I was still growing in Christ and advancing in the church. I began getting more responsibilities and ministries. Unfortunately, I was still on the roller coaster of victory and defeat. **I voluntarily** removed myself from active ministry on a number of occasions in order to focus on my struggle and overcome it. I refused to allow myself to return to active ministry until I was certain that I had this issue beat. Each time when I attempted to gain victory through one of the above "solutions", it gave me a temporary yet certain *sense* of victory. Then I would consider the forgiveness and grace that God showed to David and Peter, allowing them to get back up from their falls and return to their office and active ministry. When I felt that I was ok, I would do the same.

Unfortunately, during these periods of "victory" I was merely holding my breath, hoping the temptation would not flare up again. I did not understand *how* I was overcoming; I just knew that I was. I was like an unskilled boxer who haphazardly knocks down a superior opponent, but has no idea how to do it again when his rival gets back up. That's the problem with man's remedies; they do not *biblically* explain the how and the why of overcoming a stronghold, nor do they have any power to sustain one's victory. Inevitably, my stronghold would rise back up, the fight would resume, and I'd step down from ministry yet again.

In the end, my sin got the best of me. Simply looking at visual images was not enough to satiate the overwhelming temptation. Regrettably, I fell into the sin of adultery.

I finally reached the point where I could take it no longer. Something was broken in my life, but I didn't know what, and I couldn't minister in a clear conscience any more. Though I had won many battles and had wonderful periods of sustained victory, I was losing the war. I got my ministerial license and wrote "VOID" across it in large letters with permanent red marker. I brought it to my pastor's house with all of my church keys, confessed the particulars of my sin, and removed myself from ministry altogether. I had no intention of returning (albeit, for a very brief stint I did reluctantly return while things were sorted out).

What followed was a very dark and searching period of my life. I laid aside every form of ministry, and sought the Lord like never before. It had become very clear to me that man's solutions to sin were utterly useless—I would not turn to them again. Instead, I made a decisive conclusion to only seek victory in the word of God.

This was an intense purging process. I had to unlearn a host of religious ideologies, frames of thought, and popular "Christian" concepts. The truth of God's Word crushed every unbiblical idea that I ever had about overcoming sin. But, the Lord didn't merely teach me how to overcome *sin*; He taught me how to overcome *me*. God's Word completely renovated and restructured me as Christian—and it still is. The Lord brought me into the refining fires of His furnace, nourished me with truth, upheld my in His grace, stayed me by His love, and empowered me by His Spirit.

Carried Away Into Captivity

From the onset of my ordeal I viewed my miserable failures and losses as being similar to Israel's punishment and captivity due to their sin. Because of Israel's sin, God allowed wicked nations to come and defeat His people on multiple occasions. This occurred several times during the period of the judges as well as during the time of the kings. Ultimately, the temple was destroyed and they were taken captive, away from their homeland. Families were torn apart, multitudes were slain, and they were forced to languish in captivity to godless kingdoms. These dark times were periods of deep refining, followed by repentance, revival, and restoration.

My period of "captivity" was undeniably the darkest, most unspeakably grievous period of my life. I spent over two years away from my home church, tormented by a relentless grief that pursued my life like a hunter following the blood trail of a fatally wounded deer. Nevertheless, the Lord surrounded me with many godly saints who encouraged me and stood with me. They were bright lights within the opaque darkness of my ordeal.

However, in spite of the priceless support given by these saints, it still wasn't enough. No one fully understood the multifaceted, complicated variables of my situation, and no one had the deep, perplexing answers that I sought— though I did have a few of Job's friends who thought they did. The black, emotional abyss into which I'd fallen was too deep for anyone to reach me. Sometimes, God brings you to a place where only He can truly help you. The Lord brought me to the place of impossibilities that He might show me that *"with God all things are possible."*

The Lord became my everything! He became the very breath of my lungs, the smile on my face, the hope in my heart, my will to put one foot in front of the other, the joy in my soul, and the peace of my mind. I sought the Lord with all my being in His Word and in prayer. I had heard virtually everything that man had to offer; I'd heard it for years…and I'd heard enough! It was like a broken record of the same overused and misapplied scriptures. I knew 1 John 1: 9, I'd heard 1 Corinthians 10: 13, and I was well acquainted with 1 Corinthians 6: 18-20, along with all the other *usual scriptures*. I needed more! I needed answers! And the Church didn't have them. I needed to hear from God himself.

Many things in my situation made no sense to me. Christ had been my everything! I longed for Him, His Word, and His will more than anything else in this world. My highest desire was to have a healthy, Christ-centered home. I relentlessly tried to overcome sin and be a fruitful servant of Christ. I'd been an astute student of the Word — I had a lot of it "hid in my heart". The Lord was my everything, and I earnestly tried to seek and live for Him, but I failed…bitterly! And no one, (that I knew of), had the answers! Why couldn't I fully overcome my stronghold? I knew God's Word hadn't failed; I was missing something, but I didn't know what. I only knew that God had the answers, and I was desperate to find them — and I did.

Lessons in the Valley

After Judah's wretched failures and subsequent captivity in Babylon, God gave them a promise. "*11For I know the thoughts that I think toward you, says the* LORD, *thoughts of peace and not of evil, to give you a future and a hope. 12 Then you will call upon Me and go and pray to Me, and I will listen to you. 13 And you will seek Me and find Me,* **when you search for Me with all your heart.** **14 I will be found by you, says the** LORD, **and I will bring you back from your captivity**" (Jeremiah 29: 11-14).

Verse 11 is a favorite memory verse of many Christians, but few Christians know the context or the circumstances of this verse. Few Christians connect this promise to a people who had sinned miserably and suffered severe consequences as a result. Fewer still realize that this promise has a condition attached to it. The promise of verse 11 is conditioned upon seeking the Lord with *"all your heart"*. And even though this promise is specifically to Judah, it was written for our learning. It shows the immeasurable grace and compassion that God has for His people, even in their worst state.

As a matter of fact, God gave this promise to His people long before they had fallen. King Solomon made this request to the Lord when he dedicated the temple.

"When they sin against You (for there is no one who does not sin), and You become angry with them and deliver them to the enemy, and they take them captive to the land of the enemy, far or near; [47] *yet when they come to themselves in the land where they were carried captive, and repent, and make supplication to You in the land of those who took them captive, saying, 'We have sinned and done wrong, we have committed wickedness';* [48] *and when they return to You with* **all their heart and with all their soul in** *the land of their enemies who led them away captive, and pray to You ...then hear in heaven Your dwelling place their prayer and their supplication, and maintain their cause,* [50] *and forgive Your people who have sinned against You, and all their transgressions which they have transgressed against You..."* (1 Kings 8: 46-50).

I determined to seek the Lord *with all my heart,* not knowing that I was following the instructions of this scripture. I was no longer academically studying scripture to learn doctrine, put it into practice, and regurgitate it for others. My study became a lot more personal. I immersed myself in the scripture in order to get to know my God more intimately; to learn His heart, His mind, and His ways, along with His truths. I sought to learn all that He said about sin, bondage, chastening, forgiveness, victory, restoration, and everything else related to my situation. King David said, *"if I make my bed in hell, behold, thou art there."* My failures brought me down to what seemed to be the very bottom of hell...and I found David's words to be true. God met me where no one else could, and blessed me beyond a measure that I could ever imagine.

Like Jacob wrestling with the Angel, I wrestled with God throughout the dark night of my experience until I began to see the light of day. I told Him, *"I will not let you go until you bless me!"* He knocked my hip out of joint and changed my name. I walked away with a different stride and a new identity.

I was in a deep valley surrounded by insurmountable mountains. I must have surveyed these mountains hundreds of times to find a way out, but there was no way of escape. However, the Lord was in the valley with me. He nursed me back to health with marvelous truths that drew me closer to Him and answered virtually all of my perplexing questions. His truths were like keys methodically unlocking the myriad shackles that had bound me up in merciless, unresolved grief, stress, fear, doubt, and bondage. One by one, I surmounted the mountains with a strength outside of myself. But I was not getting stronger in the valley; I was getting weaker in the valley—I was dying. And every time a part of me died, a new spiritual strength came to life within me.

Andrew Murray captured this truth in his book "Absolute Surrender":

A man must learn to say: "I give up everything. I have tried and longed and thought and prayed, but failure has come. God has blessed me and helped me, but still, in the long run, there has been so much sin and sadness." What a change comes when a man is thus broken down into utter helplessness and self-despair and says, "I can do nothing!"…"in the beginning of the faith-life, faith is struggling. But as long as faith is struggling, faith has not attained its strength. But when faith in its struggling gets to the end of itself, and throws itself upon God and rests on Him, then joy and victory come."[3]

The founder of the Christian and Missionary Alliance, A. B. Simpson, expressed it the following way:

"God often has to bring us not only into the place of suffering, and the bed of sickness and pain, but also into the place where our righteousness breaks down and our character falls to pieces in order to humble us in the dust and show us the need of entire crucifixion to all our natural life. Then, at the feet of Jesus we are ready to receive Him, to abide in Him, depend on Him alone and draw all our life and strength each moment from Him, our Living Head.

It was thus that Peter was saved by His very fall and had to die to Peter that he might live more perfectly to Christ. Have we thus died, and have we thus renounced the strength of our own self-confidence?"[4]

Unfortunately, I had to experience years of this futile struggle before I reached the end of myself and found this victory. But when the Lord made me free, I knew it immediately. I still remember sitting in my office studying when it came to me. It was as if I'd found the final part of a ten thousand-piece puzzle. I realized the simplicity of victory. I could finally say, along with all of those other riveting testimonials, *"The Lord just took the desire away!"*

I remember thinking to myself, "I don't need this internet filter anymore. I can save some money!" I cancelled it that very hour. I didn't even wait a few months to see if my deliverance was real—I simply knew. I was no longer blindly holding my breath, anxiously waiting to see if the temptation would rise up again with vengeance. I finally understood the how, the why, and the what of total liberation. I was free and I understood how I was made free!

Exhuming Truth from the Tombs of Modern Thought

Perhaps this was God's providential plan all along. Many of us have heard the testimonies of those who'd struggled with addictions for many years, and at the moment of salvation had them taken away. But, of all the stories *that I've heard*, none of them were able to open the Word of God and *accurately* explain how someone else can obtain that same freedom. The Lord took me down the long road to this freedom, and I earnestly sought Him for, not only the victory, but complete understanding — and He gave it to me.

After about two years of *only* seeking the Lord through His Word, I reached a solid point of strength and understanding. I kept notes and a journal of everything the Lord had taught me while in the valley. It was then that I set my heart to read some of the writings of God's servants who've proven themselves to be men of God indeed. Andrew Murray's book, *"Absolute Surrender"*, had sat on my shelf for years; it was the first book I read after I'd overcome.

What I read stunned me. Every page captivated me. He described my entire Christian journey: my conversion, my progression, my struggle, my death, and my overcoming, victorious restoration. He described many of the things that I had learned at the feet of the Lord in the valley — truths that many in the modern church have long forgotten. I highly recommend that you get a copy of Murray's book if you desire further instruction on how to enter the Spirit-filled, overcoming life.

After this book, I began to read and listen to many of the other great servants of the Lord from yesteryear. I've always been very cautious about checking my biblical conclusions with Bible teachers who I respect. I found that the understanding of how God delivers us from the bondage of sin was well known, experienced by, and regularly taught by many saints through the years. Unfortunately, much of this spiritual wisdom has been lost in the convoluted smorgasbord of biblically-distorted, psychology-based, modern, man-made solutions.

The modern church has largely looked to the world for solutions to sin—problems that God alone can address. Sin is not a habitual behavior problem, an addiction, or a chemical imbalance. It cannot be managed through systematic step programs. It cannot be fought off through carefully selected memory verses. It cannot be rooted out by an accountability partner. Sin is a spiritual catastrophe that condemned a third of the angels to hell, ruined the whole human race, and cast the entire creation into disorder! Sin is a spiritual issue that only God Himself can deal with, and He confronted this great evil with His own blood on the cross. Christ not only completely delivers us from the condemnation of sin, but He completely frees us from the control of sin. Any other solution is a brash mockery, a diabolical diversion, and a man-made fraud!

Let's Get Back To the Basics of God's Word

The Lord has filled me with an overwhelming passion to minister to others the same truths and insights that delivered me out of an impossible stronghold. No doubt, there are scores of people who are facing various, spiritually debilitating strongholds. Unfortunately, many of these poor souls are trapped in the frustrating guessing game of where to turn for answers. Various man-made solutions have used the Bible like a Trojan Horse to infiltrate the church. Many honest, well intentioned Christians are running to these "solutions" only to find, at most, an illusion of victory, but typically, no victory at all.

I do not have all the answers, nor do I claim sinless perfection. Nevertheless, the Lord has afforded me decisive victory over a stronghold that once seemed impossible to overcome. His truths concerning how to obtain victory are clearly laid out for everyone who *honestly* seeks them *to obey them*. *God will not instruct those who are not willing to obey His instruction.* The Lord led me back to the sheer basics of scripture—pure waters that have long been soiled by the refuse of man's wisdom. It is to the thirsting heart that I hope to offer undiluted truth. God help me.

Spirit-filled victory is only given to those who long for it, and seek the Lord with all their heart to obtain it. It's not given to those who merely feel bad about their sin, but are not willing to offer themselves up to God so that He may empower them. Time is out for games. No more fad solutions. No more programs. No more Christian psychology. God longs to make us free more than we long to be made free! He's clearly laid out this pathway to Spirit filled victory within His word; it's for us to earnestly seek it and surrender to it. The challenge is indeed stern, but it's the sternness of a loving Father who knows better than His wayward children and wants the best for them.

God is the God of victory and restoration; He is ever seeking to bind up, strengthen, and recover *all* of His sheep. Christ doesn't abandon a single, solitary sheep—in spite of how often they've strayed…70 times 7! God knows how to heal every wound and mend every bone that has been broken. Furthermore, God knows how to make us *"free indeed"* from sin. We've forgotten that Christ is the *"savior of sinners"* through and through, and He doesn't need the unbiblical, demonstrably inadequate "solutions" of man to do so. The Lord has made me *"more than a conqueror"* (Romans 8: 37), and I know beyond a shadow of a doubt that He will do the same for you.

By God's grace and the guidance of the Holy Spirit, I trust the insights and instructions in this book will provide any struggling soldier with a wealth of truth that will enable him or her to overcome any number of spiritual strongholds. I'm not talking about eking out a marginal victory that is a struggle to maintain. I'm talking about learning from experience that *"The battle is the Lord's!"* —we need only surrender to and rest in Him, and watch Him fight on our behalf. My story is a testimony to the amazing grace and everlasting mercies of God, and if you follow closely, yours can be as well.

In the following chapter we'll lay a firm foundation for you to stand on. Do not gloss over it; read it carefully. It's imperative that your faith be firmly settled before we move on into the battle. The lack of assurance is the Achilles tendon of struggling soldiers. More than anything else, *"the Accuser of the brethren"* seeks to cut this tendon and destroy our faith. Let's get your spiritual footing stabilized before we move on to the path of victory.

CHAPTER 2

ASSURANCE

Confirming and Building Our Assurance

One of the greatest distresses of the struggling Christian is in the area of their assurance. Sin bludgeons the assurance of a saint; especially if the sin is of the viler sort and habitual in nature. The Apostle Peter urges us to keep away from fleshly lust because they *"war against the soul"* (1Peter 2: 11). Every time we sin, it damages several aspects of our inner person: our joy, our peace, our hope, our faith, our love, our strength, and our zeal, among other things. Put together, when these elements of our soul are imperiled, it wreaks havoc on our assurance.

When we are not assured of our complete acceptance in Christ, it cripples our spiritual progress. Therefore, it is critical to build the assurance of the struggling Christian *first* in order to bolster their strength for the battle. The *"hope of salvation"* is your song, and the *"joy of the Lord is your strength"* — you will need both of these if you expect to overcome. Doubt, discouragement, and depression create a fertile environment for strongholds to flourish in. The goal of this chapter, beloved Christian, is to encourage and build you up with *truth*. You've likely been beaten up long enough — directly and indirectly — by yourself and others. Now it's time for building and healing.

However, it would be naïve to assume that every professed Christian who's struggling with an issue has actually been born again. God forbid that I should offer the truths of assurance to a person who has never actually been saved. It could be that they're struggling because their faith was poorly founded to begin with. Fortunately, the truths that assure a struggling Christian will also give the accurate knowledge of salvation to the struggling *professed* Christian.

Let's Make Sure Our Foundation Is Firm

The problem with many is that they've placed their faith in Christ, but they haven't mustered up the gumption to fully rest in Him. The certainty of their assurance is often undercut by a "but" — "I know that I'm saved, but..." This nagging "but" may be present in a person's mind for several reasons. As previously mentioned, a struggle with sin is one of the most common reasons for uncertainty. However, another reason for the "but" is ignorance of many of the foundational truths concerning salvation.

Our salvation is wholly and solely grounded in the ***person*** and ***work*** of Christ. Jesus is the Christ; God in the flesh; the Son of the Living God — ***this is the person of Christ.*** He came into this world fashioned as a man for one chief purpose: *"This is a faithful saying, and worthy of all acceptance, that Christ Jesus came into the world to save sinners"* (1Timothy 1: 15). He accomplished this mighty work of salvation by allowing Himself to become the substitute for all sinners. He gave Himself to be offered up as a sacrifice for the sins of the world. When condemnation and death was our just due, He was slain in our place on the cross. He was buried in a borrowed grave for three days, and on the third day He rose from the dead with the life-creating, resurrection power of God Almighty — ***this is the work of Christ.***

Having completely paid the penalty for our sin through His *"work"*, He offers full salvation — forgiveness of all sin and eternal life — to all who believe on Him out of a genuine, repentant, committed heart. The individual who has such faith has been born again. When a person is born again they receive a new heart — the spirit within them is no longer dead to God. It has been made alive in Christ, for Christ Himself, the Lord of Life, dwells within them now.

Dear reader, do you have this kind of faith in the Person and work of Christ? I'm not asking you whether you've made a profession of faith some time in the past. Millions are hanging on to a past profession, yet little to nothing has changed in their present thoughts and actions before God. Do you *presently* have a living, conscious, committed faith in the Lord Jesus Christ? Not a faith that only comes to mind on Sunday morning or when someone starts talking about religion. Do you have a conscious faith that stirs a hunger and thirst within you to seek and know the Lord? If so, be encouraged; this is one of the chief evidences that you have a new, born again nature within you. If not, examine what I've written about the person and work of Christ, and salvation. Then take a moment in prayer to affirm your faith before the Lord.

If I'm A "New Creature in Christ", Why Do I Still Sin?

A person may ask, "If a Christian is a born-again, new creature in Christ, why do they still sin?" That's a good question. Only the spirit within a Christian has been born-again, not their whole being. *"That which is born of the flesh is flesh [our biological birth], and that which is born of the Spirit is spirit [our new birth]. ⁷Do not marvel that I said to you, 'You must be born again."* (John 3: 6-7). Unfortunately, we still live in the fleshly body that is dead to God and bound to sin. *"If Christ is in you, **the body is dead because of sin**, but the Spirit is life because of righteousness"* (Romans 8: 10). It'll be at the return of Christ that we'll be resurrected and transformed — body, soul, and spirit — into new, sinless, glorified beings. But until then, we are bound within these sinful bodies, and as long as we are in this fallen flesh, we'll have to contend with sin.

The origin of sin *within a Christian* is described in the New Testament as coming from the *flesh*. Paul called it *"law of sin which is **in** my members"* (Romans 7: 23). The flesh is made up of the yet unconverted psychological and physiological aspects of a Christian — the *natural mind* and the *physical body*. Paul calls it the *"flesh"*, the *"carnal mind"*, our *"mortal body"*, our *"members"*, and this *"body of death"* (Romans 6-8). Since these have not been born again, the scripture teaches that the psychological, natural mind must be renewed and the sinful deeds of the physical body must be crucified (Romans 8: 12-13 & Romans 12: 1-2). Ephesians 2: 3 expresses this truth more succinctly.

*"**A**mong whom also we all once conducted ourselves in **the lusts of our flesh**, fulfilling the desires **of the <u>flesh</u> and of the <u>mind</u>**, and were by nature children of wrath, just as the others."*

Having this understanding gives us important insight into the dynamics of what's going on within us when we're wrestling with temptation. Every Christian has experienced the inner struggle of conflicting desires. When faced with a temptation of any sort, our flesh is often intrigued or aroused by it. Our natural mind often begins to rationalize and scheme to find ways to fulfill its desire, looking for loopholes in the truth.

For instants, the whisperer justifies their gossip by claiming to spread sensitive information *"for the sake of prayer"*; hence they devise a religious excuse to justify their sin. If the temptation is one that promises some form of physical satisfaction, the impulses, hormones, drives, and chemicals of our fleshly body begin to exert their pressure on us as well. However, the conscience of the Christian — which is rooted in their spiritual, born-again heart — is staunchly resistant against the temptation. Moreover, the Holy Spirit brings His conviction to bear on the mind as well. Hence, the inner conflict ensues.

When the flesh (i.e., the *"carnal mind"* and *"mortal body"*) is aroused with temptation, the spiritual nature is often overwhelmed, and if it's not empowered by the Holy Spirit, it often loses the fight, and the Christian commits the sin. Our fallen flesh and our natural mind have years of experience in fulfilling their ungodly desires. But our born-again nature starts out immature, and does not know how to yield to the power of the Holy Spirit yet. We often find ourselves saying, *"Lord, I know I shouldn't do this! I don't want to do this! But I don't know how to stop! God help me!"* This is the new nature within us crying out for help. God knows that multitudes of Christians have found themselves within this seemingly inescapable vortex of temptation. *"The* [born-again] *spirit is willing, but the flesh is weak."*

The spiritual nature of a Christian experiences deep agony when it falls to the strength of the flesh. This is because it has been recreated in righteousness and indwelt by the Holy Spirit; therefore, it longs for righteousness. Paul describes this bitter struggle in Romans 7: 22-24:

*"I **delight** in the law of God **according to the inward man**. 23 But I see another law in my members, warring against the law of my mind, and **bringing me** [his spiritual nature] **into captivity** to the law of sin which is in my members [his flesh]. 24 O wretched man that I am! Who will deliver me from this body of death?"*

(Before we move on, allow me to express two important points. First, the "mind" of verse 23 speaks of the spiritual mind. The next chapter, Romans 8, explains the difference between the "carnal mind" and the spiritual mind of the new nature (Romans 8: 6). *It's in Roman's 8 that Paul explains how to live in Spirit-filled victory — the victory that he **presently** lived in.*

The second point is this: **Paul was not presently living as the utterly defeated Christian personified in Roman's 7!** *A misunderstanding of this truth has far reaching implications. There were times in my life when I desperately wanted to use "Paul's struggle" as an excuse to take a lax approach to my struggle, but an honest and contextual understanding of this scripture never allowed me to do so. My understanding of this scripture is validated by some of the foremost teachers and commentators on the book of Romans, such as Dr. Martin Lloyd Jones and Dr. James Montgomery Boice. Others such as Dr. R. A. Torrey also have concluded that Paul is not speaking of his **present** condition. Much more can be said of this, but for the sake of brevity, I'll forgo.)*

Notice the agony of the defeated Christian that Paul personifies in Romans 7. Observe how the new nature is brought into *"captivity"* to the *"law of sin"* within its fleshly *"members"*. There is no grief as bitter as this experience! The spiritual, new nature within a Christian longs to be saved from *"this body of death"*! The new nature never says, *"Well, if you can't beat 'em, join 'em."* A prisoner of war is not the same as a traitor. The born-again nature may be weak and unable to overcome the flesh, but again, it *never* embraces the sin. The spiritual nature within a Christian can *never* be at peace with *any* sin.

If a professed Christian can be at peace with *any* sin, it's either because they're so carnal that they have no spiritual sensitivity, or they don't have a new nature at all—they're still spiritually dead. An unregenerate person sins without a conscience toward God. According to Paul, the person who's spiritually dead lives *"in the futility of their mind, 18 having their understanding darkened, being alienated from the life of God, because of the ignorance that is in them, because of the blindness of their heart; 19* **who, being past feeling,** *have given themselves over to lewdness, to work all uncleanness with greediness"* (Ephesians 4: 17-19).

Someone may argue, *"Well, I know some lost individuals who feel bad about their sin."* Here's the vital distinction between a Christian who grieves over sin and a lost person who feels bad over sin. A lost person feels conviction according to their own preferred moral principles. Ever since Adam ate from the *"tree on the knowledge of good and evil"*, man has had a sense of right and wrong. Man is profoundly religious. From Cain who murdered Abel over a religious sacrifice, to the religious Pharisees who crucified Christ, to the religious ruler who'll promote the Antichrist, man is hell-bent on his own religious morals. However, while the lost person feels conviction over their own preferred morals, the Christian feels conviction over God's standard of righteousness as it is revealed in the Bible. This is because their very nature has been recreated in the image of Christ and indwelt with the Spirit of God.

Can you commit *any* sin without *"feeling"* a conviction to repent? If so, that's not a good sign. However, if you've been born-again, the Spirit of God dwells within you, and *all sin* will be an unbearable grief to you — unless you quench the conviction. However, this burden over sin does not automatically give us the power to cease from all sin; we still have to grow. Just like a baby must grow and mature, born-again Christians must grow as well. The first step of our growth is a new heart — a born-again, Christ-filled spirit that longs for righteousness. If indeed you have a hunger and thirst for righteousness within your heart, God has promised to fill this hunger. Unfortunately, just like natural babies, spiritually immature Christians are very prone toward stumbling and soiling themselves.

God's Great Compassion Toward His Struggling Children

The child of God is just that — a "child *of* God", and that's how God sees us. Since God has given us a new, born-again heart, *"God has sent forth the Spirit of His Son into* [our] *hearts, crying out, "Abba, Father!"* (Galatians 4: 6). When a Christian falls, God doesn't see a wicked, sinning heathen; He sees a fallen child because He looks at our heart. *"For as the heavens are high above the earth, so great is His mercy toward those who fear Him;* [12] *As far as the east is from the west, so far has He removed our transgressions from us.* [13] *As a father pities his children, so the LORD pities those who fear Him"* (Psalm 103: 11-13). Christ came to save us from sin, not to beat us over the head every time we fall. Many Christians feel that God has forsaken them because of their many failures. This is how Israel felt after they'd fallen many times into the same sins and were being chastised by God. But listen to how God responded to them:

"Zion said, "The LORD has forsaken me,
And my Lord has forgotten me."
[15] *"Can a woman forget her nursing child,*
And not have compassion on the son of her womb?
Surely they may forget,
Yet I will not forget you.
[16] *See, I have inscribed you on the palms of My hands;"* (Isaiah 49: 14-16).

What loving mother would forget her newborn baby who is still nursing? God says that they'll forget their precious little infant before He'll forget us. This is because our names are inscribed upon His nail-pierced hands as a memorial of His great work of redemption that has paid the penalty of our sin. Rest your faith here. Resist every *feeling* that tells you that God's unsearchable love is too good to be true. God forgives all of His children *equally*. Unfortunately, many of us are under such a weight of misinformed condemnation, we often feel just like *"Zion"* — forsaken and forgotten. But God never forgets or condemns His own. Instead, He stands guard against the Wicked One who perpetually condemns us.

"But, what if my sin has causes severe consequences to myself and others? How can God still love me if this is the case? Surely, He must push me away in anger!" If this is your concern, let me tell you the tale of two sons.

There was a father who had a well behaved son. He told his son not to play in the street. One day, while his son was playing in the yard, a car jumped the curb and hit the boy, severely injuring him. Now, let's get this same father and give him a son who is prone to mischief. One day, this son decided to ignore his father's rule, and began playing in the street. A distracted driver hit the boy and severely injured him.

Now, let's consider some questions. Which son would the father respond faster to? Would he rush to help his obedient son, but wait for his television show to finish before getting up to help his naughty son? In which scenario would the father dial 911 faster? Which son would the father pursue better treatment for? Which son would the father exhibit more compassion for? To give an answer to these hypotheticals would be an insult to the common sense of the reader.

Is God not an infinitely better Father than the absolute best of earthly fathers? Does the love of man rival the love of God? Does a candle rival the Sun? If an earthly father, *"being evil"*, would show such compassion to his son who, while in disobedience, suffered severe consequences, how much more does our Heavenly Father do so. The only difference between the two sons is that one son can have the confidence of knowing that his suffering was of no fault of his own, while other son would have the shame of knowing that his suffering was due to his misbehavior. Yet, neither son should doubt the unconditional love of their father, and the immutable security of their relationship. Beloved reader, neither should we doubt these things concerning our Heavenly Father.

Christ Is Our Advocate and High Priest

Every sense of accusation and condemnation is of the Devil. Christ, our Advocate, stands up for us against the accusations of the Enemy. Zechariah gives us a glimpse into God's courtroom and allows us to see our *"Advocate"* silencing the *"Accuser of the brethren"*.

*"Then he showed me Joshua the high priest standing before the Angel of the LORD, and Satan standing at his right hand to oppose him. ² And the LORD said to Satan, "The LORD rebuke you, Satan! The LORD who has chosen Jerusalem rebuke you! Is this not a brand plucked from the fire?" ³ Now Joshua was clothed with **filthy garments**, and was standing before the Angel. ⁴ Then He answered and spoke to those who stood before Him, saying, "**Take away the filthy garments from him**." And to him He said, "See, I have removed your **iniquity** from you, and I will clothe you with rich robes"* (Zechariah 3: 1-4).

Christ literally fights on our behalf beloved Christian—whether the Devil's accusations are 100% true, half-true, embellished, or outright lies, our Divine Advocate defends us. In the case of Joshua, his *"filthy garments"* represented his *"iniquity"*, which means that Satan's accusations were true! However, when God declares us to be righteous, nothing in all of creation can bring a charge against us.

"Who shall bring a charge against God's elect? It is God who justifies" (Romans 8: 33). Notice the reason that Paul gives for why a charge cannot be leveled against one of God's children. Paul didn't say that we cannot be charged with sin because we have great morals and "clean livin!" No! The reason we are above reproach before the eyes of God is not found within us—it's found in Christ! God has *justified* us in Christ—declared us righteous!

At this very moment, Christ is perpetually praying for us. As it is written in Hebrews 7: 25, *"Therefore He is also able to save to the uttermost those who come to God through Him, since He always lives to make intercession for them."*

Believe it or not, in spite of all our sinful failures, Christ is on our side. Since He lived in human flesh, He can *"sympathize with our weaknesses"* because He was *"in all points tempted as we are, yet without sin"* (Hebrews 4: 14-15). The Lord purposely lived in the frailty of human flesh so that He could experientially understand and empathize with us. This empathy that He gained in His humanity lets us know that we can always come to him, in spite of what we've done, and He'll always understandingly welcome us back.

In fact, like the reception of the prodigal son, God invites us to *"come **boldly** to the throne of grace, that we may obtain mercy and find grace to help in time of need"* (Hebrews 4: 16). This is by no means an excuse for us to take sin lightly. It is the will of God that we *"may not sin. [but] if anyone sins, we have an **Advocate** with the Father, Jesus Christ the righteous. ² And He Himself is the **propitiation** for our sins, and not for ours only but also for the whole world"* (1John 2: 1-2).

A Sin Debt Paid In Full Allows For Perpetual Forgiveness

The question is often asked, *"What if the person commits the sin again?"* The answer is simple; what if a person commits *any* sin again? — they repent, confess, accept forgiveness, and move on. How can Christ offer us such unlimited forgiveness? The answer is because He is our *"propitiation."* This word speaks of **"satisfaction."** It means that the justice of God the Father has been *thoroughly satisfied* in the sacrificial work of His Son. This means that God's justice has been satisfied toward all sin — even yours and mine.

For this reason, God grants us perpetual forgiveness. Furthermore, He commands us to perpetually forgive one another.

"Then Peter came to Him and said, "Lord, how often shall my brother sin against me, and I forgive him? Up to seven times?" ²² Jesus said to him, "I do not say to you, up to seven times, but up to seventy times seven" (Matthew 18: 21-22).

*"Take heed to yourselves. If your brother sins against you, rebuke him; and if he **repents**, forgive him. ⁴ And if he sins against you seven times in a day, and seven times in a day returns to you, saying, 'I **repent**,' **you shall forgive** him"* (Luke 17: 3-4).

God is not giving us a forgiveness quota in these verses. The number seven in the Bible is universally understood to stand for completeness. If there's any question about how much the Lord forgives us, it is swiftly answered in these verses. God commands us to forgive perpetually, and it's impossible for us to out-forgive God! Indeed, the model prayer in which the Lord taught us to request *"daily bread"*, by implication He also taught us to pray for daily forgiveness (Matthew 6: 9-18 & Luke 11: 1-4). The Lord literally invites us to come to Him for forgiveness every single day! So why do we so squeamishly approach the One Who invites us to come *"boldly"* into His Presence?

I've often heard individuals make the thoughtless and absurd assertion that, *"If someone sins and then repents of it — if they commit the same sin again, then their repentance wasn't genuine the first time."* This is what happens when we lean on our own understanding; this is foolish reasoning. Christ says that a person can sin and genuinely *"repent"* seven times in a single day! Everyone who's spiritually awake enough to recognize their own sin has experienced the frustration of stumbling into a sin, being deeply grieved and repentant because of it, and then in a moment of weakness, being drawn back into the same sin. This is common to the Christian experience. Unfortunately, many who have displaced God's righteousness with man's selective morality do not realize how much they themselves sin.

It's very disturbing to see professed Christians scoff at these scriptures on forgiveness. This insolent hubris is a clear indication that such persons have absolutely no concept of their own sinfulness (in spite of how piously they may say, *"I'm only a sinner saved by grace."*). Every single blood-bought Christian should be rejoicing with exuberant joy at the truth contained within these scriptures! When an individual derides the great compassion revealed within these verses, they're exhibiting their glaring ignorance to the fact that *they too* need this much forgiveness! If *God's* holy justice has been thoroughly satisfied through the blood of Christ, who do we make ourselves out to be when we, in our own self-righteous sense of justice, refuse to be satisfied? But praise God, He is satisfied!

Just-if-I'd Never Sinned

Let's explore this great truth of justification a little more. Many people get anxious and confused because they look at the quantity and severity of their sins. They feel that there may be a heavenly Sin-o-Meter that is tallying their sins. This is not how it works. The Christian is expected to grow and mature so that the quantity and severity of their sin is greatly diminished. However, the moment a Christian is born-again, they are completely saved from the condemnation and penalty of sin — sin cannot even touch them in their new, spiritual nature. If it could, then *one sin* would condemn us to hell, for *"whoever shall keep the whole law, and yet stumble **in one point**, he **is guilty of all**"* (James 2: 10).

The work of Christ has redeemed us from the Law of Moses. The law accuses, condemns, and kills. The law not only details and identifies our sins; it invigorates our sinful tendencies and executes justice against us when we sin. *"For apart from the law sin was dead. ⁹ I was alive once without the law, but when the commandment came, sin revived and I died. ¹⁰ And the commandment, which was to bring life, I found to bring death"* (Romans 7: 8-10).

For this reason the Law has become a curse to us. *"For as many as are of the works of the law are under the curse"*, but *"Christ has redeemed us from the curse of the law, having become a curse for us"* (Galatians 3: 10-13). Christ's redemption has made it so that we *"are not under law but under grace"* (Romans 6: 14). Therefore, the Christian is bound under an entirely different governing principle in God's eyes — grace.

When a Christian sins, there is no longer any law to condemn them. We have been delivered from the bondage of the merciless justice of the law. Our relationship with God has been translated from one of a law-breaking fugitive under the judicial law, to that of a child of the Heavenly Father who is always viewed through the eyes of grace and handled with the hands of love.

*"When the fullness of the time had come, God sent forth His Son, born of a woman, born under the law, ⁵ **to redeem those who were under the law, that we might receive the adoption as sons.** ⁶ And because you are sons, God has sent forth the Spirit of His Son into your hearts, crying out, "Abba, Father!" ⁷ Therefore **you are no longer a slave** (under the law) **but a son** (under grace), and if a son, then an heir of God through Christ"* (Galatians 4: 4-7).

Again, we are under an entirely different governing principle before the eyes of God — the principle of grace. Sin is not judicially measured nor is it tallied within God's administration of grace. Justice can never touch the child of God, because God's justice has been satisfied — *propitiated* — in Christ. Remember, every sin is *"deserving of death"* in God's eyes (Romans 1: 28-32); therefore, *any sin* would damn us if God's grace had not freed us from the law — *any sin!* If the justice of the Law touches a single born-again Christian, then the work of Christ was not finished on the cross, and we are *all* lost.

To reinforce this glorious truth, consider the words of Paul:

*"The law brings about wrath; for **where there is no law there is no transgression**"* (Romans 4: 15).

And again;

"Sin is not imputed when there is no law" (Romans 5: 13).

Do you understand what you just read? God does not impute (charge, account, *tally*!) sin to the account of those who are not under the Law. This, again, is the doctrine of *"justification"*. However, this truth did not originate in the New Testament. The Apostle Paul quoted the words of King David in order to lay the foundation for this wonderful truth:

"Blessed are those whose lawless deeds are forgiven,
And whose sins are covered;
⁸ Blessed is the man to whom the LORD **shall not impute sin**" (Romans 4: 7-8 & Psalm 32: 1-2).

Do you know the circumstances in David's life when the Lord gave him this revelation? David had just committed adultery with another man's wife, got her pregnant, and then had her husband murdered in order to cover up his sin! But David repented bitterly before His God, and it was in David's brokenness that God revealed to him this glorious truth called ***"justification".*** None of David's sins were charged against Him — they were blotted out! He didn't even need to offer a sacrifice — and this was the Old Testament! *"For You do not desire sacrifice, or else I would give it"* (Psalm 51:16). If there's any question as to whether God's justification extends to what man has classified as *"gross sins"*, those questions are immediately answered in the grace shown to David.

Since we are no longer under Law, sin *cannot* be judicially imputed to us. As I mentioned earlier, we must determine to rest our faith in these truths in spite of our feelings that tell us that they're too good to be true. Feelings can lie; God can't! God's grace is indeed true, and it is truly "Amazing".

Wonderful grace of Jesus,
Greater than all my sin;
How shall my tongue describe it,
Where shall its praise begin?
Taking away my burden,
Setting my spirit free;
For the wonderful grace of Jesus reaches me.

Wonderful the matchless grace of Jesus,
Deeper than the mighty rolling sea;

Higher than the mountain, sparkling like a fountain,
All-sufficient grace for even me;

Broader than the scope of my transgressions,
Greater far than all my sin and shame,
O magnify the precious Name of Jesus.
Praise His Name!

Not Judicially Judged, but Parentally Paddled

The struggles and failures of our *sinful flesh* do not in any way alter the justified status of our *born-again nature*. This is because these two natures are on two thoroughly different and divergent wavelengths. The inner nature of a Christian is almost just as grieved at the sins of the flesh as the Holy Spirit Who dwells within him. However, do not assume that God takes it lightly when we allow our flesh to bring us *"into captivity to the law of sin which is in* [our] *members."*

Our Heavenly Father does not cast us away because we are weak and struggling; however, He will chasten us out of love. Consider 1 Corinthians 11:32: *"When we* [Christians] *are judged, we are chastened by the Lord,* **that we may not be condemned** *with the world."* Let this priceless truth sink in.

Although the context of this verse is the "Lord's Supper", Paul is stating a universal truth in this scripture. The worst that can happen to a child of God is some form of chastening, up to and including an early death—a death that brings us home to Heaven with the loss of rewards and the shame of having failed our Lord. However, seal this truth in your heart—the child of God can *never* **"be condemned with the world."** Do you see how God separates His *parental* discipline from His *judicial* justice? There is *"***no condemnation** *to those who are* [truly] *in Christ Jesus"* (Romans 8: 1).

However, we should never take God's grace for granted; we should always repentantly confess our sins and seek to walk upright again. Consider the words of Charles Spurgeon:

"It is quite certain that those whom Christ has washed in His precious blood need not make a confession of sin, as culprits or criminals, before God the Judge, for

Christ has forever taken away all their sins in a legal sense, so that they no longer stand where they can be condemned, but are once for all accepted in the Beloved; but having become children, and offending as children, ought they not every day to go before their heavenly Father and confess their sin, and acknowledge their iniquity in that character? Nature teaches that it is the duty of erring children to make a confession to their earthly father, and the grace of God in the heart teaches us that we, as Christians, owe the same duty to our heavenly father. We daily offend, and ought not to rest without daily pardon."[5]

The Reason That *"Nothing Shall Separate Us From The Love Of Christ."*

Allow me to conclude this section with a final point. For many years, I would read the end of Romans 8 and not find the comfort that it promised. *"For I am persuaded that neither death nor life, nor angels nor principalities nor powers, nor things present nor things to come, [39] nor height nor depth, nor any other created thing, shall be able to separate us from the love of God which is in Christ Jesus our Lord"* (Romans 8: 38-39). The reason I didn't find comfort in this scripture is because "sin" wasn't listed among the things that cannot separate us from the love of Christ. I've even heard preachers point out this obvious omission. They concluded that certain vices could indeed separate a person from the love of Christ.

When I set my heart to earnestly seek the Lord, He opened my eyes to see the whole truth contained within these scriptures. We often have a problem of taking things out of context. If we simply read the preceding verses we will understand the depths of God's grace.

*"What then shall we say to these things? If God is for us, who can be against us? [32] He who did not spare His own Son, but delivered Him up for us all, how shall He not with Him also freely give us all things? [33] Who shall bring a charge against God's elect? It is God who **justifies**. [34] Who is he who **condemns**? It is Christ who died, and furthermore is also risen, who is even at the right hand of God, **who also makes intercession for us**"* (Romans 8: 31-34).

Do you understand what you just read? There is not a soul in Heaven, on earth, or in hell who can bring any charge against God's children. Why? Because we never mess up? No! Because God has *justified* us! Sin *cannot* be imputed to us. Neither is there any being in Heaven or on earth who can *"condemn"* a child of God. Why? Because Christ bore our condemnation on the cross! He is our *propitiation* — justice has been satisfied! He's interceding for us at this very moment. God is *for* us, not against us!

Now, this is what the Lord revealed to me. The reason that Romans 8: 35-39 is even possible is because of the marvelous truths of Romans 8: 31-34. God *doesn't need* to put "sin" on the list of things that cannot separate us from the love of God, because He thoroughly dealt with the issue of sin in verses 31-34. As a matter of fact, verses 35-39 of Romans 8 *would not even be possible* if God had not first dealt with our sin! The *only* thing — and I repeat, *"the only thing"* — that can separate a human being from God is *sin*; therefore, God had to deal decisively and conclusively with the sin issue first — as described in verses 31-34. And if God has utterly eradicated sin through the work of Christ, there is **absolutely nothing else** in all of creation that can separate us from the love of God — verses 35-39! Do you understand?

When you feel condemned, dear brother — when you feel condemned, dear sister, I assure you that that condemnation is not coming from God. Condemnation comes from the *"Accuser of the brethren"*. Conviction comes from the Holy Spirit. What's the difference? Condemnation fills us with hopeless guilt and pushes us away from God — like Judas. Conviction fills us with grief and remorse over our sin, and draws us back to God — like Peter. And, in spite of how many times we foul up, our Heavenly Father is always waiting to receive us back to Himself so that He can lift us up again in His boundless grace — 70X7! Nothing can separate us from His everlasting love.

Heart Check

Dwell on the things that you've learned in this chapter, and determine to completely rest your faith in these truths. Do not listen to your emotions. Do not *try* to believe these things. Learn to simply *rest*. Do not allow the Deceiver to convince you that God's grace is too good to be true. God's word is clear and it is indeed true. Settle your faith in this harbor of grace, drop the anchor of your soul here, and never again sail in the wavering seas of doubt and fear. Faith is a decision to rest, and though anxious feelings may try to disturb this rest, shoo them away and lay your head once again in the bosom of *Truth*.

There's so much more that I could say about our assurance, but enough has been said already. However, I sternly warn you that you do not attempt to rest in an assurance that is not rightfully yours. These truths and promises are for born-again children of God, not presumptuous professed Christians.

Examine your faith to make sure it is genuinely settled on and committed to the Person and work of Christ alone for salvation. Examine your heart to see if you truly have a hunger and thirst for Christ. Here is a good way to gauge your heart.

Having heard the wonderful assurance that the Christian has in Christ, are you now compelled to become lax in your faith? Does it cause you to take sin less seriously? Are you less concerned about following the Word of God and the Will of Christ? Does it compel you to use *"grace"* as an excuse to defy God's revealed will? If so, this could very well be a reflection of your true heart—a heart that is yet unregenerate and dead to God. However, if learning of God's great grace toward you has stirred a joyful zeal within you, and revived a love for Christ that longs for His Word and His will, then be of good courage, your heart is right before God.

"It is not my aim to introduce doubts and fears into your mind; nay, verily, but I shall hope the rather that the rough wind of self-examination may help to drive them away. It is not security, but carnal security, which we would kill; not confidence, but fleshly confidence, which we would overthrow; not peace, but false peace, which we would destroy. By the precious blood of Christ, which was not shed to make you a hypocrite, but that sincere souls might show forth his praise, I beseech you, search and look, lest at the last it be said of you, "Mene, Mene, Tekel: thou art weighed in the balances, and art found wanting." __Spurgeon.[5]

I close this chapter with the immortal words of the Apostle Paul and Christ our Lord: *"If anyone does not love the Lord Jesus Christ, let him be accursed"*; However, *"Grace be with all those who love our Lord Jesus Christ **in sincerity**. Amen."* (1 Corinthians 16: 22 & Ephesians 6: 24). And Christ defines this love as follows: *"He who has My commandments and keeps them, it is he who loves Me"* (John 14: 21). Do you have a heart of love for Christ that seeks to obey Him? If so, that's a very good sign. But, *how* do we obey Him? The Bible is clear on the subject of justification, but what about sanctification—how do we overcome sin and live righteously? We'll explore that in the next chapter.

CHAPTER 3

THE FORGOTTEN TRUTH OF SANCTIFICATION

> *"If you seem to have so much fighting to do, it may be because you did not have one sharp, decisive battle to begin with. It is far easier to have one great battle than to keep on skirmishing all your life. I know men who spend forty years fighting what they call their besetting sin, and on which they waste strength enough to evangelize the world.*
>
> *Does it pay to throw away your lives? Why not have one battle, one victory and then praise God. There is labor to enter in. The height is steep;* ***the way of the cross is not an easy way. It is hard to enter in, but having entered in, there is perfect rest.*** *And when he giveth you rest from all your enemies round about (Deuteronomy 12:10). May God help us and give us His perfect rest.*
>
> *O come, and leave thy sinful self forever*
>
> *Beneath the fountain of the Saviour's blood;*
>
> *O come, and take Him as thy Sanctifier,*
>
> *Come thou with us and we will do thee good."* — A. B. Simpson[6]

Over the years I've discovered that most relatively sound Christians are very dogmatic concerning the doctrines of salvation. We vigilantly hold to the testimony that we are saved by grace alone, through faith alone, in Christ alone. Most Christians know how easy it is to rattle off a host of scriptures to reinforce and expound upon this truth. To these glorious truths we do not and dare not waver or sway an inch to the left or to the right.

Unfortunately, this is where most of us stop. The Christian life has been reduced down to a sound confession of faith and a handful of "essential doctrines". I call this *"Threshold Christianity."* As long as we make it through the threshold — we've said the sinner's prayer and the preacher has declared us "Saved!" — we settle down into a self-satisfied, haphazard Christian walk that often lacks urgency, purpose, and zeal. The hunger and thirst to advance to higher levels of spiritual power and sanctification has been notably absent among many. Tozer wrote the following:

"How tragic that we in this dark day have had our seeking done for us by our teachers. Everything is made to center upon the initial act of "accepting" Christ (a term, incidentally, which is not found in the Bible) and we are not expected thereafter to crave any further revelation of God to our souls. We have been snared in the coils of a spurious logic which insists that if we have found Him we need no more seek Him. This is set before us as the last word in orthodoxy, and it is taken for granted that no Bible-taught Christian ever believed otherwise."[7]

This stunted spiritual reasoning has crippled the growth of not a few Christians. We pride ourselves in having the doctrines of *salvation* nailed down, but when it comes to the doctrines concerning *sanctification,* it has been a virtual free-for-all within the church. This doctrine has been left open to a grab bag of religious ideas. If a person were to go to 100 different churches and ask the leadership of how we are to overcome sin and live the resurrection life of Christ, it's likely they'd get nearly 100 different explanations.

The church has been inundated with a host of man-made solutions to sin. Desperate Christians are running two and fro, frantically trying to gain victory over their besetting sin. This was my case for many years. I had a profound ignorance of the biblical fundamentals of sanctification. And every straw of hope I grasped for only added to the confusion. Multitudes of struggling Christians in churches across America are searching for answers in an ecclesiastical system that doesn't have any. This is because the church has largely pawned off this cardinal responsibility to a host of psychology based, man-made solutions and para-church ministries (i.e., addiction ministries outside of the local church). We have all but abandoned and forgotten what the scripture teaches us about sanctification.

The late David Wilkerson, a true servant of God, is well known for his evangelistic outreach to the street gangs of New York. The movie, *"The Cross and the Switch Blade"*, tells the story of how Wilkerson led the violent gangster, Nicky Cruz, to Christ. Wilkerson planted a church right in the midst of Times Square on Broadway, and spent his life reaching out to the gangs, drug addicts, and prostitutes of New York. His ministry, known as "Teen Challenge", spread throughout New York and across the world.

"Teen Challenge has grown to include 173 residential programs and numerous evangelism outreach centers in the United States and 241 centers in 77 other countries. The program's cure rate of 86% has been recognized and substantiated by the U.S. Government's National Institute on Drug Abuse."[8] But, unlike most ministries, Wilkerson didn't resort to man's methods to deliver those in bondage. In a sermon he preached titled, *"Not With the Sword of Man"*, he lambasted the churches trust in the arm of the flesh:

"God says 'you have revolted against me.' God considers it a revolt among His people when they believe that through their own power they trust in the strength of the flesh; they trust in man and his methods to deliver them from the powers of darkness. We have our own chariots today. We have our own horses today. These are the vehicles through which we try to achieve victory over the flesh. We've got books by the thousands on "how to." How to improve the flesh. How to charm the flesh. How to subdue the flesh. How to submerge the flesh. Ten ways to get victory over loneliness. Six ways to find a new wife or a new husband. AA's got 12 steps to victory over alcoholism. They've got all of these man-made tapes and seminars. Folks, we've got it coming out our ears! People running everywhere to find and lean on some man. Leaning on the arm of the flesh, looking for a word, looking for man, looking for a vehicle, looking for something to deliver them from their bondage!"[9]

This is the ecclesiastical atmosphere that most struggling Christians find themselves rummaging through. The sin management racket has been marketed to the religious consumer like an over-the-counter drug—so many options to choose from, and the average customer doesn't know which one is best. And like the average drug, it only relieves the symptoms of the problem; it doesn't cure the problem. In a few months the sickness returns, so we run back to the drug store to try a new product. For many Christians this back-and-forth gets old—really old! They often conclude that struggling with sin is just a normal part of Christian life. So, they shrug their shoulders, misapply grace, offer up a pre-planned confession, and prance along in barren bliss.

But by God's grace, what I've come to experience and understand is that it is *not* normal for a Christian to continue struggling in sinful bondage—and it's certainly not normal for them to unrepentantly revel in it. It is understandable for a Christian to struggle when they are a babe in the faith, but babes are expected to grow up. And this growth is not supposed to be haphazard, nor is it to be left to the "eeny, meeny, miny, moe" of man's quasi-biblical solutions. *The Scripture clearly teaches how a believer is to overcome sin through sanctification. The doctrine of sanctification is in essence as clearly taught within scripture as the doctrine of justification.* If a Christian simply follows God's Word concerning sanctification, overcoming sin and growing in Christlikeness will be the *normal* outcome.

I want to stress that final point without an ounce of ambiguity; overcoming *all patterns* of sin — yes, even overcoming strongholds — is supposed to be a *normal* part of Christian growth. Victory over sin is not a dynamic marvel that only a few saints are graced with; it comes standard with everybody who trusts the Savior to *"save His people from their sins."* Hearing that a saint has overcome some destructive vice should not be a novelty, it should be the norm.

The pursuit of sanctification has been reduced to a gamble; a frustratingly endless game of trying one "solution" after another. To make matters worse, it's impossible for man's solutions to achieve the biblical goal of sanctification. Any "success" achieved through one of man's solutions is like putting home-plate on first-base and calling a base hit a homerun! We've changed the goal. We've lowered the bar to a level that is attainable by religious, natural man. The religious goal of man is not the same as the spiritual goal of God. Man's goal is typically to achieve a good showing of external moral behavior. God's goal is Christlikeness. The difference between the two is immeasurable. An unregenerate pagan can achieve man's goal. Only the Holy Spirit can enable a surrendered Christian to *successfully* pursue God's goal of Christlikeness.

But very few Christians understand how to grasp and walk in the power of the Holy Spirit. So day after day, month after month, and year after year, we stumble along in the same sin. We grasp at every self-help rope we can reach, only to find that none of them are attached to a secure Anchor, so we inevitably fall again. The frustrating cycle of defeat becomes so common that we eventually lower our expectations, and accept defeat as the norm. This is the spiritually impaired frame of mind that multitudes of Christians are presently living in.

The Fatalistic Mindset of Perpetual Defeat

Many well-meaning Christians will often describe the church like a hospital. *"The church is like a hospital for broken people. We're all broken. We all have struggles. We need to encourage each other and hold each other up."* These are very comforting, encouraging, and reassuring sentiments. More importantly, they're all true. Unfortunately, many of us stop right here.

When Jesus described Himself as a Doctor with patients (sinners), not only was He being compassionate toward them, He was also calling them to *"repentance"* (Matthew 9: 9-13). Christ gives us a picture of a true spiritual hospital. He didn't merely comfort His patients; He sought to make them well. Unfortunately, many churches today are more like a hospice than a hospital. We're constantly comforting people in their sin, but we have no vigilant urgency to help them overcome their sin. This is because many of us no longer take sin seriously.

This has greatly crippled the church. Our life cannot be filled with sin and filled with the Holy Spirit at the same time. We cannot allow ourselves to get used to sin, and still expect to be used by the Holy Spirit with any degree of consistency or effectiveness. We've become so accustomed to being comforted in our sin that we've gotten comfortable! I don't want to be perpetually comforted in my sin! I want someone to take me by the hand, and with gracious longsuffering, show me from the Word of God what it takes to be an overcoming, victorious Christian.

No one wants to be anesthetized on a hospital gurney for the rest of their days, when they can become healthy, strong, and able to take life by the horns? We cannot do both. Either we're being overcome by sin and of little use to God, or we're overcoming sin and greatly used by God. *"I know men who spend forty years fighting what they call their besetting sin, and on which they waste strength enough to evangelize the world."* – A. B. Simpson[6]. It's one or the other; sinfulness or usefulness.

Wilkerson, in a sermon titled, *"Releasing the power of the Holy Ghost"*, said the following of many Christians. *"They come and claim to be saved, and they go year after year and there's no victory in their life; they still fight a lust problem, they're fighting sin all their life, and* **they finally come to the conclusion that that's the way the Christian life is lived**...*they're still weak after ten years...fifteen years, twenty years, they're still indulging in the same things and they have no victory."*[10]

At the Keswick Convention of 1963, the late pastor of Moody Church in Chicago, Alan Redpath, sternly challenged his hearers concerning sin within the church. In a sermon titled, *"Restoring the Breach"*, he gave us a snap-shot of the pervasive nature of sin within the church over half a century ago.

"We are here to face just this. Not a secondary issue, but the priority need of our day to get right with God, for that is the key to healing every other wrong. For this, there is a price to pay. It is pictured in this chapter, where the people to whom God spoke were maintaining an active outward form of religion, without any basic reality. They had to be shown that the only way of experiencing the blessing of God was the way of forsaking of sin. The operation of the grace of God in a life is never in conflict with the demands of His holiness. If sin is to be forgiven, it must be forsaken. **The tragedy is that so many of us have learned to live with sin.**

The call – the urgent call, the national call, the personal call, is to repentance in the church; to face the jealousy, discord and sin within our own ranks; for in days like these we cannot afford the luxury of civil war or the tragedy of personal defeat in life. 2 Chronicles 7:14 still rings down the centuries.

This is an intensely personal matter for us all. To get right with God must have repercussions in every area of life, for Christianity in its application is not selfish but selfless. To restore a clear line of communication with the throne in heaven by repentance and confession is to be assured of the inflow of Holy Spirit life from God Himself. For, what I forsake, He forgives; what He forgives, He cleanses; what He cleanses, He fills; and what He fills, He uses."[11] – It's one or the other; sinfulness or usefulness.

R. A. Torrey was a helper and protégé to D. L. Moody. In 1912 he founded the Bible Institute of Los Angeles, which later was renamed Biola University. In 1915 he became the first pastor of the Church of the Open Door, which was later pastored by the renowned Dr. J. Vernon McGee. He said the following concerning sin.

"Some go so far as to maintain that this is the normal Christian life, that one must live this life of constant defeat."[12] — What Torrey described as *"some"* nearly a century ago, would now be *"many"*.

Zac Poonen, a pastor from Bangalore India, gives the following illustration concerning how most Christians handle sin. A test was given to patients in an insane asylum to see if they were improving. A faucet was turned on in a room, and a mop and bucket were placed next to it. Patient was then placed in the room and told to mop up the water. If the patient began mopping without turning off the faucet, it was clear that he needed to stay there a little longer. However, if the patient turned off the faucet then began mopping, it was evident that he was thinking a bit more clearly.[13] Many Christians are constantly running to 1 John 1: 9 in order to perpetually mop up *habitual* sins, but they never turn off the faucet. Most don't even realize the faucet of *habitual sins* can be turned off! They've come to believe that it's perfectly normal for a Christian to struggle in *bondage* to sin.

Andrew Murray, the great South African missionary and man of God, described the different stages of the struggling Christian in his book, "*Absolute Surrender.*" In the following quote, he describes the second stage of the Christian's struggle.

"He begins to see such a life is impossible, but he does not accept it. **There are multitudes of Christians who come to this point**: *"I cannot"; and then think God never expected them to do what they cannot do. If you tell them that God does expect it, it appears to them a mystery. A good many Christians are living a low life, a life of failure and of sin, instead of rest and victory, because they began to see: "I cannot, it is impossible." And yet they do not understand it fully, and so, under the impression, I cannot, they give way to despair. They will do their best, but they never expect to get on very far."*[14]

Many Christians have continued in sin for so long that the conviction of the Holy Spirit has been completely quenched. For some, their conscious has become seared to such a degree that they no longer recognize their sin. This is where many find themselves today. The concept of biblical sanctification has been all but forgotten, and our understanding of sin is in stark conflict with God's truth concerning sin.

The book of Judges says the *"everyone did what was right in his own eyes."* Many *misread* this verse as saying *"everyone* ***knowingly*** *did what was wrong in the eyes of God."* No. This verse is speaking of a people who were doing *what they considered to be right according to their own understanding*, and not according to the Truth. Such is the present state of much of the church. We've so abandoned God's truth concerning sin, that it has become accepted, normative, and essentially interwoven within the fabric of what's perceived as normal Christianity.

The great spiritual sage and writer, A. W. Tozer, was often described as a modern day prophet (an identity that he did not take upon himself). His writings have ministered to serious minded Christians for nearly over 70 years.

Dr. Stuart Briscoe wrote, *"Those who drink deeply of [Tozer's] writings are refreshed and nourished. We need invigorating draughts of Tozer today!"*[15] Ravi Zacharias said of Tozer's writings, *"I've read and re-read [Tozer's] books, and each time sense a hushed silence. It is the silence that has heard from God."*[15] Warren Wiersbe described Tozer in the following way; *"If a sermon can be compared to light, then A.W. Tozer released a laser beam from the pulpit, a beam that penetrated your heart."*[15] Leonard Ravenhill put it more pointedly; *"I fear that we shall never see another Tozer. Men like him are not college bred but Spirit taught."*[15] Tozer described 3 classes of sin. In the following quote, he explains the second class.

"Within the precincts of religion are sometimes found certain sins which I want here to mention. These may be classified under three heads: Sins committed out of weakness, respectable sins more or less allowed by everyone, and sins that have been woven into the religious fabric until they have become a necessary part of it.

Sins of the second category are those that exist with the sanction of or at least the connivance of the church, such as pride, vanity, self-centeredness, levity, worldliness, gluttony, the telling of "white" lies, borderline dishonesty, lack of compassion for the unfortunate, complacency, absorption in the affairs of this life, love of pleasure, the holding of grudges, stinginess, gossiping, and various dirty habits not expressly forbidden by name in the Scriptures.

These sins are so common that they have been accepted as normal by the average church and are either not mentioned at all or referred to in smiling half-humor by the clergy. *While not as spectacular as a roaring weekend drunk or as dramatic as a violent explosion of temper,* **they are in the long run more deadly than either, <u>for</u> they are seldom recognized as sin and are practically never repented of.** *They remain year after year to grieve the Spirit and sap the life of the church, while everyone continues to speak the words of the true faith and go through the motions of perfunctory godliness, not knowing that there is anything wrong."*[16]

Tozer penned these thoughts roughly 70 years ago. In the present day, this unchecked malignancy of flagrant sin has grown exponentially, and it has festered like a disease within the church. On many occasions I've watch in despair as Tozer's words were fleshed out within the body of Christ. I've seen the abject apathy and the *"half smiling humor"* of the clergy toward sin. This widespread ecclesiastical *"connivance"* with sin is treachery against the Lord and Head of the church, and a dereliction of duty toward the wayward flock. I've listened to church leadership casually declare that certain sins were no longer sin; therefore, they refused to even acknowledge them. They concluded rather that these sins were *"just people being people"*. Eli is in the clergy, the lamps have been snuffed out, *"Ichabod"* is written over the steeple, and no one knows *"that there is anything wrong."*

The *"fatalistic mindset of perpetual defeat"* thrives in atmospheres where sin is predominately comforted, yet rarely confronted. It flourishes in environments where we make excuses for unrepentant sin. I refused to allow myself to fall into these frames of mind, and this determination played an integral role in my victory over my stronghold. I never got comfortable in my sin, and I never made excuses for it! And this was in spite of the fact that I was surrounded by the rhetoric of giftwrapped excuses. *"Remember, Paul had his struggles in Romans 7." "Paul had his thorn in the flesh in 2 Corinthians 12."*

My fleshly mind desperately wanted to accept these contortions of truth, but my inner man never had peace with it. So I searched every facet of these scriptures (as well as others like them) in order to see if bondage to sin was something so normal that even the great Apostle Paul was a defeated Christian (let no one deceive you; the personality of Romans 7 is an *utterly* defeated Christian!). A simple surface reading of the text seems to reveal that Paul is speaking of himself *in his present state*; however, an honest and earnest study of the text *and the context* plainly reveals otherwise.

I wish I had the space to break down these scriptures for you. However, if you want to understand this scripture, read Romans 6: 1 through 8: 14, and read the entire book of Galatians. Study them. Then study them again. And again. You'll discover that Paul is teaching the *exact opposite* of sinful defeat being the norm. Paul's primary and conclusive point in these scriptures is that we're able to overcome all bondage to sin by the power of the Holy Spirit!

Every once and a while I got discouraged and overwhelmed with the despair of feeling that I'd never overcome. This sense of hopelessness usually came after fall, or during an intense inner struggle to avoid a fall. Nevertheless, I always recovered, and renewed my determination to overcome. For some reason, I always had faith that I'd one day be delivered. As a matter of fact, just between you and me, I used the name *"overcomer"* as a username and password for many applications *years before* I actually overcame! I simply knew that victory was possible, and I had a stubborn faith that never allowed me to quit.

This is the faith-filled mindset that we must have in order to achieve biblical sanctification. The whole of the Christian life, from stem to stern, is a life of faith. When we trust in the Lord for salvation, we are expected to have *"full assurance of faith"* (Hebrews 10: 22) that He has actually saved us. It's the same for sanctification. God promised victory over the power of sin *just as surely* as He promised salvation from the penalty of sin. Why trust one promise but not the other?

I'll tell you why; because one promise we take seriously, and the other we don't. One promise we deem to be essential, and the other we brush off as being nonessential. One promise has very simple to understand conditions, and the other has conditions that are a bit more complex. Add to this the fact that man has introduced countless alternative ideas for sanctification, and what we have is a convolution of confusion. So, let's clean house. Let's wipe away all of the dry-erase marker ideas of man, so that all we're left with is the Permanent Marker Truths of God's Word. Let's get back to the pure and simple basics of the Truth. How exactly do we pursue biblical sanctification?

One Way for Salvation; One Way for Sanctification!

So, what does God's word say about sanctification? Let me give you one of many scriptures. *"Walk in the Spirit, and you **shall not** fulfill the lust of the flesh."* (Galatians 5: 16). Notice that this scripture does not say, *"Walk in the Spirit, and you shall not fulfill **your one particular besetting sin**."* It doesn't say, *"Walk in the Spirit, and He'll give you the ability to strategically master a few nasty social vices."* It doesn't say, *"Walk in the Spirit, and He'll make you externally **'clean!'**"* It doesn't say, *"Walk in the Spirit, and you'll overcome your generational curse."* It doesn't say, *"Walk in the Spirit and get an accountability partner, and they'll help you to feel too guilty to sin."* No! *"Walk in the Spirit, and **you shall not fulfill** [any of] the lust of the flesh!"* Well, what are the lusts of the flesh?

Two verses after the Apostle tells us that if we *"Walk in the Spirit"* we won't *"fulfill the lust of the flesh"*, he spells out for us what the lusts of the flesh are: *"Now the works of the flesh are **evident** [manifest, obvious, open for all to see], which are: adultery, fornication, uncleanness, lewdness, [20] idolatry, sorcery, hatred, contentions, jealousies, outbursts of wrath, selfish ambitions, dissensions, heresies, [21] envy, murders, drunkenness, revelries, **and the like**"* (Galatians 5: 19-20).

"And the like!" — This is not an exhaustive list of *"the lusts of the flesh"*! God is making a clear and fundamental promise here; that if we simply *"Walk in the Spirit"*, He will deliver us from *all bondage* to *all sin*! Now, listen closely to what the apostle is saying here. If we ***"walk in the Spirit"*** we'll overcome sin; Paul is speaking of a *"walk"*, not a one-time deliverance. So, what happens if we stop walking in the Spirit? The answer is obvious; we'll start walking in the flesh again. What happens when we walk in the flesh? We sin. Adopt this principle as a spiritual red-flag: if I am committing any sin, by definition, I am no longer walking in the Spirit, but in the flesh. As long as we're walking in the Spirit, we'll both recognize and overcome sin; however, the moment we stop walking in the spirit, we'll again become prone to sin.

As my new-man gains dominance over my old-man, my walk in the Spirit becomes more consistent, and with it, my victory over sin. This does not mean that we'll ever reach sinless perfection in this life; however, it does mean that we'll have power over habitual bondage to any sin. The power is not found within my new-nature; rather, it is found within the Holy Spirit Who I am yielding to. God, Himself, literally delivers us from the power of sin. The *"battle [truly] is the Lords!"* We cease from our own efforts, yield ourselves to His Spirit, and He does the sanctifying.

Unfortunately, this is not the goal of many churches. The entire evangelical system of Christianity has been flooded with an endless variety of man's solutions to sin. Man's wisdom concerning sanctification has so utterly eclipsed God's truth concerning sanctification that few of us find it. So, when someone is struggling with sin, we either makes excuses for the sin, or we toss them a church platitude, or we point them to a religious self-help book or a program.

But, it never crosses our mind to tell them (or ourselves), *"The reason you're struggling with sin is because you're not walking in the Spirit; you're walking in the flesh. If you were walking in the Spirit, on the authority and promise of God's word, you would not be struggling with any sinful bondage. It's not about trying to sanctify one area of our life by wrestling with one sin. That's foolish! It's about walking in the Spirit of the only One who can truly and fully sanctify us. Let me take you by the hand, and guide you and train you in the Spirit filled walk."*

Now, let's be honest about this. Most Christians prefer to be emotionally aroused by the Spirit, even in the more conservative evangelical churches. However, very few Christians truly want to yield themselves to the authority of the Holy Spirit. It's too scary. It infringes too much into our comfort zone. It tramples on our individualistic independence as American citizens. It threatens our right to pursue the American Dream—to be anything *we want* to be. It doesn't fit on the agenda of our desired lifestyle. It dethrones us as lord over our own life. So we reduce the standards of sanctification, and make up quick-fix alternative solutions to clean ourselves up according to our own standards.

This is a fundamental and spiritually crippling error in judgment. It's rooted in the Serpentine lie that God has left the concept of sanctification up for grabs, open to the highest bidder, open for suggestion, open to whatever convincing opinion comes down the pike, open to the ever changing drawing-board of man's religious ideas! God didn't say, *"Now that I've saved you, clean yourself up however you see fit." "Give it your best shot." "Any idea you come up with is ok with me." "Better yet, just wait 1800 years until the humanistic atheists invent psychology, then you can mix My truth with their 'science', and they'll help you overcome your sins one by one. And for those of you who live before secular psychology is invented; well, you're just screwed!"* No! God gave us a divinely established means of Holy Spirit empowered, thorough sanctification in His word! Yet, few Christians realize that God has already spoken with timeless, absolute authority on this issue.

The truths concerning *salvation* are absolute and immutable. In the same way, the truths concerning *sanctification* are absolute and immutable. It is complete error to say that a person can be saved through some other means than faith in the Lord Jesus Christ. It is equally complete error to say that a person can be *sanctified* through some other means than Christ our sanctifier working through the Holy Spirit. Any other means of being saved falls short of true salvation, and any other means of cleaning ourselves up falls short of true sanctification.

False Gods and good works cannot *save* us. Equally, programs or psycho-religious self-help books cannot *sanctify* us—not even of one sin! And, if we do manage to "defeat" one sin through a program, it is not the sanctification of Christ, but the religious effort of man to clean himself up. He can stand up in front of the church and tell the congregation how long he's been *"clean"*, yet not be an inch closer to the Spirit filled walk! The "success" is no better than that of a common Pharisee—the Holy Spirit did not empower it.

God is not going to empower someone who refuses to walk in His Spirit, and chooses rather to clean himself up in the power of the flesh. *"Are you so foolish? Having begun in the Spirit* [salvation], *are you now being made perfect by the flesh* [sanctification]" (Galatians 3: 3). Paul later explained to the Galatians that we must perfect ourselves by walking *"in the Spirit"*. We start in the Spirit, and we continue in the Spirit. Or as Paul put it, *"If we live by the Spirit* [i.e., if we've been made alive in the Spirit]*, let us also **walk** in the Spirit"* (Galatians 5: 25).

Another stumbling block for us is rooted in the mentality that I referenced in the beginning of this chapter – *"Threshold Christianity."* This mentality so focuses on the finished work of salvation, that every other aspect of the Christian life seems insignificant and optional. And since salvation occurs in a moment, we expect sanctification to be swift. *"Just ask the Lord to take the temptation away, and 'Poof', it'll be gone!"* *"Just follow these 12 steps or 40 days and you'll have that thing beat!"* It's nonsense! Salvation occurs in a moment; sanctification is a lifetime. This bears repeating: *"Salvation occurs in a moment; Sanctification is a lifetime."* Salvation is an act of faith. Sanctification is a *walk* of faith. *"**Walk** in the Spirit…"*.

This being so, the explanation of sanctification is a bit more involved and extensive than the explanation of salvation. Salvation is by grace through faith, and this faith is rooted in the Person and work of Christ. Sanctification, however, involves not only internal faith, but external surrender (Not "works"; "surrender"; there's a difference). And this surrender must be guided by and empowered by the Holy Spirit.

Trying to clean ourselves up in the flesh is actually counterproductive – it does more *spiritual* harm than good. Any religious progress by the power and wisdom of man reduces our dependence on the power and wisdom of God. Let me repeat this just in case you missed it: *"Any religious progress by the power and wisdom of man reduces our dependence on the power and wisdom of God."* Moreover, any attempt to clean ourselves up in the flesh is not only an arduous task, but an impossible task. It is a perpetual struggle that only produces the rotten fruit of a few selective traits of surface morality.

"Sanctification is the gift of the Holy Spirit, the fruit of the Spirit, the grace of the Lord Jesus Christ and the prepared inheritance of all who enter in. It is the obtainment of faith, not the attainment of works. It is divine holiness, not human self-improvement or perfection. It is the inflow into man's being of the life and purity of the infinite, eternal and Holy One. It is the bringing in of God's own perfection and the working out of His own will.

How easy, how spontaneous, how delightful this heavenly way of holiness! Surely it is a "highway" and not the low way of man's vain and fruitless mortification. It is God's great elevated railway, sweeping over the heads of the struggling throngs who toil along the lower road when they might be borne along on His ascension pathway by His own almighty impulse. It is God's great elevator carrying us up to the higher chambers of His palace, without arduous efforts, while others struggle up the winding stairs and faint by the way." — A. B. Simpson[17]

So, how do we walk in the Spirit? Where do we start? How does a fallen human being, bound within a corrupted, fleshly *"body of death"*, limited by a natural, earthbound mind, *"Walk in the Spirit"* of God Himself, and overcome the bondage of sin?

Our problem is too big for a program! Our problem is too massive for a psycho-religious self-help book! Our problem is too extensive for a few memorized scriptures that pertain to our particular hang-up! Our problem is too complicated for an accountability partner! Our problem is too deep for a Christian psychologist to root out! Our problem is too entrenched for the absolute best solution that fallen man could ever possibly muster up! The only Being Who is capable of conquering, not only the penalty of sin, but the power of sin, is God! Until we accept and surrender to this truth, we'll continue to run down every useless rabbit trail and moral mirage that Satan set's before us!

Is Sanctification By Works Or By Grace?

Let's take it from the top. Sanctification comes from the Greek word *"hagiazo"* (Strongs #37). It means *"to make holy"*, to *"purify or consecrate"*. Simply put, it means to make a separation from that which is bad unto that which is good. Hagiazo comes from the root word *"hagios"* (Strongs #40). Hagios is the Greek word for *"holy"*. This same Greek word is used for *"saint"* or *"saints"*. Therefore, to be a *saint* literally means to be a *holy* one — one who is separated from sin unto God. All Christians are saints in their spiritual standing. This means that all Christians have already been sanctified — set apart — unto God in Christ. However, sanctification is also a process. We are both called and expected to take part in the process of sanctification. How is this accomplished; by us striving and strategizing in the flesh? No. By Grace.

"For sin shall not have dominion over you, for you are not under law but under grace" (Roman 6: 14).

What in the world does this scripture mean? I've read it thousands of times, and I've heard it quoted, taught, or preached just as many times, yet I've never heard a satisfactory explanation. The reason that many cannot fully grasp this verse is because we've adopted a very limited, powerless, vague concept of grace. *"Grace is unmerited favor." "Grace is getting something that you don't deserve."* These definitions are both good, but they do not capture the all-encompassing, divinely effectual sufficiency of God's grace for every aspect of the Christian's life. Our abbreviated concept of grace does nothing to help us understand this verse in question. God's grace does many things—better yet, *everything* for us in the Christian life. However, our present concern is how God's grace applies to sanctification.

This logically brings us to the next question. How do we access and appropriate this sanctifying grace of God? Many Christians are swift to quote 1 Corinthians 1: 30; *"But of Him you are in Christ Jesus, who became for us… sanctification."* We've become very adept at quoting promises, but very inept at appropriating them. I recall a professed Christian who struggled with bondage to sexual sin. Unfortunately, he fell for the popular deception that says, *"Since Christ is the One who sanctifies us, we don't need to do anything. Just trust Him to do it all for us."* Suffice it to say, he's still in bondage.

The ridiculous assumption is that we should just sit on our hands and trust Christ to do everything. Many Christians are infringing the requirements for salvation into the jurisdiction of sanctification. Salvation is by grace, *"not of works"*. Sanctification is by grace as well; however, instead of freeing us from works, it empowers us to live righteously.

*"Therefore, having these promises, beloved, let us **cleanse ourselves** from **all filthiness** of the **flesh and spirit**, perfecting holiness in the fear of God"* (2 Corinthians 7: 1).

The scripture is clear; God expects and commands us to *"cleanse ourselves from all"* sin—not just from the obvious sins of the flesh, but also from the not-so-obvious sins of the spirit. *"But, that's impossible!"* you say. I agree. *"That's unreasonable!"* you say. It sure is! But, you cannot say that it's unbiblical. So, what do we do with this? Do we shrug it off and dismiss it with a false interpretation and misapplication of grace? God forbid! Instead, we must yield ourselves to the One whose grace enables us to do the impossible. How do we access and appropriate this overcoming grace?

An important thing that we must understand about grace is that grace is just a word. Grace is nothing more than an abstract concept by itself. In order for grace to sanctify us it must have power. The power behind grace is the Holy Spirit. Indeed, *all grace* is administered the Holy Spirit. We're saved by grace, but this salvation is *"through the washing of regeneration and renewing of the Holy Spirit"* (Titus 3: 5). Grace is the free gift, and the Holy Spirit is the one who administers the gift. Without the Omnipotent Holy Spirit, the grace for salvation is impotent.

This is true concerning all of the grace that God has made available to His children. God's grace toward us goes far beyond salvation; salvation just the beginning. Peter says that God *"has **given** to us **all things** that pertain to life and godliness, through the knowledge of Him who called us by glory and virtue, ⁴ by which have been **given** to us exceedingly great and precious promises, that through these you may be partakers of the divine nature."* (2 Peter 1: 3).

Though the word *"grace"* is not mentioned in these verses, the word *"given"* immediately tells us that these verses are all about God's grace. What has He given us? *"All things that pertain to life and godliness."* Not only that, He's *"given"* us God-guaranteed *"promises"* that we'll *"be partakers of the Divine Nature"*; i.e., Christlikeness! God has *"given"* (past tense) us everything that we need to successfully live the Christian life and grow like Christ! So why are so many of us having such a difficult time living the Christian life?

Let's look again at the teaching of the Apostle Peter. God has *"given"* us everything that we need for the Christian life and for Christlikeness. But, just because we have it, doesn't mean that it automatically changes us. Immediately afterward, Peter told his readers that *"also for this very reason* [since God has given us all that we need], ***giving all diligence*** [make an earnest effort to], *add to your faith virtue… knowledge… temperance… perseverance… godliness… brotherly love…and…*[sacrificial, agape] *love."* These are the stepping stones of Christlikeness.

So, even though we've been *"given"* everything that we need, we're still called to ***diligently*** pursue and apply these things to our lives. Grace is like all of the capabilities of a smartphone. Many of us have smartphones. At our finger tips are countless apps and capabilities, *freely* available for our use. However, many of us only use a tiny amount of these capabilities because we're either ignorant of them, or indifferent toward them. Just because we've been *"given"* a million capabilities in our smart phones doesn't mean that we're actually using them. We have to *diligently* learn how to use what has been *"given"* to us. This is grace.

A good working definition of grace would be, *"Grace is all of God's sufficiency freely given on our behalf for all of our needs and responsibilities"* — first for salvation, then for everything else. Grace is not given to us to avoid the responsibilities of the Christian life; it's given to us to fulfill the responsibilities of the Christian life. This bears repeating: *"Grace is not given to us to avoid the responsibilities of the Christian life; it's given to us to fulfill the responsibilities of the Christian life."*

Author and Bible teacher, the late Jerry Bridges, explained the efficacious nature of grace in a message he titled, *"Four Essentials to Finishing Well."*

"The same apostle who said, 'I have fought the good fight. I have finished the race. I have kept the faith.' Also said in another context, 'But, by the grace of God, I am what I am.' Paul attributed all of his endurance, all of his faithfulness, to the grace of God. And so as we look at our responsibility today, I want you to keep in mind that we are able to fulfill that responsibility only by the grace of God.

Now the grace of God is often misunderstood. I think one of the most common understandings of the grace of God came from a Campus Crusade staff member when I asked a group of them one day, 'if you were to go out on your campus and just randomly select students and ask the question, 'what do you understand the grace of God to be.' One of the Crusade staff members said they would say, 'Grace is God cutting me some slack.' Grace is God letting me get away with a few things. That's the furthest thought from the grace of God.

The grace of God comes to us through Jesus Christ, but the grace of God is more than just God's kindness and benevolent feeling toward us. The grace of God is dynamic. The grace is God in action for our good. And so when the Apostle Paul said, 'By the grace of God I am what I am', **he was speaking about the empowering of the Holy Spirit that God, in His grace, supplies to each of us as we seek to live for Him.**

And so, please keep in mind as we look at our responsibilities, that we carry out those responsibilities only by the grace of God."[18]

Oswald Chambers puts it another way.

"Every time I obey, absolute Deity is on my side, so that the **grace of God** *and natural obedience coincide."*[19]

Let's consider a scripture that's often misunderstood. The following scripture is typically applied to our justification in Christ; however, the apostle is actually teaching about how the Holy Spirit enables and empowers us to overcome sin and walk in righteousness. This Divine empowering is the grace of *"God in action for our good."* Let's look at it.

*"For what the law **could not do in that it was weak through the flesh**, God did by sending His own Son in the likeness of sinful flesh, on account of sin: He condemned sin in the flesh, ⁴ that the **righteousness** [righteous deeds] **of the law** might be fulfilled in us **who do not walk according to the flesh but according to the Spirit"*** (Romans 8: 3-4).

There are two Greek words for *"righteousness"* in the New Testament. Dikaiosune, which is found about 100 times in the N.T., means equity of character. This is the righteousness that we receive in justification; God declares us righteous (dikaiosune) in Christ. Then there's dikaioma, which is found only 10 times in the N.T. This word literally means *"equitable **deeds**."* This is the word for *"righteousness"* found in the above scripture.

Furthermore, this scripture is obviously not talking about justification, because this *"righteousness"* is promised to those who *"walk according…to the Spirit."* Sound familiar? The righteousness of justification is for those who *"believe"* on Christ; the "righteous deeds" of sanctification is for those who *"walk in the Spirit."* Trying to keep the law in the strength of the flesh is impossible; however, if we walk in the Spirit, He literally gives us the grace that we need to keep the "righteous deeds" of the Law.

Now, this may confuse some people. Many Christians have misunderstood how the law relates to the Christian. Some feel that since we're not "under the law", we can ignore it altogether. No! This simply means that we're no longer under the condemnation and bondage of the Law. Those who are in Christ are set free from the Law because Christ has fulfilled the law on their behalf. However, Christ having fulfilled the law doesn't mean that we can simply shrug it off; instead, it means that we should submit to the Spirit of Christ Who dwells within us so that He can establish the "righteous deeds" of the Law in our lives.

Someone may say, *"I thought we weren't under the law."* It's true, we're not *"under"* the bondage and curse of the law (Galatians 3: 10-14), doomed to try to keep it in the strength of the flesh. Instead, God has *given* us His Holy Spirit, as well as a spiritual new nature which has the law written within it. The Holy

Spirit literally gives us the grace that we need to walk according to the righteous law that our heart's already long to obey. News flash! Murder is still a sin! Worshiping false God's is still a sin! Theft is still a sin! Adultery is still a sin! And these only scratch the surface of all the sins that God spells out in the New Testament. We're not free to sin now that we're under grace; instead, we're made free from sin by the enabling grace of God, and the power of the Holy Spirit.

Let's take two scriptures that we've already considered and put them together.

*"For sin **shall not** have dominion over you, for you are **not under law** but under grace."* This is the very same truth as, *"Walk in the Spirit, and you **shall not** fulfill the lust of the flesh. 17 For the flesh lusts against the Spirit, and the Spirit against the flesh; and these are contrary to one another, so that you do not do the things that you wish. 18 **But if you are led by the Spirit, you are not under the law** [but under the grace that the Spirit supplies]"* (Galatians 5: 16-18).

Notice the *"shall not's"*. Notice how the Holy Spirit and Grace are essentially used interchangeably. These scriptures are two sides of the same coin. God is not giving us two conflicting ways to overcome sin; He's giving us the same truth from two different angles. All grace is administered by the Holy Spirit.

So, how do we access this Spirit empowered grace. We must back up a couple of verses in Romans 6 in order to find the answer.

*"Do not let sin reign in your mortal body, that you should obey it in its lusts. 13 And do not present your members as instruments of unrighteousness to sin, **but present** [or "yield'] **yourselves to God** as being alive from the dead, and your members as instruments of righteousness to God. 14 **For** sin shall not have dominion over you, for you are not under law but under grace."* (Romans 6: 12-14).

R. A. Torrey, in his book, *"How To Obtain Fullness of Power"*, explained this scripture the following way:

*"'Yield yourselves unto God' – the whole secret is found in those words. The word translated 'yield' would be interpreted as 'present.' It means to put at one's disposal. 'Put yourselves at God's disposal' is the thought. **In other words, surrender yourselves absolutely to God** – become His property – and allow Him to use you however He wills."*[20]

Grace is imparted when self ends and faith begins. Let that sink in for a moment. *"Grace is imparted when self ends and faith begins."* This is an immutably established Truth; *"God resists the* [self-sufficient] *proud, but **gives grace** to the* [self-surrendered] *humble"* (James 4: 6). This divine principle encompasses the whole of the Christian walk. Whenever we selflessly humble ourselves before God, He gives us grace for whatever we need.

This is first true for salvation. When a person finally realizes that there is absolutely nothing good within them*selves*, and there is absolutely nothing they can do to ingratiate them*selves* to God, they will count them*selves* as utterly bankrupt, cast them*selves* down at the foot of the Cross, and utter the seven words of the penitent publican, *"God, be merciful to me, a sinner!"* To which the Lord Jesus Christ graciously responds, *"I tell you, this man went down to his house **justified** [made righteous!]"* (Luke 18: 14).

The same is true for sanctification. *"Grace is imparted when self ends and faith begins."* . Sanctification is not accomplished by us trying to wrestle with sin in an attempt to clean our lives up. It's definitely not accomplished by us cleaning up the sins that the religious *self* doesn't like, and tolerating the sins that *self* is comfortable with. We cannot attain biblical sanctification through our strategizing, scheming, psychological manipulation, or any other device manufactured by man. This is fleshly, futile, and foolish (Galatians 3: 3). Instead, sanctification is accomplished by us abandoning our own ability to clean ourselves up, and —*not sitting on our hands,* but— surrendering our*selves* by faith completely over to the Lordship of Christ. When we do so, the Lord Himself sanctifies us completely by the power of His Spirit.

> *"The reason some of us have not entered into the experience of sanctification is that we have not realized the meaning of sanctification **from God's perspective**. Sanctification means being made one with Jesus so that the nature that controlled Him will control us. Are we really prepared for what that will cost? **It will cost absolutely everything in us which is not of God.**"* —Oswald Chambers[21]

Herein lies the answer of how we obtain victory over bondage to *all sin.* It's not our victory; it's God's victory. When we try to overcome sin on our own, we are attempting the impossible. The sins are too many, and too deeply entrenched within our flesh. We cannot help but to be selective and woefully inept in our efforts at victory. However, if we give up the fight, and give ourselves over to Christ, the Savior and Sanctifier of sinners, He will do a thorough work of sanctification within our life.

So, where do we start? Does the scripture give us any direction concerning how we are supposed to yield ourselves to the Lord so as to obtain His empowering grace? It absolutely does!

*"Then Jesus said to those Jews **who believed Him**, 'If you abide in My word, you are **My disciples indeed**. ³² And you shall know the truth, and the truth shall make you free… whoever commits sin is a **slave** of sin…Therefore if the Son makes you free, you shall be free indeed"* (John 8: 31-36).

This is the life that Christ calls all believers to enter into — the life of a disciple. The call to be a disciple of Christ is a call to the consecration of ourselves to God. It's not a call to good works. It's not even a call to service. It's a call to follow Christ, surrendered to His Lordship — good works and service will follow. This is the doorway to the grace that we need in order to obtain biblical sanctification. This is the only God ordained means to being made *"free indeed"* from the *"slavery"* of sin.

*(Before we move on, allow me to make a critical insight. The reader may be wondering how we went from walking in the Spirit to overcome sin, to following Christ to overcome sin — which one is it? It's both. Before the cross, Christ called us to follow Him in His physical person. However, in John chapters 14-16 He explained that He would be sending the Holy Spirit to take His place. Therefore, the **"follow Me"** before the Cross is the same as **"walk in the Spirit"** after Pentecost. I'll explain this further in the 6th chapter.)*

After we've *"believed"* on Christ, He calls us to abide in His word as *"disciples indeed"* in order to obtain complete freedom from the slavery of sin. Now, I strongly warn you; do not allow the *"threshold Christian"* mentality to undermine this clear truth spoken by our Lord! The scripture is clear; after we've believed on Christ, we are squarely called to follow Him. *"As you therefore have received Christ Jesus the Lord, so walk **in** Him"* (Colossians 2: 6). And just as the scripture is clear concerning what it means to believe on Him for salvation, it is also clear on what it means to follow Him for sanctification.

Notice again that I've said nothing about serving Christ, or doing good works for Christ — my sole focus is on *following* Christ; there's a world of a difference. Most Christians want to put the cart before the horse. We're typically very eager to serve Jesus; however, very few of us want to surrender to Him as Lord of our lives. We're all too eager to be a busy-body Martha, but very few of us want to abide in His presence as a Mary (Luke 10: 38-42). Doing good works for Jesus has a tendency to scratch our religious itch. However, yielding to Christ so that He can do a good work within us requires the abnegation of self —

this is where most of us dig our heels in. So, our first steps on the road to sanctification must be the steps of a consecrated disciple. God Himself will perform the actual work of sanctification. He will make us *"free indeed"* from the slavery of sin.

"*Consecration is our part, sanctification is God's part.*" — Oswald chambers[22]

"*Walk in the Spirit*" is our willful consecration to Him. "*You **shall not** fulfill the lust of the flesh*" is God's power to sanctify and make us free.

"*Consecration is taking Jesus fully in exchange for our own miserable lives...The moment we consecrate ourselves to Him, He consecrates Himself to us.* ***Thereafter the whole strength of His life and love and everlasting power*** [i.e., His grace] ***is dedicated to keep and complete our commitment to Him and to make the very best and most of our consecrated lives.***" — A.B. Simpson[23]

Getting To the Root of Our Problems

The very word "*consecration*" can be very intimidating for most of us. But what exactly does it mean? The primary issue with man's methods is that they tend to focus on the branches, but they never get to the root. Consecration addresses the root of all our problems. The great evangelist Andrew Murray put it the following way:

"*We perhaps think of individual sins that come between us and God. But what are we to do with that **self-life which is all unclean — our very nature**? What are we to do with that flesh that is entirely under the power of sin? **Deliverance from that is what we need**.*"[24]

This is a major misconception within the church; we focus so much on different individual sins that we often miss the root of our sinful proclivities — the self-nature. God's goal for us is not that we should overcome a few "major" sinful vices in order to become "clean", decent people with good values. I know Muslims who are clean and decent! I know atheists who are clean and decent! God's goal is to get at that deceptively deluded self-nature within us, and replace him with the nature of Christ. But, if we're not willing to yield ourselves up to

Him, we'll be left to our own misguided understanding and efforts to contend with sin.

Trying to tussle with certain select sins is like a man who has a large weed growing in his yard. He decides that something must be done about it, so he marches up to it and looks it over. He notices one of the leaves is larger and uglier than the other leaves. In a courageous show of righteous indignation, he grabs the leaf and plucks it off! Satisfied with the results, he pats himself on the back and strolls back into the house for some well-deserved rest. It's easy for us to see the absurdity of this man's reasoning, but few understand that this is the very manner in which most Christians confront their sin. We have entire books and programs on how to master one single doggone, stupid sin! It's a mockery of truth and a first-class fraud!

This is one of the most critical lessons the Lord taught me. His Word began to cleanse away all of the unbiblical ideas that I'd had about overcoming sin. The Holy Spirit began to get to the root of all my issues — me! And as I learned to completely yield and surrender my *self* to the hands of the Vine Dresser, I watched as He snipped off my sinful branches one by one. I cannot count the number of times when I was struck with the realization that certain issues, which once were thorns in my side, hadn't even crossed my mind for months — even years! I learned to focus my eyes on the Lord and seek Him with all my heart, and He dealt with my sins...and still is! I learned from experience that *"the battle"* truly *"is the Lord's."*

I challenge you, dear reader, to completely change your paradigm about sanctification. Striving and strategizing against sin is not the answer; rather, seeking and surrendering to the Sanctifier of sinners is the answer. Our multitude of biblically compromised methods and programs for overcoming certain sins will only afford us a bootlegged rendition of patchwork sanctification. They'll *never* deliver us from sin and make us like Christ. Christ promises to make us *"free indeed"* if we abide in His word as *"disciples indeed."* He calls us to simply focus on and follow Him, and in the process, He'll deal with our sin. This is one of the biggest difficulties of the self-nature; for the self-nature is used to focusing on *itself*.

The Depraved Morality of the Self-Oriented Mind

Self is the root influence behind the sinful flesh. Self is the natural you and the natural me. It is our natural personality, our logic, our wisdom, our understanding. It is our individuality that we've obtained from Adam and Eve that believes it has *"the knowledge of good and evil."* Self is what causes us to *"turned, every one, to his **own** way."* Therefore, trying to overcome sin and live the Christian life with the wisdom and strength of our religious self-nature — in spite of how moral we become — is a fool's errand.

That's why scripture teaches that the mind must be renewed and brought into alignment with the Spirit of God. But this can be tricky. According to Paul, the fleshly mind is also bent on seemingly *good* fleshly things. Satan loves good morals and "clean livin'!" He's a strong proponent of Judeo-Christian values. It's the fleshly mind that believes good works and keeping the tenants of the law will somehow bring sanctification. The fleshly mind not only loves sin, but it also loves boasting of its own "cleanness." Cain's offering, no doubt, looked a lot more pleasant and decorative than Abel's. All of Christ's accusations against the scribes and Pharisees were in relation to their *good* works — He never accused them of any vile, fleshly sin. The self-oriented, fleshly mind cannot be trusted. That's why God tells us not to *"lean on our own understanding"* (Proverbs 3: 5-6).

The natural, fleshly mind is on a completely divergent, unbridgeable wavelength with the Spirit of God. This is why it is critical that we do not attempt to live the Christian life according to our *"carnal mind"* because it is *"enmity against God; for it is not subject to the **law of God**, **nor indeed can be**"* (Romans 8: 7). Man's understanding, even in his most wholesome thoughts, falls drastically short of God's Truth. The difference is *literally* as vast as that which was between Christ and the Pharisees! The Religious Right within the U.S. is not the model for Christlikeness; far from it — Christ is. And it is only as we seek the face of Christ — *according to the Word* — that we are made free from *all* sin and transformed into His image.

Back to Basics: The First Three Steps Toward Spirit-Filled Victory

In order to lead me to biblical, Spirit-filled victory, God had to bring me back to the simple basics of the word of God. God's way is not unique and novel. If you want unique and novel, man has a million intriguing ideas for you.

Our problem is that many of us are like the Syrian general, Naaman. He wanted the prophet Elisha to perform a visually spectacular miracle to heal his leprosy. Elisha gave him something basic and nonsensical to do. Naaman got huffed about it and stormed away. But his servant cooled him down, and persuaded him to simply obey. Obedience would require faith in what made no sense to the natural mind; nevertheless, he trusted and obeyed — and was healed.

Too many of us want God to give us a dog-and-pony show in order for us to embrace His way of doing things. We want some academic scholar to give us a logical explanation to our sin, and to provide us with some manageable steps to fix our problem. God gives us Truth — Himself — and tells us to follow Him into the uncomfortable, the unexplainable, and the unknown.

"The truth shall set you free!" This is one of the most commonly quoted biblical phrases among Christians and non-Christians alike. And just like every other Bible verse that has been denigrated to a cultural cliché, it has been torn out of context and over *misused* to the point that it's lost all of its potency. Yet this scripture in question is the very heart and soul of God's promise that He would deliver us, not simply from the penalty of sin, but from the power of sin in our lives. Let's put it back into the context where it belongs.

*"Then Jesus said to those **Jews who believed Him**, "If you abide in My word, you are My **disciples indeed**. 32 And **you shall know the truth, and <u>the truth shall make you free</u>.**" 33 They answered Him, "We are Abraham's descendants, and have never been in bondage to anyone. How can You say, 'You will be made free'?" 34 Jesus answered them, "**Most assuredly, I say to you, whoever commits sin is a <u>slave of sin</u>**. 35 And a slave does not abide in the house forever, but a son abides forever. 36 **Therefore if <u>the Son makes you free</u>, you shall be free indeed**"* (John 8: 31-34).

This is the only path to thorough, Holy Spirit empowered, victory! It is when a Christian literally gains an intimate, transformative knowledge of the *"Truth"* — Who is *"The Son"* — that they are made free from *all bondage* to *all sin*. However, we can only gain this intimate knowledge of Christ through the process of continuing in His Word as a *"disciple indeed."* Some Christians experience immediate victory, while for others it may take years, but in both cases the individual is adequately emptied of self-sufficiency and filled with the power of Christ. The Christian who reaches this stage of growth is enabled to overcome even the most deeply entrenched stronghold.

Very few Christians truly immerse themselves into what Christ's call to discipleship truly means for us, and how it relates to sanctification. Remember, to be sanctified simply means to be "set apart". Christ calls us to be *set apart* unto Himself as *"disciples indeed"*, and He performs the work of sanctification within us. Christ's universal call to discipleship is the key to the whole Christian life. It's not new, but it's true; it's not novel, but it's vital. Many may talk about discipleship with deep emotions, intensity, and sincerity (as I once did), but few truly immerse themselves into the actual reality of following Christ as a true disciple.

Unfortunately, many professed Christians have viewed Christ's call to follow Him as undesirable and too difficult. Others, in a show of profound ignorance of the Word, have dismissed it as legalism. As I mentioned in the beginning of this chapter, since sanctification does not fall within the category of doctrines necessary for salvation, it is dismissed as optional and approached haphazardly.

The very concept of being a disciple of Christ has been profoundly distorted within the minds of many modern Christians. I cannot begin to count the number of times I've spoken with and heard Christians arguing that discipleship is *"not necessary for salvation"*. The *"threshold Christian"* mentality has all but destroyed our motivation and desire to be *biblical* disciples. However, the *"threshold Christian"* fails to understand that the conversation is no longer about salvation; it's about sanctification — growth, fruitfulness, and power!

The person who refuses to follow Christ as a *"disciple indeed"* is like a young man seeking to get on the high school football team. The coach, who graciously accepts everyone on the team, immediately puts the young man's name on the roster. He's on the team! But, then the coach says, *"If you want to play, you have to read the playbook, learn the rules, and come to practice, etc."* The young man haughtily says, *"Well, did I need to do those things to get on the team? You're being legalistic! You're trying to add to my requirements for joining the team!"* So he neglects these basic fundamentals of learning the game. But when game day comes, he throws on his uniform and runs out on the field! Many Christians are being busybodies for Christ just like this young man — fumbling the ball, running in the wrong direction, and amassing penalties. And tragically, most believe they're living the *normal* Christian life!

It's like a child who's born into this world by two gracious parents. Eventually, his parents come to him and say, *"We want you to start using the potty, learning your abc's and 123's, primary colors, doing your chores, dressing yourself, manners, school, etc."* The child smugly responds, *"Well, did I need to do those things to be born? You're being legalistic! You're trying to add to my requirements for birth!"* Naturally, the child grows up to be an undisciplined, unkempt, uneducated, failure—who believes he's succeeding!

There are a million scenarios that can illustrate this basic principle of life. There are no disciplines of life—whether they be games, sports, academic, musical, theatrical, professional, or simply growing into a mature, productive adult—where we can join it freely, neglect the established training and preparation procedures, and yet leap right into "game" and expect success! Furthermore, we *cannot* make up our own rules based on our own understanding, our own feelings, and our own comfort levels, and expect to excel in *any* discipline. Yet this is what most Christians have done with the most important *discipline* that prepares us for the most complicated and difficult; rather, *impossible* undertaking a sinful being could ever pursue—being conformed into the image of Christ who is the image of the Living God!

A person *cannot* become a *"disciple indeed"* by haphazardly living the Christian life. Modern discipleship has been reduced to a few guys or gals getting together for a coffee, a meal, or an outing; talking about life, talking about sports, talking about the latest entertainment, talking about the Bible, confessing faults to an accountability partner, praying, and then parting until they meet again in a week. However, God gives us very clear, definitive principles to follow if we expect to truly follow Christ. Having been a Christian for over 20 years, and having seen countless methods of discipleship promoted in numerous churches, I've *rarely* seen it patterned soundly after Christ's command – *"deny yourself, take up your cross, and follow Me."* **This three part call provides us with the most descriptive and definitive principles for how we are to follow Christ as a *"disciple indeed"*. These are the first three steps toward Spirit-filled sanctification.**

This is how Christ trained and built up His disciples, and this is how He squarely *commanded* them to train up *every* new Christian. If final words mean anything, Christ final words should mean everything! *"Jesus came and spoke to them, saying, "All authority has been given to Me in heaven and on earth.* [19] *Go therefore and* **make disciples** *of all the nations… teaching them to* **observe** **all things** *that I have* **commanded** **you***"* (Matthew 28: 18-20).

How is it that so many of us can look at this *command* given by The One who has *"All authority…in heaven and on earth"* and dismiss it as an optional, modifiable suggestion? We show more regard to the person leading a game of "Simon Says" than we do to the *"King of Kings and Lord of Lords!"*

Renounce the satanic lie that dismisses discipleship as being unnecessary and optional. Of course it's not necessary for salvation, but the conversation is no longer about salvation, it's about sanctification! And the plain biblical truth is this: discipleship is absolutely essential for sanctification and the entire Christian walk. "**<u>Whoever desires to come after me</u>** (i.e., "whoever wants to follow Me.", "Whoever wants to grow in Me.", "Whoever wants to advance in the Christian faith."), *let him deny Himself, and take up His cross, and follow Me."* He doesn't say, *"Whoever desires to come after me, however you chose to do so is ok with me!"* Unfortunately, this is what multitudes of Christians are doing. This is what I unwittingly did for many years!

The Lord calls us to follow Him on **His terms**; therefore, His first command for prospective followers is *"deny yourself"*. The Christian who attempts to "follow" Christ without yielding to this essential first step is following Christ on their own terms, and therefore not consistently following *Him* at all. Self is still lord.

This is why many of us do not have the grace that we need to victoriously and fruitfully live the Christian life — we're not sufficiently yielded to the One Who is the Source of all enabling grace. We haven't truly denied ourselves. We haven't truly put off the old man. We haven't truly reckoned ourselves dead. We haven't given up yet. We still think there's something profitable in our own understanding and strength toward spiritual progress. There's not! God tells us to kill the old man — not to salvage the "good" parts of him — kill him! In order for God to sanctify us (i.e., set us apart to Himself), He must strip us of our fallen, corrupted self-nature! *"Grace is imparted when self ends and faith begins."*

Decisively and Resolutely Relinquish Self

Most Christians avoid Christ's unapologetic call to discipleship because the first two commands cut us right to the heart — deny yourself and take up your cross. Death must come before resurrection, and we love ourselves and this world too much to accept this.

Oswald Chambers, author of *"My Utmost For His Highest"*, wrote the following concerning how Christ's call to discipleship is essential for sanctification:

*"**Sanctification requires our coming to the place of death**, but many of us spend so much time there that we become morbid. There is always a tremendous battle before sanctification is realized — something within us pushing with resentment against the demands of Christ. When the Holy Spirit begins to show us what sanctification means, the struggle starts immediately. Jesus said, "If anyone comes to Me and does not hate . . . his own life . . . he cannot be My disciple" (Luke 14:26).*

*In the process of sanctification, the Spirit of God will strip me down until there is nothing left but myself, and that is the place of death. Am I willing to be myself and nothing more? Am I willing to have no friends, no father, no brother, and no self-interest — simply to be ready for death? **That is the condition required for sanctification**...This is where the battle comes, and where so many of us falter. We refuse to be identified with the death of Jesus Christ on this point. We say, "But this is so strict. Surely He does not require that of me." Our Lord is strict, and He does require that of us.*

*Am I willing to reduce myself down to simply "me"? **Am I determined enough to strip myself of all that my friends think of me, and all that I think of myself? Am I willing and determined to hand over my simple naked self to God? Once I am, He will immediately sanctify me completely**, and my life will be free from being determined and persistent toward anything except God (see 1 Thessalonians 5:23-24).*

*When I pray, "Lord, show me what sanctification means for me," He will show me. **It means being made one with Jesus. Sanctification is not something Jesus puts in me — it is Himself in me** (see 1 Corinthians 1:30)."* [25]

This is what God calls us to — being stripped of self and wholly separated unto Christ. This Calvary road cannot be taken in the strength of impassioned emotions and deep sincerity — these can sway with the winds of life's circumstances. This road can only be taken by resolutely, committed faith. An unquestioned, resolved belief that *"you died, and your life is hidden with Christ in God"* (Colossians 3: 5). An unquestioned, resolved belief that your entire soul — mind, will, and emotions — must to be retaught, redirected, and renewed according to every Word that proceeds out of the mouth of God. An unquestioned, resolved belief that this world is not your home, and anything in it that draws you away from Christ must be on the chopping block. An unquestioned, resolved belief that you are a new, resurrected, creature in Christ, and your allegiance is to His kingdom and Lordship. *Absolute surrender to Christ.*

No More Halfhearted Efforts

Christ's call to follow Him is a package deal, not a buffet — we can't pick and choose the parts of the call that we like and snub what we don't like. We cannot obey one or two aspects of the call and expect to grow into a flourishing, strong, overcoming Christian. What's my point?

If I deny myself without taking up my cross and following Christ, I become a self-absorbed, navel-picking, ascetic. If I take up my cross without the other two I become an antisocial, legalistic, party-pooper. And if I follow Christ without the first two I become a wavering, stumbling, self-willed, double-minded, worldly, self-righteous, *mis*representative of Christ. Many Christians are trying to do this last one and getting these very results. If we simply followed Christ according to His three part call, instead of using Him as a life-coach for our self-diagnosed, compartmentalized personal problems, *all* of our other problem areas would be resolved.

It's become trendy in popular Christianity to call ourselves "Christ followers", and this is great! But if we're not also self-deniers and cross-bearers, we're fooling ourselves! And, although many Christians passionately embrace the *idea* of denying self and taking up the cross, the depths of what this truly means has been all but lost in the materialistic, self-centered western church.

It is imperative that we earnestly seek to embrace and surrender to every aspect of Christ's call to follow Him as *"disciples indeed"*. No more halfhearted efforts; it's all or nothing! The reason for this is because the three part call of Christ directly challenges the 3 great enemies within our stronghold. Consider the following insights: In the chapter containing *my story* I defined what a personal stronghold is. There are three enemies that we contend with when trying to overcome a stronghold in our life: the flesh, the world, and Satan.

The three part call of Christ directly confronts the three enemies of our soul. *"Deny yourself"* confronts the flesh. *"Take up your cross"* confronts the world. And *"follow Me"* confronts the Devil. I'll explain each one of these in detail in the following chapters. Again, the call is a package deal; you cannot leave a single part out if you expect to get thorough, solid, and consistent victory over your strongholds.

Fear Not, For **I AM** With You

I believe it's needful here to add a little comfort and grace to this call. Although the Lord is very direct and unapologetic in what He demands of those who follow Him, He is still a God who is longsuffering, gentle, and patient. He understands our weaknesses and has identified with every one of them. He knows how deeply entrenched we are in our own understanding and the ways of the world.

The process of conforming a sinner into the likeness of Christ will not be finished overnight—nor in a lifetime. When a person commits to follow Christ, God commits to helping them every step of the way. *"Draw near to God, and He will draw near to you"* (James 4: 8). It's like a father helping his toddler learn to walk. He stays close by, constantly encouraging the child's progress, and lifting him up every time he falls.

God doesn't expect us to run overnight. The disciples followed Christ for three years before they were sent out as apostles. Paul spent three years alone with God in Arabia before he exploded on the scene in the power of the Holy Spirit—and even still, none of them arrived. God is a wise Father who knows how to start us out on the rudimentary levels that best suit us. But it starts with us committing ourselves to taking the first three steps—deny yourself, take up your cross daily, and follow Christ.

It's important where and how we start. If we start in the wrong direction, we'll go in the wrong direction, and we'll end up at the wrong goal.

Many Christians who start wrong end up like the individuals described by A. B. Simpson in the beginning of this chapter; *I know men who spend forty years fighting what they call their besetting sin, and on which they waste strength enough to evangelize the world."*

I started my Christian life as one of these persons. If the Lord hadn't redirected my life I would have remained in this doleful state. However, as the Lord began to retrain me in the truth, He compelled me to unlearn many of the unbiblical ideologies that have permeated much of modern Christian thought. The idea of completely surrendering myself to Christ as a *"disciple indeed"* was intimidating in the beginning; however, the more I pursued Him, the more I learned of His great compassion, patience, and enabling grace. The Lord's call to discipleship is not an arduous call, especially when our knowledge of His love for us nourishes our love for Him, and when we realize that His grace is there to help us every step of the way.

Just consider how Christ was with His disciples, and you'll know how He'll be with you. **After they committed to following him**, they still stumbled and blundered all along the way. Yet He never forsook them; on the contrary, He forsook those who *made excuses* about following Him (Luke 10: 57-62). Every once and a while, He'd rebuke them for their unbelief, but he never lingered in the past—He always helped them to press forward. Even after Peter's grievous sin of denying Him, Christ didn't expose him or rebuke him. Peter was already repentant; you don't scold a repentant person—they've already beaten themselves up enough. Christ simply asked him of his love and encouraged him to continue on. It was never a question of Christ's love for him; rather, of his love for Christ.

Ask yourself this same question: Do you love Christ? Not with a soupy, sentimental, or even passionate love. Do you love Him with a settled, resolved, sacrificial love? A love that is ready and willing to offer oneself up in order to follow hard after Him. A love that the Apostle John defines as not *"in word or in tongue, but in deed and in truth"* (1John 3: 18). Jesus said, *"If you love Me, keep My commandments"* (John 14: 15), and His first command to every believer is to follow Him as a disciple indeed—this is the *beginning* of the Christian's walk. Leaping over this and trying to live the Christian life is like a student leaping over med school and trying to do surgery. But if he goes to school, he'll be taught the basics step by step. And under the guidance of The Wise Instructor, he'll reach milestone after milestone of spiritual growth.

Surrender to God; He Knows What He's Doing

Christ's call to discipleship is very much like Mr. Miyagi's training of Daniel Larusso in the iconic film, "The Karate Kid". It may not make much sense having to do the proverbial "wax on, wax off", but once you've adequately submitted to the Lord's training, you'll be a highly-skilled warrior, able to take on and route any stronghold! God's "training" wonderfully enables us to master every issue we face, because it's literally Him overcoming in us.

Stop putting so much time and energy into trying to fix your own problems. God doesn't want us trying to fix our pet-peeve problems; He wants to fix us altogether! Chop off one branch—alcohol, drugs, anger, sex--and there are multitudes of branches still lingering. The Pharisees managed to chop off virtually all of the sinful branches in their lives, but they failed to recognize the thick trunk of proud, self-sufficient, self-righteousness they were living in. They were so busy cleaning the *"outside of the cup"* that they were blind to the foul, self-centered inside (Matthew 23: 25).

We can modify our behavior, manipulate our thought patterns, memorize particular scriptures, get biblical counsel, speak self-help mantras, get accountability partners, and the whole shebang, but it will all be in the power of the flesh. Moreover, it will never bring us into the Spirit filled life—a life of progressively growing into the likeness of Christ. The church needs to get this point!

R. A. Torrey brings this point home:

"Only when we put away our own righteousness will we find the righteousness of God…Only when we put away our own wisdom will we find the wisdom of God…And only when we put away our own strength will we find the strength of God…Emptying must precede filling. Self must be poured out so that Christ may be poured in."[26]

Never forget this essential principle: *"Grace is imparted when self ends and faith begins."*

What about you? Do you simply want God to help you with a personal, habitual sin, or do you want Him to fill you with the power of His Spirit and completely transform your life? I hope that this stirs a passion in your soul. It's my prayer that you discover *experientially* what I discovered; *"the battle is not yours, but God's"* (2 Chronicles 20: 15). And the only way that God will take up this battle on our behalf is if we get out of the way. Let's move on to the next chapter and learn what it means to *"deny yourself"*.

"I know men who spend forty years fighting what they call their besetting sin, and on which they waste strength enough to evangelize the world

Does it pay to throw away your lives? Why not have one battle, one victory and then praise God…

0 come, and leave thy sinful self forever…" __A. B. Simpson[27]

CHAPTER 4

"DENY YOURSELF"

The Making of a Conqueror

A flame began to grow within the heart of the Egyptian prince. Although he had been treated with all the pomp, privilege, and promise of royalty, his soul was bound in the chains of his kin. He was a powerful prince in the greatest kingdom on earth; certainly he could do something to relieve his people. But the *stronghold* of their situation was too massive, complex, and impenetrable. Nevertheless, when he could bear it no longer, he decided to act!

"By faith Moses, when he became of age, refused to be called the son of Pharaoh's daughter, choosing rather to suffer affliction with the people of God than to enjoy the passing pleasures of sin, esteeming the reproach of Christ greater riches than the treasures in Egypt; for he looked to the reward" (Hebrews 11: 24-26).

Watching the oppression of his own people burdened the heart of Moses so much that he attempted to deliver them with *his own strength and wisdom*. His killing of the Egyptian seems to have been an attempt to gain the trust and allegiance of the Children of Israel. Certainly, he wasn't trying to single handedly defeat the entire Egyptian kingdom! Perhaps if he could win his people over and rally them, he could insight a rebellion. But instead of gratitude and loyalty, he got their envy and contempt. Fear drove him into the backside of the desert, where for 40 years his proud self-sufficiency was crushed and humbled.

His heart was right. He chose to identify with God's people and sought to deliver them. But he attempted this feat in his own strength, on his own terms, with his own strategy. When God puts a strong conviction on our heart about a matter, it is essential that we seek Him and completely rely on His sufficiency to prevail. By the time God was finished with Moses, his regal, Egyptian trained, affluent self-sufficiency was transformed into, *"**Who am I** that I should go to Pharaoh, and that I should bring the children of Israel out of Egypt?"* (Exodus 3: 11). Now, this humbled, emptied vessel was ready for God to use him to deliver His people from the most powerful *stronghold* on earth.

"I Must Decrease…"

This principle of man decreasing in order for God to increase is played out throughout the scripture. It is essential for every battle that we face as Christians. Unfortunately, our old self is extremely stubborn and resilient. It is convinced that it can somehow help God in the battle. But the Bible clearly teaches, and multitudes of testimonies have shown, that man has to come to the end of himself before he can experience a decisive, resolute, and sustained victory over any stronghold. Most of us are used to hearing the testimonies of those who've *unwittingly*, *haphazardly* and *reluctantly* come to an end of self; however, God teaches us in His word that we are to intentionally pursue selflessness.

The Lord Jesus, no doubt, had this in mind when he uttered the first step in His call to discipleship—"deny yourself". As long as the old, fleshly self is strong, the new, spiritual self is weak. This is law of the natures within us.

To deny one's self does not mean that we simply try to resist certain sins, nor does it mean that we try to avoid certain comforts or pleasures—it goes deeper. It deals with the root and fertile soil where our sin springs up within us—the proud, fallen, spiritually confused *self*. No gardener merely plucks the leaves off of the weeds, but he pulls them up from the root. Weeds will continue to grow if the roots are not pulled; even so, sin will continue to torment us if self is not relinquished. Most Christians are constantly tearing at leaves and wondering why the weeds keep growing back.

In his classic devotional, "My Utmost for His Highest", Oswald Chambers wrote the following:

"It is not a question of giving up sin, but of giving up my right to myself, my natural independence, and my self-will. ***This is where the battle has to be fought.*** *The things that are right, noble, and good from the natural standpoint are the*

very things that keep us from being God's best. Once we come to understand that natural moral excellence [such as the external morality of the Pharisees] *opposes or counteracts surrender to God, we bring our soul into the center of its greatest battle. Very few of us would debate over what is filthy, evil, and wrong, but we do debate over what is good. It is the good that opposes the best.* **The higher up the scale of moral excellence a person goes, the more intense the opposition to Jesus Christ** [The Pharisees optimized this fact]. *"Those who are Christ's have crucified the flesh . . . ."* **The cost to your natural life is not just one or two things, but everything.** *Jesus said, "If anyone desires to come after Me, let him deny himself..."* (Matthew 16:24). *That is, he must deny his right to himself,* **and he must realize who Jesus Christ is before he will bring himself to do it** [This is key!]. *Beware of refusing to go to the funeral of your own independence.*

The natural life is not spiritual, and it can be made spiritual only through sacrifice. If we do not purposely sacrifice the natural, the supernatural can never become natural to us. There is no high or easy road. Each of us has the means to accomplish it entirely in his own hands. It is not a question of praying, but of sacrificing, and thereby performing His will."[28] — Read this again and let it sink in.

The Thorough Depravity of Self

Our self-nature is a multifaceted, complex nature. It is the root of all of who we are in our natural state. At first glance it doesn't seem all that bad — we tend to like ourselves. But, a deeper look discovers the abominable nature of the thoroughly rebellious, depraved, proud, self-centered disposition within us.

It is often taught that God is so holy that Satan couldn't even get away with the tiniest sin of lifting up his own self will. But Satan's sin was no small sin; it was the birth of the root and core of every abomination and atrocity that a creature is capable of committing. It was the deification of self. When Satan rose up and began to declare, "I will..., I will..., I will..." it was a direct affront and challenge to the sovereignty of the I AM!

To assume Satan's sin was small is to assume a lethal virus is small when it gets into the blood stream. That microscopic virus may seem small, and the subsequent symptoms of the illness may seem big, but understanding tells us that the virus is the *root* and *source* of all the vile symptoms that appear in the flesh. Furthermore, it is futile and foolish to only treat the external symptoms while ignoring the virus within. Kill the virus, and the fleshly symptoms fade and vanish away.

Satan tempted Eve with the same self-glorifying lure. He diminished God's authority by questioning His Word concerning sin, and exulted man's authority by promising that we would be like God, *"understanding good and evil."* Our first parents defied God and self-consciousness was awakened—they understood they were naked and covered themselves. Then self said within *himself, "I will ascend to the throne of my own heart. I will rule alone as sovereign there. I will reign according to my own understanding. I will be like the Most High over my own life."* From that point on it was written in scripture, *"Everyone did what was right in their own eyes."*

When we seek to follow Christ, it's imperative that He cuts right to the root of all our problems—the self. If He can extract the virus of self out of us, then He can reclaim the throne of our heart, and have greater sway and power over our lives. His goal is to draw us away from the independence of self and into a place of absolute dependence on Him*self*. The Christian who ignores or skims over this essential stage of growth and seeks to *follow Christ* is doomed to a frustrating life of perpetual blundering, stumbling, and straying. And the greater tragedy is when they become so comfortable within them*selves* that they don't even notice the problem.

Take time, dear reader, to consider this unapologetically lengthy, quote from A. W. Tozer's essential book, "The Pursuit of God"—another book that I highly recommend. Read slowly through it and let it sink in.

"There is something more serious than coldness of heart, something that may be back of that coldness and be the cause of its existence. What is it? What but the presence of a veil in our hearts? A veil not taken away as the first veil was, but which remains there still shutting out the light and hiding the face of God from us. It is the veil of our fleshly fallen nature living on, unjudged within us, uncrucified and unrepudiated. ***It is the close-woven veil of the self-life which we have never truly acknowledged…an enemy to our lives and an effective block to our spiritual progress…***

It is woven of the fine threads of the self-life, the hyphenated sins of the human spirit. **They are not something we do, they are something we are, and therein lies both their subtlety and their power.** *To be specific, the self-sins are these: self-righteousness, self-pity, self-confidence, self-sufficiency, self-admiration, self-love and a host of others like them. They dwell too deep within us and are too much a part of our natures to come to our attention till the light of God is focused upon them. The grosser manifestations of these sins, egotism, exhibitionism, self-promotion, are strangely tolerated in Christian leaders even in circles of impeccable orthodoxy. They are so much in evidence as actually, for many people, to become identified with the gospel.* **I trust it is not a cynical observation to say that they appear these days to be a requisite for popularity in some sections of the Church visible. Promoting self under the guise of promoting Christ is currently so common as to excite little notice...**

...To tell all the truth, it seems actually to feed upon orthodoxy and is more at home in a Bible Conference than in a tavern. Our very state of longing after God may afford it an excellent condition under which to thrive and grow.

Self is the opaque veil that hides the Face of God from us. It can be removed only in spiritual experience, never by mere instruction. *As well try to instruct leprosy out of our system. There must be a work of God in destruction before we are free. We must invite the cross to do its deadly work within us. We must bring our self-sins to the cross for judgment.* **We must prepare ourselves for an ordeal of suffering in some measure like that through which our Savior passed when He suffered under Pontius Pilate.**

... It is never fun to die. To rip through the dear and tender stuff of which life is made can never be anything but deeply painful. Yet that is what the cross did to Jesus and it is what the cross would do to every man to set him free.

Let us beware of tinkering with our inner life in hope ourselves to rend the veil. **God must do everything for us. Our part is to yield and trust. We must confess, forsake, repudiate the self-life, and then reckon it crucified. But we must be careful to distinguish lazy "acceptance" from the real work of God. We must insist upon the work being done. We dare not rest content with a neat doctrine of self-crucifixion.** *That is to imitate Saul and spare the best of the sheep and the oxen. Insist that the work be done in very truth and it will be done. The cross is rough, and it is deadly, but it is effective. It does not keep its victim hanging there forever.* **There comes a moment when its work is finished and the suffering victim dies. After that is resurrection glory and power, and the pain is forgotten for joy that the veil is taken away and we have entered in actual spiritual experience the Presence of the living God."**[29]

Pause and ponder.

As mentioned earlier, self has many facets to it. Its tentacles manipulate every thought process and subsequent action we engage in. So, how do we identify the self-nature? I do not attempt to give an exhaustive list of the attributes of self, but to give an overview and idea of what the self-nature is so that we can recognize it and learn what it means to deny it.

An Overview of the Self-Nature

The Apostle Paul said, *"I have been crucified with Christ; it is no longer I who live, but Christ lives in me"*, and again *"you died, and your life is hidden with Christ in God"* (Galatians 2: 20, Colossians 3: 3). Our self-nature is a residual product of our old Adamic nature. If a person has been born again, that old Adamic man is dead. Unfortunately, the fleshly hungers and carnal thought patterns are still very much alive within our self-nature.

So what's the difference between our old man who died and our present self-nature who's still alive and kicking? Our old man is like a country that has been completely defeated in war; their government has been toppled, and a formal surrender has occurred. The war with that nation is *officially* over. Our self-nature is like the scattered loyalists and insurgents who refuse to give in. Even though their country no longer belongs to them, they've dug in, and they will not surrender without a fight. Even so, even though our old man is officially dead, there are remnants of his nature entrenched within our fleshly minds and members. These fleshly insurgents will retake the government of your life if you allow them. Complacency is not an option. The Lord calls us to deny the insurgency of our self-nature so that He can reign alone on the throne of our heart. But, in order to deny our self, we must learn who our enemy is — as the old adage goes, "know your enemy".

Another way to view it is to consider a child who's grown up in an abusive home. You may remove a child from an abusive home in a moment, but it'll take years to remove the effects of that abuse from the child's mind and character. Being in a new environment may have *saved* the child from the destructive abuse of a bad parent, but it does not automatically save the child from destroying their own lives due to the effects of that abuse. Our old man is crucified with Christ the moment we're saved, but it'll take years to root out the lingering self-nature that he left behind. Even so, we must learn to identify and deny our fleshly self-nature lest we destroy our spiritual progress within this life.

What does it mean to deny yourself? First, to "deny" means to reject, put away, or disown. Self-denial can also be seen as letting go — simply refusing to hold on to the old you. To deny yourself means to *let go* of your own self-understanding, your own self-glory, your own self-strengths, your own *ideal* self-image, your own self-will, and surrendering yourself to Christ as Lord of all of who you are.

*"The weakest saint **can experience the power of the Deity of the Son of God** if once he is willing to '**let go.**' Any strand of our own energy will blur the life of Jesus. **We have to keep letting go**, and slowly and surely the great full life of God will invade us in every part, and men will take knowledge of us that we have been with Jesus."*[30] — Oswald Chambers

Let's look more closely at these different elements of self-denial.

Deny your own self-understanding: This is a critical first step. *"Trust in the Lord will all your heart, and **lean not on your own understanding**"* (Proverbs 3: 6). *"For My thoughts are not your thoughts, Nor are your ways My ways,"* says the LORD. *"For as the heavens are higher than the earth, So are My ways higher than your ways, And My thoughts than your thoughts."* (Isaiah 55: 8-9). The natural mind cannot figure out the thoughts and ways of God — in spite of the lofty PhD's it may have. Denying our limited and distorted understanding is a critical first step. It primes our hearts and minds to be open and submissive to the truth of God.

When Adam and Eve first sinned, they ate of the *"Tree of the **Knowledge of Good and Evil.**"* Ever since then man has been imprisoned to the belief that he can decide what is good or evil, what is right or wrong, what sins are "major" and which ones are "minor", and what is best for his own life — God is no longer needed. Determining and judging between good and evil is the sole prerogative of God. That's why judges in the Bible were called *"elohim"* — one of God's names. Referring to the judges in Psalm 82: 6, God said, *"You are gods."* When Adam and Eve acquired the knowledge of good and evil, God said, *"Behold, the man has become like one of Us,* [how so?] ***to know good and evil***" (Genesis 3: 22). Therefore, when we take it upon ourselves to measure and determine good and evil with our own understanding, we're usurping a prerogative that solely belongs to God.

The first thing that sin distorted within us was our own understanding of God, ourselves, and the whole creation. This fallen understanding is the cornerstone of all sin because it falls short of the truth of God and the Truth about God. And sin, by definition, means to "fall short". As long as we lean on our own understanding, we will *always* fall short of God's truth into our own *convincing* deceptions.

Furthermore, our own understanding is the basis for all our doubts. Doubts are simply inverted beliefs. We doubt God when we begin to *believe* something else besides God's plain truth. We never stop believing something. When we choose to believe one thing, we by default doubt the opposite of that thing—and vise versa. Therefore, when we believe our own understanding, we doubt God's truth—and vice versa. That's why scripture adjures us to *"trust [have faith] in the Lord with all your heart"*, and not to *"lean on your own understanding."* Notice, our own understanding is both the opposite of, and the opponent of faith.

*"Let no one deceive himself. If anyone **among you** (Christians) seems to be wise in this age, let him **become a fool** that he may become wise. ¹⁹ For the wisdom of this world is foolishness with God"* (1 Corinthians 3: 18-19). —Deny your own self-understanding.

Deny self-glory: This is the first and most insidious sin. Satan desired glory when he attempted to usurp the throne of God. Since the beginning of time, man has longed for glory, credit, worship, praise, recognition, popularity, adoration, vindication, and the like—and he'll do anything for it!. He has been deceived into believing in his own intrinsic importance. This is self-idolatry. God wants to be the I AM of our life—a constant, sovereign presence. But our pride declares within himself, "*I* AM," and God is only for circumstantial purposes such as troubles to be delivered from or blessings to be delivered.

How we respond to this truth will determine the very nature that we're walking in. Satan was a created being who sought to lift himself up in order to obtain glory. Christ was the Creator who humbled Himself down in order to identity with the feeble, frail flesh of humanity. God calls us identify with the mind of Christ (Philippians 2: 1-11). Even after being cast out of heaven and destined for the lake of fire, Satan still had a deranged lust for glory: *"All this authority I will give You, and their glory; for this has been delivered to me, and I give it to whomever I wish. ⁷ Therefore, if You will worship before me, all will be Yours"* (Luke 4: 6-

7). The *"god of this world"* was willing to give up everything for worship. Many of us go through painstaking measures to obtain the same.

We are called to lay our own desire for glory and sense of importance at the feet of the Lord. Paul said, *"… if anyone thinks himself to be something,* **when he is nothing***, he deceives himself"* (Galatians 6: 3). David captured it more poetically: *"Behold, thou hast made my days as an handbreadth; and mine age is as nothing before thee: verily every man at his* **best state** *is altogether vanity* [emptiness]*…Surely every man walks in a vain show…"* (Psalm 39: 5-6). — Deny self-glory.

Deny self-strength: This includes all forms of strength: physical strength, strength of personality, leadership strengths, social strengths, strength of status, strength of intellect, strength of resources, and so on. Man is obsessed with his own strength — especially in the church! We are desperate to give some degree of credit to the strength and ability of man. Paul, however, was the opposite of this. Consider what Paul said about his earthly strengths.

"If anyone else thinks he may have confidence in the flesh, I more so: ⁵ circumcised the eighth day, of the stock of Israel, of the tribe of Benjamin, a Hebrew of the Hebrews; concerning the law, a Pharisee; ⁶ concerning zeal, persecuting the church; concerning the righteousness which is in the law, blameless.

⁷ **But what things were gain to me** [my earthly strengths]**, these I have counted loss for Christ***. ⁸ Yet indeed* **I also count all things loss** *for the excellence of the knowledge of Christ Jesus my Lord, for whom I have suffered the loss of all things, and* **count them as rubbish** [literally *"dung"*; feces!]*, that I may gain Christ"* (Philippians 3: 4-8).

I've heard sermons on how God chose Gideon's 300 men because they were *alert and watchful* when they drank water — as if 300 *"alert and watchful"* soldiers could defeat tens of thousands of enemy soldiers! Preachers have attributed Paul's usefulness to his theological brilliance and great training in the law under Gamaliel — Paul called His credentials *"dung!"* (Philippians 3: 8). I've yet to hear the credentials of stinking fishermen trumpeted from the pulpit — Christ called four of them and one Pharisee (Paul). Others have given credit to Moses's training in Egypt as part of the reason God used him. What part of Egypt's pagan training did *God need* in order to use Moses? What training did Joseph need in order to become second to Pharaoh as ruler of Egypt? What about Daniel in Babylon and Persia?

The common denominator with all who were greatly used in the Bible is faith in the Lord God, in whom is all power and wisdom; their fleshly strengths were a matter of indifference. Sometimes God may have used their strengths, but He did not *need* them. Furthermore, He only used their strengths when they were humble enough to still give Him the glory.

"*²⁶ For you see your calling, brethren, that not many wise according to the flesh, not many mighty, not many noble, are called. ²⁷ But God has* [purposely] *chosen the foolish things of the world to put to shame the wise, and God has chosen the weak things of the world to put to shame the things which are mighty; ²⁸ and the base things of the world and the things which are despised God has chosen, and the things which are not, to bring to nothing the things that are, ²⁹ **that no flesh should glory in His presence!**"* (1 Corinthians 1: 26-29).

God does not *need* our strength in any form or fashion. If He needed it, then we could take some of the glory, and God will not share His glory with anyone. God's will is to have us stripped of all creature strength that we might be filled with His all sufficient power. It's not that we refuse to use our strengths and talents; instead, that we refuse to put our trust in them to the degree that we lose sight of our *constant dependence* on the Lord. We lay them at the feet of Christ and follow His lead as to how, when, and if they should be used. We completely surrender our profoundly insufficient 5 loaves and 2 fishes to Christ, and He *"is able to do exceedingly abundantly above all that we ask or think, according to the power that works in us"* (Ephesians 3: 20).

Many of us run in our own strength to do something for Jesus like a five year old running to cook breakfast for his parents. Although it's cute and admirable, it often ends in a big mess. The Lord calls us to take His yoke upon us, and to walk with Him at His pace and direction; not to plow our way forward in in our own strength and abilities. Our puny, finite strengths do not impress God; instead, God is moved by a trusting heart that leans wholly on Him. *"For the eyes of the LORD run to and fro throughout the whole earth, to show Himself strong on behalf of those whose heart is loyal to Him"* (2 Chronicles 16: 9).

We've read what Paul had to say about his earthly strengths; what did he have to say about his weaknesses?

*"And He said to me, "My grace is sufficient for you, for **My strength is made perfect in** [your] **weakness**." Therefore most gladly I will rather boast in my weaknesses, that the power of Christ may rest upon me. Therefore I take pleasure in*

*infirmities, in reproaches, in needs, in persecutions, in distresses, for Christ's sake. **For when I am weak, then I am strong.***" (2 Corinthians 12: 9-10). — Deny your self-strength.

Deny your own *ideal* self-image: We've become an extraordinarily vain people in western society. Our self-perception dominates our thinking and behavior at every level. It is imperative that we begin to deny our ideal self-image in order for us to start growing into the image of Christ.

We've been inundated with a host of "ideal images" within both the church and popular culture around us. Consequently, most of us are striving to obtain or maintain some image that we've come to admire or envy — a movie star, a family member, a great religious leader, popular friends, a philanthropist, a motivational leader, or one of many other popular cultural personalities. Unfortunately, *it's extremely rare* to see a Christian seeking to follow the ultimate *ideal* image, namely, Christ. We need to abide in His word to accomplish this — wearing a WWJD bracelet and following our own personal concept of Jesus won't cut it.

One of the hardest things for us to deny about ourselves is the ideal image that we've erected in our minds. Unfortunately, this is also one of the biggest barriers to the Holy Spirit filling us and transforming our character. He will not strong-arm us. However, God is not trying to change our personality; instead, He wants to transform our character and disposition so that Christ shines *through* our individual personality.

This is not accomplished by us cherry-picking a handful of scriptures that have some of Christ's *preferred* character traits, and then trying to *act* them out. Let go of the control over your own character development. God is the potter, not us. A child doesn't govern their own character development; children want to be thugs, rock stars, teen idols, and superheroes. Instead, the child is expected to *surrender* to his parent's authority, and in doing so, over time he develops good character. A thug is far from a parent's ideal for their child, yet immeasurably further is our *best* conception of ourselves compared to God's ideal for us.

Let go of what *you* envision yourself to be. If you have low self-esteem, be very cautious. This often leads to self-pity. Self-pity will drown you in your own misery, obscure reality, and quench the Holy Spirit's influence in your life. Self-pity is murmuring of the soul. It's rooted in envy, covetousness, and thanklessness; all of which are sin. "*I wish I had another person's personality,* qualities, looks, position, privileges, body, relationships, etc." When the Children of Israel murmured about their pitiful situation in the wilderness, God didn't say, "There, there. I understand. It'll be ok." —He judged them! Self-pity consumes you with the longings of the god of self, and murmurs against the true God for not giving you the life that you wanted. Now, this is not the same as casting our burdens on the Lord; He invites us to do this. Self-pity is being so absorbed with our own issues that we spurn the Lord who could resolve our issues.

Stop trying to be somebody and accept the fact that you really are a nobody—a *"vain show"*! I understand that this will not be easy, because the person with low self-esteem desperately longs to be a somebody in the eyes of the world—earnestly seek to *"let go"* of this longing. The liberation and peace you'll experience is indescribable. Then the Lord won't need to break down the man-made image that you've erected within yourself. Remember, it took God 40 years to empty Moses of his identity as prince of Egypt! Self-pity brings us into the bondage of perpetually worrying about the myriad ways that we perceive others as better, or better off than ourselves. Let it all go and pursue the fullness of your identity in Christ alone.

If you have high self-esteem, humble yourself in brokenness before the Lord. Make it your earnest pursuit to seek the face of God so that He may establish your character as He sees fit. In spite of how highly you esteem yourself, your *"self"* is still at enmity with Christ. It's just as difficult, if not more difficult, for a person with high self-esteem to grow into the image of Christ as it is for a person with low self-esteem.

You may feel, *"Well, I'm a wonderful person; many people like me. Doesn't that mean I'm shining the light of Christ?"* No! Your "wonderfulness" is not equivalent to Christlikeness. As Oswald Chambers put it; *"What a wonderful personality! What a fascinating man! Such marvelous insight! What chance has the Gospel of God through all that?"* Self-confidence (in spiritual matters) is one of the primary hindrances that keeps a person from denying self and yielding to Christ—they're too confident in their depraved self-nature! Cast off the self-deifying phrase, *"That's just how I AM!"* If how *you are* is not like *Christ is*, you're still filled with self and walking at enmity against Christ. Learn to let go of your ideal self-image and humble yourself on the wheel of the potter.

"A disciple is not above his teacher, but everyone who is perfectly trained will be like his teacher" (Luke 6: 40). — deny your ideal self-image.

Deny your own self-will: "*For I have come down from heaven, not to do My own will, but the will of Him who sent Me…I can of Myself do nothing. As I hear, I judge; and My judgment is righteous, because I do not seek My own will but the will of the Father who sent Me*" (John 6: 38, 5: 30).

Christ the Lord is our perfect example for everything that pertains to the Christian life. From start to finish the Lord's life was perfectly centered in the midst of the Father's will. He never deviated a micrometer to the right or the left, in thought, word, or deed. Now, as the risen Lord of Life, He calls us to deny our own self-will and submit to His Lordship.

The primary thing that makes denying our self-will difficult is that we don't want (will) to do it. What we *want* is for things to be done according to our will. In her devotional book, "Each New Day", Corrie Ten Boom wrote of our need to surrender our self-will to the Lord:

"So often we do not live as richly as is possible because our unwillingness to yield stands in the way. Yield! What God does not have at His disposal, He cannot sanctify. Let His will be your will, His way your way, and all insufficiency and earthly ineptitude will be met by the sufficiency of His grace.

Make me a captive, Lord, And then I shall be free; Force me to render up my sword, And I shall conqueror be. I sink in life's alarms when by myself I stand; Imprison me within Thin arms, And strong shall be my hand. – George Matheson.

Lord, make me willing to be made willing to do Your will."[31]

This is likely the most vital aspect of self-denial. This is where the battle is won or lost. The bottom line is do you actually *want* to overcome sin and become a Spirit-filled, vibrant, fruitful follower of Christ? Unfortunately, many people, just like the rich young ruler, look at the demands of Christ, and walk away discouraged because they do not want (will) to surrender to the Lordship of Christ.

"*…why do you call Me 'Lord, Lord,' and not do the things which I say?*" (Luke 6: 46). Deny your self-will.

Begin Rooting Out Self

This is not an exhaustive explanation of every aspect of self that we must learn to deny. Rather, it is an overview of the chief aspects of our fleshly selves, and what it means to deny them. Denying yourself is all about purposefully letting go of the fallen traits of the old, fleshly you, and resolutely embracing the Christ-like traits of the new, true you. It's all about putting off the *"old man"* so that we can put on the *"new man"*.

Get out of the carnal habit of saying, *"That's just how I AM!"* Many American Christians are proud of their individualism. If "how you are" is at odds with the Character of Christ, you're living according to your fallen self-nature. Stop justifying yourself and deny yourself! Learning to deny yourself will be a lifetime pursuit. The Holy Spirit will unveil to you more and more of your *self* as you yield to Him. There will be blurred graduation points as you progress to deeper levels of self-denial and Christ-like growth.

Denying Self Must Be Done Intentionally and Patiently

The key to denying yourself is not memorizing all the aspects of self — it is *slowing down and waking up*. It's learning to pause and consider the motive behind every significant thought, word, action, and endeavor. It's about learning to walk in step with Christ. We don't need to memorize every aspect of the self-nature; we just need to focus on Christ. If we live our lives *"looking unto Jesus"*, all of our self attributes that are contrary to Him will become glaringly apparent. Focusing on our self-nature is just as unproductive and detrimental as focusing on our sin.

The more that we come to know Him — the truth — the more we'll see aspects of our *self* that are not like Him. This is where the battle must be fought and won. Will I stubbornly say, "Well, that's just how I am?" Will I lazily slouch back into my comfortable, self-oriented way of thinking? Or, will I deny myself and surrender to Christ? It is recognizing that God doesn't think like us; therefore, our common sense may not always be right. Learn to slow down. Jesus was never in a rush, and he never operated according to his own *self-centered,* common sense — and no doubt He had a lot more sense than all of us.

The world prizes assertive, quick-thinkers—people who are fast on their feet. We love to exude the image that we have it all together. Common sense is king in our culture, but "common sense" is often merely an acceptable phrase for our *"own understanding."* God wants us to slow down and consider His Truth at every turn. This is how Jesus lived. We are no longer earthly creatures and citizens of this world; we're new creatures in Christ and citizen of New Jerusalem. Learning to live on earth according to the Spirit of God will take time and commitment. No baby began sprinting the moment they learned to walk. We are learning to walk according to an entirely new nature—*"See then that you walk circumspectly* [carefully]*, not as fools but as wise"* (Ephesians 5: 15).

Don't be like Martha, anxiously busying herself to do something for Jesus; instead, be like Mary who *"sat at Jesus' feet and heard His word"* (Luke 10: 39). The disciples spent three years in training, totally yielded to the Lord, before they became apostles. We never read of them huddling together and saying, "Hey, guys, let's go do something for Jesus."—they always followed close behind Him and waited on His direction. A disciple is a learner, and learners do not carelessly rush forward without looking to their Teacher. But once you've learned to walk close to Him, and have become more acquainted with His truth and sensitive to His voice, life's decisions, great and small, will become more fluid.

We are too fast paced, preoccupied, self-assured, and confident. Many of us casually cruise through life in the comfortable assurance of our own understanding. We've established appropriate, compartmentalized religious times for God, but we've given *self* lordship over all the other areas of our life. The Holy Spirit's power and victory over sin cannot be realized within us as long as we are nonchalantly walking through life according to the whims of self. This was the whole purpose of the Lord sending the Holy Spirit; that He might reign unrivaled within us. And He will not usurp the throne of our heart; we must fully surrender our *self* to Him.

A B Simpson, the founder of the Christian and Missionary Alliance and a friend of A. W. Tozar put it the following way:

"This definite, absolute and final putting off of ourselves in an act of death is something we cannot do ourselves. It is not self-mortifying, but it is dying with Christ. Nothing can do it but the cross of Christ and the Spirit of God.

The church is full of half-dead people who have been trying to slay themselves for years and have not had the courage to strike the fatal blow. **Yet if they would just put themselves at Jesus' feet and let Him do it, there would be accomplishment and rest.**" [32]

Our problem is not whether we attempt to mortify ourselves — that's impossible. The sticking point with us is abiding in the presence of our Lord and watching as our fleshly self pleads and begs for recognition and fulfillment. It's unspeakably painful to stand by and watch as your self-nature is gasping for air and clinging to life. Do not give him aid — for then you will only be helping yourself. Let him die. Let yourself die. Deny him his yearnings and do not show mercy to yourself for the excruciating pain. It will be a death in the truest sense of the word, but afterward, it will be a glorious resurrection of indescribable rest, peace, joy, and power — I tell you what I know.

The End of Self

Do you want to experience a true revival in your life? The first line of God's great promise for revival says, *"if My people who are called by My name will humble themselves…"* (2 Chronicles 7: 14). God always begins the transformation of a life by getting self out of the way. Are you ready to deny yourself? Don't expect it to be accomplished in one dynamic act of surrender. Denying self will be a lifetime pursuit — never rest content as if you've arrived. Once you've come to an end of yourself in one area, the Holy Spirit will give light on yet another self-oriented disposition. Remember, don't attempt to wrestle with your self-nature; rather, let it go — surrender it. Earnestly seek the Lord and yield yourself to His providential refining; you'll see yourself more clearly through the light of His person.

But Christ doesn't only call us to deny our self — this only addresses our inward fleshly disposition, but it does not fully address our outward lusts. Let us now turn from looking at the problem within to looking at the problem without. Our stronghold is inhabited by three enemies: our selfish flesh, the lusts of the world, and the deceptions of the Devil. Our selfish flesh, in and of itself, is lustful; however, the chief *objects* of our lusts are found in the corrupted *world* around us. In order to overcome this second enemy we must take up our cross. We'll explore this in the next chapter.

CHAPTER 5

"TAKE UP YOUR CROSS"

A Resident of Babylon, but a Citizen of Zion

As the young captive approached the city walls he was awed by the magnificent hanging gardens. But his wonder was swiftly blanketed with a heavy grief over the destruction of his homeland and desecration of the once glorious temple of the Living God. He and several other young men were selected, washed, emasculated, and prepared for the king's service. What would be expected of him? How could he worship and serve his God while subjugated under a godless king in an utterly pagan land?

Will he be asked to commit vile acts? Will he be forced to bow to idols? No. Not yet. For now, all he was required to do was to eat a daily portion of the king's food and drink. Many compromised with this seemingly harmless diet; it wasn't a "major" sin. Besides, if they didn't obey, it could cost them their life—it wasn't worth it. However, for Daniel and three others, this compromise was too great, even under the threat of death.

Daniel's heart was not in Babylon; it was dead to Babylon but fully alive to Jerusalem. No pleasure in this country could satisfy his soul. The dainties of Babylon could not supplant his devotion to Jerusalem, and death would only free his soul to rest with his fathers. In spite of his trial of captivity, this consecrated devotion was the signature of Daniel's life from youth to old age.

The wisdom that God instilled within him always eclipsed the absurd superstitions and incantations of Babylon's mystics. His devotions ascended like a rainbow from His open window, over the cesspool of Babylon's abominations, and descended into the city of the Great King. He was known and respected, yet separate from the close company of pagans — he was never unequally yoked. Whenever a mysterious issue arose, Daniel was often called upon to reflect the light of the Divine into the dark confusion of Babylon's world. Daniel lived as a citizen of Jerusalem in the kingdom of Babylon. Daniel's was the life of a cross bearer.

What Does It Mean To Take Up Our Cross?

When Jesus commands aspiring followers to take up their cross, what exactly does He mean? I've learned that taking up one's cross has three primary elements: 1. Bearing our cross by being crucified to this present world. 2. Bearing the reproach and scorn of the cross that results from living crucified to the world unto Christ. 3. Bearing our cross through times of suffering — not just suffering — *bearing our cross* through suffering. This means that we faithfully respond to and endure the trial just as Christ would.

The cross of suffering plays a pinnacle role in the development of Christ-like character within the believer. Consider how the Apostle Paul was crucified with Christ during his times of suffering, and in doing so manifest the character of Christ.

"We are hard-pressed on every side, yet not crushed; we are perplexed, but not in despair;[9] *persecuted, but not forsaken; struck down, but not destroyed —* [10] ***always carrying about in the body the dying of the Lord Jesus, that the life of Jesus also may be manifested in our body.*** [11] ***For we who live are always delivered to death for Jesus' sake, that the life of Jesus also may be manifested in our mortal flesh"***
(2 Corinthians 4: 8-11).

Notice Paul's response to suffering; *"always carrying about in the body the dying of the Lord Jesus."* He bore his cross through suffering. Furthermore, suffering, in and of itself, is not the cross; *it's our Christ-like response to suffering that is the cross.* This is the key factor that determines whether suffering makes us better or bitter. Paul patiently bore his cross through suffering; therefore, he was made better, i.e., like Christ—"*that the life of Jesus also may be manifested in our body.*" Trials are literally like refining fires that separate the impure dross of self from the pure silver of Christlikeness.

However, growing into the likeness of Christ isn't the only benefit that comes through bearing our cross through a trial. As a person bears their cross through a trial they're also simultaneously freed from sin. The Apostle Peter reveals to us how the cross of suffering delivers us from sin.

"*Therefore, since Christ suffered for us in the flesh* [the cross]*, arm yourselves also with the same mind* [i.e., take up *your* cross of suffering]*, **for he who has suffered in the flesh has ceased from sin**, ² that he no longer should live the rest of his time in the flesh for the lusts of men, but for the will of God. ³ For we have spent enough of our past lifetime in doing the will of the Gentiles — when we walked in lewdness, lusts, drunkenness, revelries, drinking parties, and abominable idolatries. ⁴ In regard to these,* **they think it strange that you do not run with them** [the cross of separation often coincides with cross of suffering] *in the same flood of dissipation, speaking evil of you*" (1 Peter 4: 1-4).

These scriptures do not even scratch the surface of all that the cross of suffering does for the spiritual development of a believer. However, we cannot manufacture our own periods of suffering—providence determines our trials. Nevertheless, we must be vigilantly resolved to take up our cross when trials come, so that we can learn the appointed lessons and receive the maximum benefit of spiritual growth during those times.

Unlike the cross of suffering, which is dependent upon unexpected, haphazard trials, we can and must take up the cross of separation at all times. Therefore, in this chapter I'm only going to cover the cross of separation. The cross of separation is essential to gaining victory over sin. This book is devoted explaining what *we are called to do* in the process of sanctification—God doesn't call us to manufacture our own trials. Furthermore, I assure you of this; if you embrace what it means to take up the "cross of separation", you will be primed and ready to bear the "cross of suffering" through any trial. Indeed, suffering is one of God's chief means of *separating* us from our attachments to this world.

Before we go on, it's important to connect how denying self and taking up our cross work together to enable us to overcome sin. Remember, self is the root of all the sin that springs up within us. Denying self progressively kills the single "virus" of all of our various sinful tendencies. However, what good is it to kill the virus if we remain in an environment that is infested with that very same virus? Our fleshly self-nature experiences the draw of temptation *from within*; however, the source of our temptations predominantly come from the innumerable snares and lures of the world around us. Denying self confronts the *felt* temptations within; taking up our cross confronts the *source* temptations without. Together, they provide us with a powerful resistance against any sin. And it's not merely that our resistance grows stronger, but our desire to sin becomes profoundly weaker.

Take Up the Cross of Separation

The Apostle Paul best summarized the "cross of separation" in Galatians 6: 14: "*God forbid that I should boast except in the cross of our Lord Jesus Christ, by whom the* **world has been crucified to me, and I to the world**." To take up one's cross is to embrace and surrender to the fact that we have died to this world.

Jesus expressed this same truth in His familiar three part call:

"*Then Jesus said to His disciples, "If anyone desires to come after Me, let him deny himself, and take up his cross, and follow Me. ^{25} For whoever desires to save his life will lose it, but whoever loses his life for My sake will find it. ^{26} For what profit is it to a man if he* **gains the whole world**, *and loses his own soul*" (Matthew 16: 24-26)?

And again, the same idea is found in John's Gospel.

"*Most assuredly, I say to you, unless a grain of wheat falls into the ground and dies, it remains alone; but if it dies, it produces much grain. ^{25} He who loves his life will lose it, and* **he who hates his life in this world** *will keep it for eternal life*" (John 12: 24-25).

In both cases it is the person who loses their life—embraces the crucifixion of the cross—who turns from the world to follow Christ. The person who tries to *save* their life is the one who is holding on to this world. These are the two options that are set before us. Either the person tries to save their life by seeking their purpose, sufficiency, and fulfillment within this world, or they lose their life by allowing themselves to be crucified to this world and finding their purpose, sufficiency, and fulfillment in Christ. The Apostle Paul chose the latter.

There was nothing inside of this world that appealed to Paul more than following hard after his Lord—the world was crucified to him. And there was nothing in Paul that yearned after the things of this world more than the things of his God—he was crucified to this world. Paul could say with the psalmist, *"Whom have I in heaven but You? And there is none upon earth that I desire besides You. My flesh and my heart fail; But God is the strength of my heart and my portion forever"* (Psalm 73: 25-26). Though Paul's body was in "Babylon", his heart was in New Jerusalem, and it showed by the things that he treasured most.

Moses was a cross bearer as well. *"By faith Moses, when he became of age, refused to be called the son of Pharaoh's daughter, ²⁵ choosing rather to **suffer affliction with the people of God than to enjoy the passing pleasures of sin**, ²⁶ esteeming the <u>reproach of Christ</u>* [the cross] *greater riches than the treasures in Egypt* [the world]; *for he looked to the reward.²⁷ **By faith he forsook Egypt***, *not fearing the wrath of the king; for he endured as seeing Him who is invisible"* (Hebrews 11: 24-27).

Unfortunately, the concept of the cross in the modern Church has been greatly distorted. We still speak of taking up our cross, but we've become very adept at using the right words, yet profoundly inept at discerning the proper meaning and application of the words.

*"All unannounced and mostly undetected there has come in modern times a new cross into popular evangelical circles. It is like the old cross, but different; **the likenesses are superficial, the differences fundamental**… The new cross is not opposed to the human race; rather, it is a friendly pal, and if understood aright, it is the source of oceans of good clean fun and innocent enjoyment. It lets Adam live without interference. His life motivation is unchanged; he still lives for his own pleasure, only now he takes delight in singing choruses and watching religious movies instead of bawdy songs and drinking hard liquor. The accent is still on enjoyment, though the fun is now on a higher plane morally, if not intellectually…*

*The new cross does not slay the sinner, it redirects him. It gears him into a cleaner and jollier way of living and saves his self-respect… Among the plastic saints of our times Jesus has to do all the dying and all we want is to hear another sermon about His dying. We want to be saved but we insist that Christ do all the dying. No cross for us, no dethronement, no dying. We remain king within the little kingdom of Man-soul and wear our tinsel crown with all the pride of a Caesar; **but we doom ourselves to shadows and weakness and spiritual sterility**."* —Tozer[33]

To further understand what it means to take up one's cross, we must consider what transpires during the actual event of a person bearing their cross to the place of crucifixion. When the condemned criminal bears up under that wooden cross beam, he realizes one thing above all else—his life is over in this *world*. He is a dead man walking. Everything in this world that once seemed important to Him is now obscured under the shadow of Golgotha. Though surrounded by scoffers, mockers, and revilers, he presses on through the humiliation and scorn—his life no longer belongs to him. It is the will of the King that he be crucified; therefore, he must indeed be crucified.

However, although the crucifixion of Rome was devoid of hope, the crucifixion in Christ is overflowing with hope and unspeakable joy—for it is always followed by a glorious resurrection. Furthermore, taking up one's cross daily, in and of itself, becomes an adventure of the inner man breaking free of the bonds of this world in order to soar at higher spiritual altitudes. When a soul captures sight of the *"joy that is set before him"*, the weight of the cross is lifted, and the road to Calvary is leveled.

In Romans 12: 1-2 we, again, see how the cross confronts conformity to this world.

"I beseech you therefore, brethren, by the mercies of God, that you present your bodies a living sacrifice, **holy***, acceptable to God, which is your reasonable service.* ² *And do not* **be conformed to this world,** *but be transformed by the renewing of your mind, that you may prove what is that good and acceptable and perfect will of God."*

We typically picture an animal on an alter when we read this scripture. Animal sacrifices are not our chief example; Christ is. Animals are *forcefully* slain then placed on an altar. Jesus said, *"I lay down My life that I may take it again.* ¹⁸ *No one takes it from Me, but I lay it down of Myself"* (John 10: 17-18). Christ presented Himself as a *"living sacrifice"* when he voluntarily bore His cross to Calvary and submitted Himself to a brutal execution. We are called to do the same.

Now, notice the connection; the offering of ourselves as a living sacrifice is a necessary prerequisite to overcoming conformity to the world. The signature evidence of this *"living sacrifice"* is that it makes us *"holy"*—separated from the influence of the world. This is the *"cross of separation."* If we no longer allow our minds to be conditioned by the world, but instead we devote ourselves more wholly to Christ and His truth, our minds will be renewed and our lives will be *"transformed"* into the likeness of Christ. It's that simple.

Jesus, **bearing his cross***, went forth to suffer without the gate. The Christian's reason for leaving the camp of the world's sin and religion is not because he loves to be* singular, but because Jesus did so; and the disciple must follow his Master. Christ was "not of the world:" **his life and his testimony were a constant protest against conformity with the world**… *Jesus would have his people "go forth without the camp"* **for their own sanctification.** <u>**You cannot grow in grace to any high degree while you are conformed to the world.**</u> —Spurgeon[34]

And, again.

"*One cannot travel two roads at once-the way of the* **cross** *and the way of the* **world***. We are not going to see much revival until we decide which road we are going to travel*" — Vance Havner[35]

Waking Up To the Hidden Snares All Around Us

The cross means sacrifice. It is a willingness to offer up everything that in any way hinders or cripples our full surrender to the Spirit of God within us. Does this mean that Christ expects us to sell all of our belongings, sever every relationship, and move into some obscure monastery in the hills? Of course not. God doesn't call us to give up things just for the sake of giving up things—that's foolish. What it means is that everything in this fallen world *that compromises our faith* is on the chopping block. Nothing's sacred! Everything's on the table— even *"your only son Isaac"* (Genesis 22: 2).

In 1 Corinthians 6: 12, Paul teaches that "*All things are lawful for me, but all things are not helpful. All things are lawful for me, but I will not be brought under the power of any.*" In other words, I will not allow anything, however *"lawful"* it may be, to have a domineering influence or sway in my life.

This is important because there are many "things" in this world that make us vulnerable to sin. Jesus said, "*If your right eye* **causes** *you to sin, pluck it out and cast it from you; for it is more profitable for you that one of your members perish, than for your whole body to be cast into hell.* [30] *And if your right hand* **causes** *you to sin, cut it off and cast it from you; for it is more profitable for you that one of your members perish, than for your whole body to be cast into hell*" (Matthew 5: 29-31).

There are two important principles here. One is that sin is so destructive that we should be willing to take severe measures in order to overcome it. However, He's obviously not encouraging self-mutilation. The other is that there are *seemingly harmless things* in our lives that *"cause"* us to sin, and even something as treasured as our proverbial "eye" or "hand" should not be left off the chopping block. This is an important point to remember. *Christ is not calling us to wrestle with sin; instead, He's calling us to seek out and eliminate the things that make us vulnerable to sin.* Many Christians already know this. However, knowing the lingo is not enough. We must diligently seek to turn the rhetoric into reality by examining our lives and seeking out what things make us vulnerable to sin.

Everything in this world—good, evil, and neutral—is arranged and orchestrated by the god of this world (Satan) in a manner to keep our hearts and eyes earthbound and spiritually obtuse. The apostle John said it best: "*We know that we are of God, and* **the whole world lies under the sway of the wicked one**" (1John 5: 19). Let that sink in. God has allowed Satan to have full sway—under His over-ruling, sovereign providence—over every facet of this world.

The most innocent, harmless "thing" in this world can be—and often is—used to draw comfortable Christians away from Christ into a harmless routine where they live out the rest of their days as tasteless salt, in useless, barren bliss.

This is one of the most important lessons that I learned—pinpointing the "harmless" things in this world that made me vulnerable to my sin and crucifying them. Picture your particular sin as a spider, and many of the "harmless", worldly influences in your life as the spider's web. Most of us are intent on avoiding the spider, yet we're often blind to the fact that we're spending large amounts of time playing in its web. A web cannot hurt you, but it can entangle you. Before we know it, we often find ourselves unwittingly tangled in some harmless worldly engagement, and the spider—the sin—is darting toward us. This is one of the Tempter's primary schemes; gently interweave his undiscerning prey within a seemingly harmless web of worldly things. A life that is filled with the world cannot be filled with Christ.

We cannot overcome bondage to sin if we do not allow ourselves to be crucified to this world. The whole world is under the sway of the Devil, so as long as any part of this world has sway over us, we too are vulnerable to the Devil's sway. Are you ready to be crucified to this world? Are you ready to be sanctified — literally *separated?* Oswald Chambers challenges us with this sobering truth:

> *"When we pray, asking God to sanctify us, are we prepared to measure up to what that really means?* **We take the word sanctification much too lightly. Are we prepared to pay the cost of sanctification? The cost will be a deep restriction of all our earthly concerns, and an extensive cultivation of all our godly concerns.** *Sanctification means to be intensely focused on God's point of view. It means to secure and to keep all the strength of our body, soul, and spirit for God's purpose alone. Are we really prepared for God to perform in us everything for which He separated us? And after He has done His work,* **are we then prepared to separate ourselves to God just as Jesus did?** *"For their sakes I sanctify Myself . . ." (John 17:19). The reason some of us have not entered into the experience of sanctification is that we have not realized the meaning of sanctification from God's perspective.* **Sanctification means being made one with Jesus so that the nature that controlled Him will control us.** *Are we really prepared for what that will cost?* **It will cost absolutely everything in us which is not of God.**"[36]

There are hidden snares all around us in this world. Most of us are walking in darkness, stumbling through life, utterly oblivious to them. Worse yet, when exposed in the light, we often shrug them off as inconsequential. We have a romanticized idea of spiritual warfare. With a flexed chest and a deepened voice, we dramatically speak of the armor of God that allows us to defeat the spiritual evils that seek to snare, deceive, trip up, and destroy us. But, this posturing is nothing more a dramatized fiction rehearsed by generation of Christians who've lost the ability to distinguish theater from real life. We have a very real Enemy who incessantly seeks to destroy us. We live in his world. We are squarely commanded to *"Be sober, be vigilant; because your adversary the devil walks about like a roaring lion, seeking whom he may devour"* (1 Peter 5: 8). **If you believe this, don't boldly say it — boldly obey it.**

So, what exactly is the world? A common response to this question is that "The world means *the world system*." This is an utterly meaningless phrase! I have no idea what it means! It's a vague, ambiguous phrase that's subject to countless interpretations. It's a nifty *nutshell* answer that gives us the appearance that we know what we're talking about. It provides us with a false sense of understanding; if we can quote an impressive definition or stick a label on something, we assume that we have a grasp of it. Tozer wrote about this tendency of ours in a work he titled "Empty Words". Evangelicalism has countless "empty words" that we're very keen at parroting, but that are no more real to us than the proverbial man in the moon. Did God leave something as serious as the world up for just anyone's interpretation? I don't think so. Let's take a closer look at the world.

Moving forward, we're going to consider 3 aspects of the world: the **things** of the world, **people** of the world, and the **philosophies** of the world. After this we're going to explore how we are to practically prepare and position ourselves to gain victory over the world.

The Things of the World

The "things of the world" is a broad category, but I'm going to narrow it down to the tangible things that we see and experience all around us. Consider the following scriptures:

*"Do not **love** the world or the **things in the world**. If anyone loves the world, the love of the Father is not in him.* ¹⁶ *For all that is in the world – the **lust** of the flesh, the **lust** of the eyes, and the **pride** of life – is not of the Father but is of the world.* ¹⁷ *And the world is passing away, and the lust of it; but he who does the will of God abides forever"* (1 John 2: 15-17).

And again,

*"Where do wars and fights come from among you? Do they not come from **your desires for pleasure** that war in your members?* ² ***You lust** and do not have. **You murder and covet** and cannot obtain. You fight and war. Yet you do not have because you do not ask.* ³ *You ask and do not receive, because you ask amiss, **that you may spend it on your pleasures**.* ⁴ *Adulterers and adulteresses! Do you not know that **friendship with the world is enmity with God? Whoever therefore wants to be a friend of the world makes himself an enemy of God**. Or do you think that the Scripture says in vain, "The Spirit who dwells in us yearns jealously"* (James 4: 1-4)?

Notice first that James and John leave no buffer zone – there is a clear line of distinction between living for God and living for the world. The two cannot be reconciled. Remember, Christ's call to discipleship puts us in direct opposition to the world. God doesn't "cross-over" into the world in order to convince people like Him.

Secondly, **it's vital to understand that the "world" and "covetousness" are intrinsically bound to one another. They're inseparable. The world, alone, is not the issue; it is our lust for the things of the world that is the issue. We cannot divorce the subject of the "world" from the lusts (or covetousness) of the world. Therefore, in order to be** *crucified to the world* **we must confront covetousness.**

Worldly covetousness severs our fellowship with God. But unlike other sins, since the objects of our covetousness are typically not sinful, we tend to continue in our worldliness, oblivious to the fact that our fellowship with God has been severed (like the Laodiceans in Revelation 3: 14-20). Money is not sinful; the love of money is. Since God is the source of our fruit and our power, how can we ever expect to obtain victory and fruitfulness as long as the things of this world are wedged between us and our God?

Taking up our cross and being crucified to this world is no minor, optional matter; it is absolutely essential for every Christian. The above scriptures give extremely serious and sobering warnings about the world. That very few western church leaders preach against the world *with the same intensity that Christ and the apostles did* is both an obvious and disturbing fact. How is it that western Christians so casually tread where the Apostles spoke with sobering urgency?

The American Dream has become the model for western Christianity; we're no longer *"sojourners and pilgrims"* – we've settled down. I remember hearing a radio program where a "Christian" author declared that his goal was to make Christians *"disciples of capitalism"*! We invest more time, energy, money, and passion in fighting for the Kindgom of America and Judeo-Christian values, than we do the *"Kingdom of God and **His** righteousness"* (Matthew 6: 33)! We've forgotten that we're here on a *heavenly visa,* and that our loyalty belongs to another Kingdom.

God says if we're a *"friend"* of the world we make ourselves an *"enemy of God"*; this is serious! So why is the "world" so misunderstood within the church? Why aren't we earnestly seeking to recognize the world and renounce it like the *faithful* church has done throughout history?

These above scriptures speak of the *"things"* and *"pleasures"* of this world that we covet. Anything in the world can be made into an idol. Idolizing a television set is just as destructive as idolizing a carved image of an imaginary god. God doesn't care what idol we commit spiritual adultery with; *"The Spirit who dwells in us* [still] *yearns jealously."* God is a jealous God. The idolatry of the Old Testament is equivalent to the worldly covetousness of the New Testament (Colossians 3: 5). And just like the children of Israel continually took idolatry lightly, the modern church has taken worldly covetousness lightly.

Worldly Covetousness: God's Chief Rival To The Throne of Our Heart

It's impossible to serve both God and worldly things. *"Do not lay up for yourselves* **treasures on earth***, where moth and rust destroy and where thieves break in and steal;* [20] *but lay up for yourselves* **treasures in heaven***, where neither moth nor rust destroys and where thieves do not break in and steal.* [21] **For where your treasure is, there your heart will be also** [i.e., your covetous, idolatrous devotion]…*No one can serve two masters; for either he will hate the one and love the other, or else he will be loyal to the one and despise the other.* **You cannot serve God and mammon** [wealth & things]*"* (Matthew 6: 19-21, 24).

The *heart* is the principle reason for why we must be crucified to this world. Worldly covetousness is the chief rival that contends with God for the heart of man. That bears repeating: ***worldly covetousness is the chief rival that contends with God for the heart of man.*** Remember what James and John said — the two cannot mix. God desires to reign unrivaled on the throne of our heart. It's not a question of whether something in the world is harmless or not; the question is, does it have more lordship over our life than Christ does? If it does, it is an idol — an idol just as abominable a Baal, for it turns us against the God we claim to serve and makes us His *"enemy!"* God takes this sin seriously; listen to Paul:

"But now I have written to you **not to keep company with anyone named a brother***, who is sexually immoral, or* <u>covetous</u>*, or an idolater, or a reviler, or a drunkard, or an extortioner –* **not even to eat with such a person***"* (1 Corinthians 5: 11).

The knee-jerk thought of the typical Christian is, *"Not even eat with the person? This doesn't seem Christ-like."* Such thinking is a product of *our "own understanding"* and *"knowledge of good and evil."* A clear-eyed look at truth often reveals a stark contrast between God's truth, and the religious norms that we've gotten comfortable with. However, although man changes, God doesn't change.

So let's consider the basic clarity of this scripture without kicking against it with our own understanding. The scripture above commands us not to company with, or even eat with an unrepentant, covetous person who calls himself a *"brother"*. How do we know that this scripture is referring to those who are unrepentant? For one, the Bible is replete with commands to forgive the repentant, and warns of severe consequences for unforgiveness. Furthermore, the context is speaking of a man who was *unrepentantly* living in adultery with is father's wife. In 2 Corinthians the man repentant and was restored.

However, the primary point that we must draw from this scripture is how seriously the Lord takes worldly covetousness. Within the western church, covetousness is rarely even classified as a *miner* sin; it's often not even recognized as sin at all! The American Dream has become so enmeshed within the western church that covetousness not only seems normal; it seems right!

Most Christians are used to the covetousness described in the Ten Commandments—an unrighteous, deliberate longing within one's heart. However, the covetousness mentioned in the above verse does not mean to covet *within one's heart*. There are two words for covetousness in the New Testament (Epithumeo and Pleonektes in the Greek); one is covetousness within the heart, and the other is covetous behavior. This verse is describing covetous behavior *[You can't exercise church discipline based on a sin that's committed within the heart; the covetousness mentioned in this scripture is a visible sin]*.

In the Greek this word for "covetousness" is a compound word that means *"holding much"* (Ekho and Pleion). However, this sin doesn't merely apply to the filthy rich. It applies to everyone who values their worldly possessions above God and above the concern of others. Such people have no interest in taking up their cross and being crucified to the world; instead, they're seeking to gain the world. Unfortunately, there is no true gain to be made; only loss.

In the Parable of the Sower, Christ explained just how destructive the things of the world are to the spiritual growth of a professed Christian:

"Now the ones [the seeds] *that fell among thorns are those who, when they have heard, go out and are choked with* **cares, riches, and pleasures of life,** *and* **bring no fruit to maturity"** (Luke 8: 14).

Christ defined the seed as the Word of God, and the different types of soils represented the different types of hearts. The heart that was filled with the "thorns" of the things of this world was choked out. It could not mature and bear the fruit of the Holy Spirit because it was more devoted to the world than it was to Christ. This is one of the chief reasons most Christians are fruitless and struggling.

In spite of these clear scriptures, many still assume that they can do both. If I could read minds, I would be almost certain that the reader doesn't *feel* that coveting after the things of the world is all that bad. God's warnings could not be more clear or more serious. He said of covetousness (Again, *"holding much"* in the Greek), *"let it not even be named among you, as is fitting for saints… for because of these things the wrath of God comes upon the sons of disobedience"* (Ephesians 5: 3-7). This is where the reader should put into practice what was taught in the previous chapter — deny your own self-understanding which trusts its own *"knowledge of good and evil."* We are not God. We must not judge sins based on our fleshly emotions, or dismiss them in the name of grace. We must judge sin solely by the truth. Remember, God alone has the prerogative to determine the seriousness of sin.

Taking up our cross and being crucified to the things of this world isn't easy. It's literally a dying experience, and dying involves bereavement and grief. But as long as the things of the world have a hold on us, God does not. Whenever I hear excuses for why people do not take the time to seek the Lord, **99% of the time** it is due to their devotion to something in this world. Worldly covetousness so fills the heart that it leaves no room for God. **No other sin so consumes every waking moment of our day as the sin of worldly covetousness**. This sin is so grievous, that it was the *sole recorded sin* of the worst church in the Bible — Laodicea.

"And to the angel of the church of the Laodicean write, 'These things says the Amen, the Faithful and True Witness, the Beginning of the creation of God: [15] *"I know your works, that you are neither cold nor hot. I could wish you were cold or hot.* [16] *So then, because you are lukewarm, and neither cold nor hot, I will vomit you out of My mouth.* [17] *Because you say,* **'I am rich, have become wealthy, and have need of nothing'** *– and do not know that you are* **wretched, miserable, poor, blind, and naked**…*Therefore be zealous and repent"* (Revelation 3: 14-19). They had thorny, worldly hearts, and therefore they could not mature and bear fruit.

The riches and wealth of the Laodiceans were not intrinsically sinful, but since they were not crucified to them, they became idols. The Laodiceans refused to take up their cross. The Lord was on the outside of the church knocking, trying to find a heart that would love Him more than this world. They assumed they could serve *"God and mammon"*, and they got the very consequences that Christ warned us about. No one is exempt from this divine law of the heart – *"you **cannot** serve God and mammon!"*

Again, how can we even begin to expect to overcome any stronghold as long as anything in this world has more of our heart than God does? God is our source of power; if we have dethroned Him for the sake of some corruptible, empty token or activity in this world, how can we even imagine that He will empower us?

I love America, and I wouldn't want to live in any other country, but the commercialism and materialism of the American dream has thoroughly infested the western church. Too many of us have failed to heed the warning that God gave to the Children of Israel:

*"Beware that you do not forget the LORD your God by not keeping His commandments, His judgments, and His statutes which I command you today, [12] lest – when you have eaten and are full, and have built beautiful houses and dwell in them; [13] and when your herds and your flocks multiply, and your silver and your gold are multiplied, and all that you have is multiplied; [14] when your heart is lifted up, and **you forget the LORD your God** who brought you out of the land of Egypt"* (Deuteronomy 8: 11-14).

The sin of worldly covetousness is as lethal as it is subtle, for it lurks within shadows of our blessings. Therefore, let's not allow ourselves to become enamored with our blessings, for God has said *" Set your mind on things above, not on things on the earth"* (Colossians 3: 2). And again, we must not be of those *"who set their mind on earthly **things**. [20] For our citizenship is in heaven, from which we also eagerly wait for the Savior, the Lord Jesus Christ"* (Philippians 3: 19-21).

Determine to take up your cross and be crucified to the things of this world. However, I cannot tell you *which* things. A person who nitpicks the *"lawful"* things in another person's life is being legalistic. It's for each individual Christian to honestly examine how the things within their own life are affecting their spiritual walk. Crucify (or at least, greatly minimize) everything in your life that has more sway, or demands more of your devotion than Christ does.

Otherwise, you'll never realize His power to overcome sin. You'll be choked out and *"bring no fruit to maturity"*.

The People of the World

We are called to turn from *closely bonded* relationships with the people of the world.

"Do not be unequally yoked together with unbelievers. For what fellowship has righteousness with lawlessness? And what communion has light with darkness? [15] *And what accord has Christ with Belial? Or what part has a **believer with an unbeliever**?* [16] *And what agreement has the temple of God with idols? For you are the temple of the living God. As God has said:...*

[17] *Therefore "Come out from among them and be separate, says the Lord. Do not touch what is unclean, and I will receive you."* [18] *"I will be a Father to you, and you shall be My sons and daughters, says the* LORD *Almighty"* (2 Corinthians 6: 14-18).

"Do not be deceived: "Evil company corrupts good habits" (1 Corinthians 15: 33).

Many assume that this only applies to the overtly wicked people of this world. This is another area where we're naturally prone to discern surface problems, but we're spiritually blinded to more sinister, subtle influences. This truth applies to every relationship between a *"believer* [and] *an unbeliever"*. This is exceptionally difficult for many of us to accept. It's hard for us to look at that sweet grandmother, that benevolent coworker, or that noble neighbor, and believe that they are of the world and under the sway of the Devil. Some of most wicked counsel has been packaged in the soft, comforting words of sweet ole grandmothers.

In fact, man's *goodness* seems to create an even deeper contempt for the Lord Jesus Christ than man's wickedness. I've witnessed to hundreds of professors and students on college and university campuses. I've witnessed to multitudes of well-off, middle class suburbanites. I've witnessed to hundreds of lower class individuals in the inner city. And I've witnessed to thousands of criminals within the prison system. I've found that the hostility toward Christ and His truth is most intense among the most educated, moral, and refined. Yet the lower you go on the social ladder, the more open hearts are to the truth. This should be no surprise to us, for this is what Christ experienced in His ministry on earth.

> *"Very few of us would debate over what is filthy, evil, and wrong, but we do debate over what is good. It is the good that opposes the best.* **The higher up the scale of moral excellence a person goes, the more intense the opposition to Jesus Christ."** Oswald Chambers.[37]

The first character trait of the Devil revealed in scripture is subtlety. We must recognize that every lost human being on earth is *"taken **captive** by* [the Devil] *to do his will"* (2 Timothy 2: 26). It doesn't matter if they're sweet, kind, religious, spiritual, wholesome, or conservative; if they are not born-again *and* seeking to follow Christ, they are under the *subtle* sway of the wicked one. Some of the most violent opposition to the Truth comes in the nicest packages.

One of the biggest lies of the Serpent that many of us have swallowed is that evil only reveals itself in overtly vile and debauched ways. The scribes and Pharisees were models of righteous character and integrity until Christ came and exposed their *hearts* and the subtlety of their hypocrisy. Outwardly, before the natural eyes of man, they looked good, but inwardly, before the eyes of God, they were evil. This is why it's critical that we use extreme caution with who we allow to have influence in our lives. Only a firm understanding of truth, and consistent walk in the Holy Spirit will enable us to identify subtle worldly deceptions.

> *"Now I urge you, brethren, note those who cause divisions and offenses, contrary to the doctrine which you learned, and **avoid them**. ¹⁸ For those who are such do not serve our Lord Jesus Christ, but their own belly, and **by smooth words and flattering speech deceive the hearts of the simple**."* (Romans 16: 17-18).

Satan chose the serpent because the *"serpent was* [already] *subtle"* (Genesis 3: 1); he operates the same way today. Satan loves to use the attractive and the appealing; *"and no wonder! For Satan himself transforms himself into an angel of light."* (2 Corinthians 11: 14).

How Should The Believer Relate To The Unbeliever?

If at all possible we must avoid any relationship where we are *"yoked"* with an unbeliever. Obviously, if we are already married to an unbeliever (or a professed believer who lives like an unbeliever), we cannot sever this relationship. To be yoked means we must be on the same page and going in the same direction like two yoked oxen. These relationships include marriage, business partnerships, closely engaged friendships, close church fellowship, and any other relationship where two or more people have significant influence in one another's life.

Listen to these words of Christ: *"Now great multitudes went with Him. And He turned and said to them,* [26] *"If anyone comes to Me and does not hate his father and mother, wife and children, brothers and sisters, yes, and his own life also, he cannot be My disciple.* [27] *And whoever does not bear his cross and come after Me cannot be My disciple"* (Luke 14: 25-27).

If most preachers were to see these *"great multitudes"* following them they would say, *"God is blessing my ministry! Hallelujah! Let's build a mega-church!"* Jesus was never interested in gaining bodies; His interest was in gaining hearts. And in order to do this, He put these "seekers" through the refining fires of a challenge that touched them right in the center of their hearts—close, treasured relationships.

Now He's getting personal. We have to be willing to put Christ before every relationship! In spite of how warm and nostalgic a relationship may feel, if that relationship is compromising our spiritual integrity, we cannot be yoked to it. Most of us have heard of the concept of "toxic friendships". These are usually easy to identify. However, for the Christian, many relationships are *spiritually* toxic. Recognizing these relationships requires a greater degree of biblical understanding and spiritual discernment.

Christians will often say, *"Well, Jesus sat and ate with sinners!"* I remember an occasion where I witlessly made this statement to justify unequally yoked relationships. The Christian I was speaking to immediately corrected me; *"No, Jesus sat and ate with repentant sinners!"* Whenever I hear a new perspective from the Bible, I don't argue against it just to be right; I shut my mouth and inquire to see if it's accurate.

Upon examining the scriptures, I found this to be so; when Jesus spent time with sinners He was ministering to them. When confronted about His involvement with sinners by the self-righteous Pharisees, Jesus explained how

He was ministering to them: *"Those who are well have no need of a physician, but those who are sick ...For I did not come to **call** the righteous, but **sinners, to repentance"*** (Matthew 9: 12). And again, in Luke 15: 1 it says that *"all the tax collectors and the sinners drew near to Him **to hear Him**."* After this verse, Jesus gave three corresponding illustrations about the *"sinner who **repents**"* (Luke 15).

Christ was like a spiritual physician to sinners. Physicians spend time with patients in order to diagnose their problems and nurse them back to health. No good physician turns a blind eye to a patient's sickness in order to keep the atmosphere lighthearted. And they certainly don't recklessly spend so much time with infectious patients that they themselves become sick! Furthermore, Christ plainly declared that He was calling these sinners to *"repentance."* Whenever Christ sat and ate with sinners, *He* was influencing them, not vice versa. They're reason for being there was to *"hear Him"*, not to hang out. *Jesus Christ **never** built a **close, involved relationship** with unrepentant sinners — neither did the Apostles.* Any other assumption of what Christ may have been doing with these sinners is sheer, unbiblical imagination.

However, it must be clarified that the Bible forbids "yoked" relationships, not general associations and neighborly friendships. You have to examine your own relationships. Is anyone drawing you away from the Word, will, and ways of God? Is anyone causing you to compromise? Is anyone tempting you toward sin, intentionally or inadvertently? If you want to overcome your stronghold, you have to put those relationships on the chopping block — crucify them. If you don't, their influence and power over you is competing with God's influence and power in your life. Furthermore, Christ says that you *"cannot"* be His disciple.

The Philosophies of the World

The philosophes of the world are closely linked to the people of the world because philosophies come from people. However, I've separated them, presenting people as *direct* influences and philosophies as *indirect* influences. Consider the following verses:

*"**Beware** lest anyone cheat you through **philosophy** and empty deceit, according to the tradition of men, according to the **basic principles of the world**, and not according to Christ"* (Colossians 2: 8).

And again,

"Let no one cheat you of your reward, taking delight in false humility and worship of angels, intruding into those things which he has not seen, vainly puffed up by his fleshly mind…[20] Therefore, ***if you died with Christ*** *[the cross]* ***from the basic principles of the world****, why, as though living in the world, do you subject yourselves to regulations –* [21] *"Do not touch, do not taste, do not handle,"* [22] *which all concern things which perish with the using – according to the commandments and doctrines of men?* [23] *These things indeed have an appearance of wisdom in self-imposed religion, false humility, and neglect of the body,* ***but are of no value against the indulgence of the flesh"*** (Colossians 2: 19-23).

Since the beginning of creation, man has been sewing together the fig leaves of philosophes, ideologies, sciences, and religions in order to improve himself. However, in spite of man's best efforts and greatest minds, all of his philosophes *"are of no value against the indulgence of the flesh."* Probably the most invasive and pervasive philosophy that has infested the modern church is Christianized psychology (and yes, I realize that psychology is technically not a philosophy. For the sake of simplicity, anything that is based within the wisdom of man, I've classified as a "philosophy").

The reader may wonder why I'm so staunchly against Christianized psychology; ***particularly and specifically when it is utilized to teach Christians how to live the Christian life and how to overcome sin.*** I categorically renounce Christian psychology because it fundamentally contradicts God's Truth in a number of essential areas; especially, as it relates to overcoming sin. Furthermore, it doesn't even work. When it does "work", it produces a distorted, *illusion of sanctification* that falls drastically short of the *Spirit-filled* sanctification promised in the scripture.

Psychology is fundamentally antithetical to God and the truth by its very design and origin. It addresses the issues of man from a strictly natural perspective; however, God addresses us *predominantly* from a spiritual perspective. When I studied psychology in college, it became very clear to me that the entire structure of psychology is purely naturalistic (interprets all things strictly from a natural perspective, and denies the spiritual), humanistic (man centered), and atheistic. Its principles, philosophes, and methodologies are irreconcilable with most biblical truth. Predictably, every book and message that I've read or heard where truth is mixed with psychology, the truth is *always* modified to fit into the scheme of man's psychology; never vice versa.

On a few occasions I respectfully challenged my professors on this matter. I told them that psychology cannot address the issues of the whole man. The science of psychology, *in its purest form*, does not account for God, the Devil, spiritual warfare, righteousness, Christ, the cross, the blood, the resurrection, this fallen world, the Holy Spirit, the sin nature, the new nature, good, evil, the spirit, the soul, truth, error, heaven, hell, eternity, or any other fundamental biblical truth. In the world of psychology, man is nothing more than a highly evolved organism that operates based on chemicals, impulses, and the accident of consciousness! You cannot Christianize this! Furthermore, **God has already given us His truth concerning how to live the Christian life and overcome sin—there is no need to Christianize this atheistic invention of man!**

How in the world can we attempt to deal with issues of sin by using a psychological construct that doesn't even acknowledge sin? Sin is not a psychological issue at its core; it's a spiritual issue. Mixing God's truth with man's psychology creates a philosophical Frankenstein that appears to have life but is intrinsically dead.

Someone may say, *"Well, I know some psychological principles that agree with the Bible."* So do I! Not too far from where I live is a "church of Satan" that has principles that agree with the Bible! Islam has principles that agree with the Bible! Here's the problem. In the few places that psychology happens to agree with the Bible, if it's already written in the scripture, obviously psychology's not needed. Nevertheless, in most cases, the concepts of psychology are in stark variance with the Word of God. These areas of agreement are Satan's lures to draw Christians into a net of spiritually stultifying deceit!

One of the Serpent's primary schemes is diluting the truth with convincing lies. No Bible taught Christian would tolerate the Truth of God's Word being diluted with the lies of a false religion. However, since psychology is considered to be a *scientific, professional* field, we've given it license to intermingle with God's Truth. What we fail to recognize is that the **premise** of psychology is based *purely* in naturalistic, humanistic atheism; therefore, all of the *"science"* of psychology is based upon these premises. These are anti-biblical beliefs and philosophies—they're not science. Science is only as good as its premise; if the premise is wrong, the science will be compromised. Evolution, for instants, begins with the wrong premises; therefore, the conclusions are compromised.

Evolution is man's attempt to explain creation without God. Psychology is man's attempt to explain the nature of humanity without God. Most *Bible-taught* Christians are wise enough to recognize the absolute irreconcilability between evolution and the truth; i.e., theistic evolution. Evolution absolutely cannot be Christianized. Unfortunately, very few Christians have the biblical discernment to recognize the absolute irreconcilability between secular psychology and the truth. It is irresponsible and dangerous to adopt a science or philosophy, which is intrinsically based upon unbiblical lies, and attempt to Christianize it.

It was a breath of fresh air for me to finally hear a biblically astute Christian psychologist speaking on the radio one day. He explained that after he'd finished his schooling in psychology, he had to throw it all away because it could not be reconciled with the Bible. He was still a Christian psychologist, but instead of forcing the Bible to fit into the mould of his psychological training, he upheld the integrity of scripture in spite of his training. No doubt, there are other Christian psychologists out there who've given God's truth priority over their schooling. Unfortunately, such individuals are a rare find.

1900 years of Christianity did not need Wundt and Freud, both godless atheists, to show us the *light* on how to live the Christian life and deal with sin! The reader may have noticed how often I confide in, and resort to the spiritual sages of the past. One of the primary reasons for this is because they lived in a time *before* psychology and modern philosophical thought had made deep inroads into our Bible colleges and seminaries. Now, don't get me wrong; there are many great Bible teachers today. Most of my rudimentary knowledge of the truth has come from modern Bible teachers. However, it goes without saying, that when it comes to the matter of overcoming sinful habits, the modern church is in a world of confusion, at the center of this confusion is Christianized psychology.

Many modern churches have forced God's Word to bow the knee to psychology. Much of our modern preaching and teaching is saturated with it. It's become easy for me to distinguish the pure word of God, from a scripture that has been contorted in order to fit into the mold of a psychological idea. In order to discern the difference, one must have a firm grasp of and love for the truth. Unfortunately, many Christians have neither; therefore, they're often *"tossed to and fro and carried about with every wind of doctrine "*(Ephesians 4: 11-15).

Many churches have adopted "biblical counseling" as an alternative to Christian psychology. This is a step in the right direction, but be cautions; the biblical counsel received is only as good as the biblical counselor. I know of a leading biblical counselor who was one of the most headstrong, self-righteous Jezebels in the Church. I know of others whose lives were filled with haughty, flagrant, unrepentant sin. They were so lifted up in pride because of their training, that they undermined the leadership within a church, causing strife and divisions. Becoming a biblical counselor is often a way for carnal Christians to make a name for themselves and gain influence. Confronting self is not the same a denying self and following Christ.

Moreover, biblical counseling is often laden with psychological methodologies and concepts as well. When researching the *"Biblical Counseling Coalition's"* assessment and treatment of sinful *"addictions"*, I discovered that their language and approach toward the issue was barely distinguishable from that of secular psychology. Absolutely nothing was mentioned about Christ, the Holy Spirit, or deliverance from the power of sin. Of all the scriptures that teach on the subject of overcoming sin, *not even one was referenced*! The official **"Biblical Counseling Coalition"** offered nothing more than rank-and-file psychology, couched in religious terms. The only sure way to overcome sin is not to run to another program, in spite of how *"biblical"* it sounds. It is to get back to the pure basics of scripture, and become a *"disciple indeed"* so that Christ Himself may make us *"free indeed"* from sin.

God's Truths have been manipulated and contorted in every way imaginable in order to fit them into the ideological systems of psychological thought. With reckless abandon we've cast out what God says about sanctification, and replaced it with the ever-growing cesspool of naturalistic, psychology based answers to man's sins and struggles. Sin, at its core, is not a physical issue, nor is it a mental issue; it's a spiritual issue. And only the Holy Spirit, working through the powerful Truth of God's Word, is capable of fundamentally transforming and empowering us at the spiritual core.

God doesn't need *any help* from the wisdom of man in the matter of saving people from the power of sin. God's Truth has already spoken to this issue! God doesn't sit down at a committee table with pea-brained man, squeamishly presenting His point of view: *"This is My idea for sanctification. What do you guys think? I know it requires a little sacrifice and commitment and all, but if anybody's got a better idea, I'm all ears. Let's put our heads together."* God's Truth stands alone without any contributions from the peanut gallery of Man's wisdom.

Christ, whose name is *"The Word of God"* and *"The Amen"*, has already spoken to the issue of sanctification. All man can do is seek to understand it; never to add to it or take away from it. No philosophy of man should be placed on the same level of inspired Truth, as if somehow it could improve upon it, clarify it, or help it in any way. *"You have magnified **Your Word** above all Your name"* (Psalm 138: 2) — no other words can share this exalted place. Unfortunately, many within the church think otherwise.

We Are Saturated In The Philosophies of This World

We are prone to embrace what makes sense to our natural understanding. But this is not how God works. From Genesis to Revelation, God's pathway to victory has always been by faith — often, faith in what seemed absurd and illogical! God's way strips man of any hope of sharing in the glory. God did not call us to psychoanalyze self; He called us to deny self. He did not tell us to conjure up some worldly philosophy in order to fix our issues; He commanded us to *"Look to Me, and be saved, All you ends of the earth"* (Isaiah 45: 22). Unfortunately, psychology is not the only worldly philosophy that influences us.

The ungodly influences of the world are all around us. We are inundated with sinful influences every waking moment of our lives. The moment we get up and turn on the TV, we're showered with the sordid lives of celebrities and sexually oriented commercials. We are bombarded with the messages of selfishness, lust, deception, rebellious children, weak fathers, feminist women, murder, saving the earth, humanism, glory-seeking, tolerance, conservatism, liberalism, celebrity worship, social justice, capitalism, socialism, pluralism, existentialism, envy, relativism, vanity, greed, worldly causes, biased science, and the list goes on — and this is just what's on TV! These messages are reinforced on the billboards, in magazines, newspapers, the Internet, and especially music! We are surrounded by the philosophies of the world.

And do not think for a moment that since you're a Christian you're not being influenced by these things. If you are not *consciously* seeking to be crucified to the world, you are being greatly influenced, and you don't even notice it. Remember, the "*whole world is under the sway of the Wicked one.*" Lucifer was the wisest being under God, and He has masterfully organized his world like a chess game, anticipating every facet of our fallen nature that he can manipulate. If he can fill our lives with good, common sense, "harmless" things and philosophies, he can keep us from filling our lives with Christ, His truth, and His wisdom—and ultimately, His Spirit and His power.

The scripture is clear, "*and **do not be conformed to this world**, but be **transformed by the renewing of your mind**.*" The transformation starts in the mind. It is a transformation from a natural mind to a spiritual mind; a self-oriented mind to a Christ oriented mind; a mind that operates according to its "*own understanding*", to a mind that thinks according to Truth; a mind that is conditioned by worldly reasoning, to a mind that is renewed to see things from an eternal perspective.

"*If then you were raised with Christ, seek those things which are above, where Christ is, sitting at the right hand of God. ² **Set** [fix, focus, align] **your mind** on things above, **not on things on the earth**"* (Colossians 3: 1-2).

Take up your cross of separation and be crucified to the philosophies this world.

How To Overcome the World — Wake Up!

Since we are so immersed within this world, how in the world are expected to overcome the influences of the world and follow Christ? Christians are commanded to be *alert, watchful, vigilant, and sober*. Consider the following scriptures:

"*Therefore **gird up the loins of your mind**, **be sober**, and rest your hope fully upon the grace that is to be brought to you at the revelation of Jesus Christ; ¹⁴ as obedient children, **not conforming yourselves to the former lusts, as in your ignorance;** ¹⁵ but as He who called you is holy, you also be holy in all your conduct,* ¹⁶ *because it is written, "Be holy, for I am holy"* (1 Peter 1: 13-16).

Holiness demands sobriety and alertness. We cannot haphazardly be holy. Consider this next verse.

*"And do this, knowing the time, that now it is high time to **<u>awake out of sleep</u>**; for now our salvation is nearer than when we first believed. ¹² The night is far spent, the day is at hand. Therefore **let us cast off the works of darkness**, and let us put on the armor of light. ¹³ Let us walk properly, as in the day**, not in revelry and drunkenness, not in lewdness and lust, not in strife and envy. ¹⁴ But put on the Lord Jesus Christ, and make no provision for the flesh, to fulfill its lusts."* (Romans 13: 11-14).

We must *wake up* before we can *"cast off the works of darkness"* and *"make no provision for the flesh, to fulfill its lusts."*

*"For the grace of God that brings salvation has appeared to all men, ¹² teaching us that, **denying ungodliness and worldly lusts, <u>we should live soberly</u>**, righteously, and godly in the present age,"* (Titus 2: 11-12).

Before we can overcome *"worldly lust,"* we must learn to live *"soberly."* I could go on, but the Bible is resoundingly clear; in order to overcome the various influences of this world, we must be vigilant, alert, watchful, and sober. The Christian life is a sober life. This bears repeating: ***The Christian life is a sober life.*** *Spiritual* sobriety is one of our most crucial defenses against the world. Notice that I didn't simply say "sobriety"; I said "*spiritual* sobriety".

Many Christians are vigilant, sober, and alert in natural things. They know how to manage their lives well, make prudent decisions, and avoid the pitfalls in life. However, any godless pagan can live with the same degree of prudence and discipline. Spiritual vigilance is on an entirely different level. The mother of the great evangelist, John Wesley, wrote to her son in order to instill within him the wisdom of how to be spiritually alert against sin. No theologian could have written it better.

"*Son, whatever weakens your reasoning, impairs the tenderness of your conscience, obscures your sense of God, or takes away your relish for spiritual things; in short, if anything increases the authority and power of the flesh over the Spirit, then that to you becomes sin, however good it is in itself.*" Susanna Wesley[38]. Read it again and take a "Selah" moment after each comma.

The common thread between everything that I had to crucify within my life was that it compromised the *spiritual* alertness of my mind. Dear reader, this is a crucial point—give strict heed to it. I had to learn how to slow down and assess how the various things in this world affected my *spiritual* sobriety.

Remember, we must earnestly consider the environments and conditions that make us vulnerable to sin. What things, activities, patterns of life, people, ideologies, and the like are suffocating you spiritually? Be crucified to them! Pluck out the *"eye"* and cut off the *"hand"* that is *causing* you to sin. Yes, it'll hurt—bad! Being crucified in any area of your life may hurt you, but sin hurts others and grieves God—who are you living for? Wake up! Be alert and watchful! Begin to deliberately consider the things, people, and philosophies of this world that compromise your spiritual alertness and stability.

Trifling In the Midst of Heated Combat

Several times in scripture we are commanded to be watchful. We are not simply called to avoid *black and white* sins—we are called to be crucified to the world altogether. The Pharisees avoided the obvious, external sins of the flesh, but they were entirely of the world. This world is not the home of the Christian. For a citizen of New Jerusalem and ambassador of Christ to live *"according to the course of this world, according to the prince of the power of the air"* (Ephesians 2: 2) **is** tantamount to high treason! Remember, *"Whoever therefore wants to be a friend of the world makes himself an enemy of God"* (James 4: 4).

We forget that we are literally in the midst of the most polarized, bitter, and fierce battle that time and creation has ever seen. The way in which many western Christians follow after the pleasure, people, and perspectives of this world is remarkable. We're on a battle field in heated combat with spiritual enemies who *sleeplessly* seek to destroy us. The casualties of this war far exceed the combined total of every war waged in the history of civilization. This fact alone should cause every one of us to reevaluate our walk. We cannot afford to whimsically stagger through the Christian life from one worldly pleasure to another, constantly using grace as an excuse to live at a distance from Christ. And after all of our excuses have been doled out, we have the audacity to wonder why God is not giving us power to overcome sin.

Western Christianity has sold out to the world of entertainment. We are so imprisoned to our lust to be amused that we cannot even stomach sitting through a two hour church service one day out of the week unless we are entertained! And after Church is over, some of the most exhilarating entertainment comes on TV, especially that which targets the *male* audience—nine hours of football, basketball, baseball, NASCAR, golf, and the like. The god of this world is very wise to target the head; get the head of the family, and you get the family.

Moreover, Sunday has the best news specials and late night TV shows. Any truth that a soul may have gleaned from the Sunday morning service has been thoroughly expunged from the heart before the day's end! Sunday has arguably replaced Saturday as the chief day in which we enjoy life's leisure's and activities. Now obviously, the Lord allows for leisure and activity, but not to the extent that our spiritual life is starved out!

Unfortunately, this is the very state of many Christians today. The world has shrunk into the palm of our hand, and with a push of an icon, we have access to millions of opportunities. It's impossible to keep up with them all! There's something new and intriguing around every turn. Every product has a latest model before the *old* model has even been figured out. Like a child who's bored with his Christmas present before the day is up, we've been stricken with an insatiable craving for the latest and greatest. And, God forbid that we miss out on the trending fads that all of our friends are into. We never outgrow the covetous mindset of the high school teen who'll *just die* if they don't get the latest shoes that all the *in* kids are getting. The adult's covetousness is simply more mature and dignified, but no less intense.

We've been conditioned to believe that if our life is not filled with the latest gadgets, and activities, and projects, and outings, and events, then we don't have a life—we're missing out. Yet, few of us pause to ask the question, *"What are we missing out on?"* The answer: *"The things of the world."* Solomon tried everything the world had to offer in his time. He indulged in everything to the fullest! And, what he discovered was that it was all *"vanity* [utterly empty]...*and grasping for the wind"*.

It's the same with us, for *"there's nothing new under the sun"*. So, what are we grasping for? Are we afraid to miss out on the world? *"The world is passing away, and the lust of it; but he who does the will of God abides forever"* (1 John 2: 17). The great missionary, Jim Elliot, said it best: *"He is no fool who gives what he cannot keep to gain that which he cannot lose."* What do you fear missing out on; the natural and the temporal, or the spiritual and the eternal? The answer *of your heart* will identify the condition of your heart, *"for where your treasure is, there your heart will be also"* (Matthew 6: 21).

My job allows me to visit many homes. I'm always intrigued by the corruptible nature of all the things that we feel compelled to accumulate. I take pictures of the *many* swimming pools that have been overrun with moss—a call them moss gardens. Damaged toys are strewn across the lawn, and weathered tarps are draped over broken ski-doos. A few times my job brought me to junkyards. I walked through the rusted, abandoned cars. I pondered them. All of these things have two things in common: at one point, a person greatly desired them, and was filled with giddy excitement to receive them, and number two, all of them are irreversibly corruptible.

The words of the Lord, though welcome on many lips, are unwelcome in many hearts: "*Do not lay up for yourselves treasures on earth, where moth and rust corrupt and where thieves break in and steal; but lay up for yourselves treasures in heaven, where neither moth nor rust corrupts and where thieves do not break in and steal*" (Matthew 6: 19-20). What will we do with these words? Will we continue to respond to corruption with new toys, and boredom with new thrills, or will we pause a moment to seek the Wisdom of Solomon and Christ.

"*Let us hear the conclusion of the whole matter:*

Fear God and keep His commandments,
For this is man's all.
14 For God will bring every work into judgment,
Including every secret thing,
Whether good or evil" (Ecclesiastes 12: 13-14).

"*Seek first the kingdom of God and His righteousness, and all these things shall be added to you*" (Matthew 6: 33).

Do you see things for what they truly are? Do you see things as God sees them? We cannot see as God sees with natural sight; only with spiritual sight—faith. Natural sight will cause us to cleave to the things of this world, leaving our spiritual nature emaciated and frail, weak and stumbling, "*wretched, miserable, poor, blind, and naked*" (Revelation 3: 17). Spiritual sight will lift our hearts to the things of God; eternal things; things that produce sustained joy instead of the transient happiness produced by corruptible things. Let the people of the world be consumed with the things of the world; let the citizens of Heavenly Zion be consumed with eternal things.

"We do not look at the things which are seen, but at the things which are not seen. For the things which are seen are temporary, but the things which are not seen are eternal" (2 Corinthians 4: 18).

"If then you were raised with Christ, seek those things which are above, where Christ is, sitting at the right hand of God. ² Set your mind on things above, not on things on the earth. ³ For you died, and your life is hidden with Christ in God" (Colossians 3: 1-3).

"Evangelical Christianity, at least in the United States, is now tragically below the New Testament standard. **Worldliness is an accepted part of our way of life.** *Our religious mood is* **social instead of spiritual**. *We have lost the art of worship. We are not producing saints.* **Our models** *are successful businessmen, celebrated athletes and theatrical personalities. We carry on our religious activities after the methods of the modern advertiser. Our homes have been turned into theaters. Our literature is shallow and our hymnody borders on sacrilege* [notice how the natural is usurping the spiritual]. *And scarcely anyone appears to care.*

We must have a better kind of Christian soon or within another half century we may have no **true** *Christianity at all. Increased numbers of demi-Christians is not enough. We must have a reformation."* __ A. W. Tozer.[39]

This was written over *half a century* ago.

My dear brother. My dear sister. I sincerely pray that you do not walk away discouraged like the "rich young ruler." Christ's call is only difficult on the sinful self and our lust for the things of this world; however, it is joyously liberating to our inner, born-again nature. The freedom that the Lord promises is for the new spiritual man, not the old fleshly man. I tell you what I know. As our spirit begins experiencing the rested peace and rapturous joy of living above the flesh and the world, the cross becomes more inviting. We begin seeing the things of this world for what they truly are; *"Vanity of vanities, all is vanity…and grasping for the wind"*; *"Wood, hay, and stubble"*; corruptible clumps of lead shackled to the wings of our spirit.

"Jesus would have his people "go forth without the camp" <u>for their own sanctification.</u> <u>You cannot grow in grace to any high degree while you are conformed to the world.</u> … *The highway of holiness is the highway of communion. It is thus we shall hope to win the crown if we are enabled by divine grace faithfully to follow Christ "without the camp."* **The crown of glory will follow the** <u>cross of separation</u>…*It is ill for an heir of heaven to be a great friend with the heirs of hell. It has

a bad look when a courtier is too intimate with his king's enemies. Even small inconsistencies are dangerous. Little thorns make great blisters, little moths destroy fine garments, and little frivolities and little rogueries will rob religion of a thousand joys. **O professor, too little separated from sinners, you know not what you lose by your conformity to the world. It cuts the tendons of your strength, and makes you creep where you ought to run.** *Then, for your own comfort's sake, and for the sake of your growth in grace,* ***if you be a Christian, be a Christian, and be a marked and distinct one!"*** —Spurgeon[40]

Stop taking the world lightly. Cast off your spiritual lethargy, rouse yourself from your worldly apathy, and take your place among the citizens of Heavenly Zion. Be watchful and alert! Stand guard against everything that compromises you spiritually. Take up the cross of separation and be crucified to this world.

Emptied In Order To Be Filled

It's time to rise up and follow on after our risen Lord. We cannot know the power of His resurrection as long as we are clinging to our *self* and to the things of this *world*. *"The world is passing away, and the lust of it; but he who does the will of God abides forever"* (1John 2: 17). So do not hold on to that which is passing away.

It is the will of God that we be crucified to this world, but being crucified is not enough. When we begin to remove the things of this world out of our lives, we create a vacuum. Vacuums must be and will be filled. Whatever is closest to us will be sucked in. It is unwise to attempt to deny self and be crucified to this world without cultivating a close walk with Christ. This would only leave us open for a host of other worldly snares and deceptions to creep in.

But, how exactly do we follow Christ? Unfortunately, many who attempt to follow Christ according to their own understanding are unwittingly and tragically following the Devil more than they are following Christ. Satan is more than willing to fill the vacuum with unbiblical, naturalistic, religious ideas, thus drawing us under his *"sway"* again. Remember; he's subtle. Therefore, in order to follow Christ, we must learn *how* to follow Him. This is what we'll consider in the next chapters.

CHAPTER 6

"FOLLOW ME" IN THE SPIRIT

The Thin Line Between Sentimentality and Spirituality

Peter had always been the one to speak for the group whenever there was something to be said. Sometimes he spoke wisely, and other times he put his foot in his mouth. But, this time Peter hit the nail right on the head, and the Lord gave him a resounding commendation. *"Blessed are you, Simon Bar-Jonah, for flesh and blood has not revealed this to you, but My Father who is in heaven"* (Matthew 16: 17). God the Father had revealed the truth of Christ's identity to him!

Up until now, Jesus was the only one who received revelations from the Father, but now God was communicating with him, Peter! Jesus had already been recognizing him as the leader among the disciples, but now the Father was showing His approval as well. Peter was growing as a man of God. His confidence began to increase. He felt that he was beginning to gain an understanding of the Lord's will.

Immediately after this, the Lord began talking about some very disturbing future events that didn't fit Peter's understanding of God's will. *"From that time Jesus began to show to His disciples that He must go to Jerusalem, and suffer many things from the elders and chief priests and scribes, and be killed, and be raised the third day"* (Matthew 16: 21). This didn't make any sense to Peter.

Since the Lord had been recognizing his leadership among the other disciples, perhaps he had some say in this matter. The Messiah wasn't supposed to die; He was supposed to overthrow the Roman Empire and reign forever. Something wasn't right! Peter was certain he had all of his doctrines correct. Maybe Jesus was beginning to worry that those who were plotting to kill Him would succeed. Sometimes discouraged leaders need a pep talk, and Peter was just the man to give it.

"Then Peter took Him aside and began to rebuke Him, saying, "Far be it from You, Lord; this shall not happen to You!" (Matthew 16: 22). The Lord's immediate response cut to the deepest part of Peter's soul with stinging force. *"Get behind Me, Satan! You are an offense to Me, for **you are not mindful of the things of God, but the things of men**"* (Matthew 16: 23). From the pinnacle of speaking for God to the pit of speaking for Satan. Peter shrunk back in stunned silence, too terrified to utter another word.

The Devil's Favorite Tools

Peter's failure should put every Christian on high alert. The final segment of Christ's three-part call is *"follow Me."* Many Christians attempt to leap over or skim through the first two commands in an effort to become "Christ followers" on fire for Jesus! But what many fail to realize is that as long as the sinful *self* and the *things of the world* are dominant in a person's life, they're child's play for the Devil.

The Serpent loves to titillate and manipulate the *fleshly self-nature* with the endless lures and philosophies of the *world*! Let me repeat that: *"The Serpent loves to titillate and manipulate the fleshly **self-nature** with the endless lures and philosophies of the **world**!"* Consequently, many professed Christians are unwittingly *following Satan* more than they are *following Christ*. Like Peter, many may even have the best intentions, but their focus is on *"the things of men"* (naturalism) instead of *"God"*, and this makes them easy pickings for Satan. Spiritual truths and eternal matters are on a completely different wavelength than our common sense and the worldly order of things. The natural cannot discern the spiritual. If Satan can keep us focused on *"the things of men"*, we'll remain blinded to *"the things of God"*, and wide open to the things of the Deceiver.

What's so enlightening about Peter's failure is that his words seemed to reveal his deep concern for Christ. He wasn't *trying* to be evil or malicious; he was simply thinking according to his natural, fleshly mind. However, little did he know that Satan was using him. It doesn't matter if we *feel* that our motives are wholesome and reasonable; if they are not according to the Truth, they could very well be of the Devil. Christians in whom *self* and the *world* are still strong are highly vulnerable to this kind of deception. Unfortunately, we don't have Christ physically standing there beside us to audibly identify the times when we're being influenced by Satan.

In John 14: 30, Jesus said, *"the ruler of this world is coming, and he has nothing in Me."* Jesus had no sin nature within Him; therefore, Satan could find nothing in Him to latch onto and successfully deceive or tempt Him. We cannot escape the fact that we have *"the law of sin which is in* [our] *members"*; however, we *can* progressively and substantially diminish the two dominant *catalysts* for sin in our lives—self and the world.

If we denounce and let go of our fleshly self, it will be much more difficult for the Tempter to persuade us to sin—*for all sin gratifies self.* If we have been crucified to this world, it will frustrate the Deceiver, who constantly dangles worldly lures and deceptions before us, hoping we'll bite. The more that self and the world are diminished within us, the less sway the Devil will have over us. This gives us more freedom to fluidly follow Christ without any snares, detours, or pitfalls.

Moving forward

Thus far we've learned what it means to deny our self and take up our cross; however, this chapter on following Christ is by far the most important. The focus of the Christian must be Christ. This bears repeating: *"The focus of the Christian must be Christ."* A person can become morbid and odd if they focus too much of their time and energy trying to deny self and crucify worldly lusts. However, if our primary focus is on *whole-heartedly* following Christ, we will, *by definition*, be deeply compelled to deny self and crucify the lust of the world. In other words, if we follow Christ in *absolute surrender*, denying self and being crucified to the world will come progressively and naturally.

The chief purpose of this book is not to merely teach you how to overcome sin; it is to instruct you on how to follow Christ by walking in the Spirit so that He Himself gives you power over sin. *This is the key difference between man's methods and God's truth.* If all you want is to suppress some annoying sin, then you don't need to read any further—the previous two chapters can help you do that. Deny yourself in certain key areas, and eliminate certain worldly things that make you vulnerable to your sin, and you'll be able to suppress any stronghold. But you won't be *made free* of it; neither will you be any closer to Christ.

In the beginning of this book, I wrote of how I cancelled my Internet filter the moment that I knew the Lord had made me free. When a person is made free, their besetting sin can be brought to them on a silver platter, and they'll be able to effortlessly resist it. This is freedom. They won't need any props or crutches to keep them from sinning. They won't need to check in with an accountability partner in order to motivate them to refrain from sin. Furthermore, they'll have a sensitivity and disdain for every other sin — they won't be *"half-baked"*; free from the sins that offend them, yet continuing in the sins that they're comfortable with. When such a person has come into an intimate knowledge of *"the Truth"* — *"the Son"* — they're not only made free from sin, but they gain the *Lord's perspective* on sin. This freedom is only accomplished as we follow Christ as *"disciples indeed."*

Moving forward, we're going to explore the vitally important question of *how* we are to follow Christ. It's not enough to simply call ourselves "followers of Christ", and then *winging it!* Our longing should be to follow Him as genuine *"disciples indeed"* according to **His definition** of what a disciple is. Remember, the first step in Christ's call to follow Him is *"deny yourself"* in order to follow Him on *His* terms. It is only then that we are promised complete liberation from the bondage of sin and the exhilarating fullness of the Spirit-filled life.

God's Model for the *CHRIST*ian

As I've emphasized throughout this book, one of the most essential truths that the reader must understand is that God's goal is to conform us into the image of His Son — I am both intentionally and unapologetically redundant on this vital matter. Every minuscule detail of our life is providentially orchestrated for this single goal, that we might be *"conformed to the image of His Son"* (Romans 8: 28-29). Unfortunately, I've discovered that many Western Christians are swift to resist this truth.

A common retort I've often heard is, *"Well, God doesn't want us to be a doormat!"* When I hear statements like this, it's as if Satan is drawing our attention away from the true character of Christ by highlighting and *misrepresenting* His less desirable character traits. I've watched the Devil snuff out many promising conversations about what it means to follow Christ by using the tongues of carnal, worldly Christians! Everyone is shaken awake for a moment, but the Wicked One immediately turns the light back off!

Like the Pharisees of old, we see a threat to our values and traditions, and put up staunch resistance. We prefer the westernized, conservative model of morality; the righteousness of Christ is an offence to us. Ironically and tragically, many who resist the Christ *of scripture* will claim that they're following Christ. However, they have unwittingly gutted and sterilized the pure, biblical conception of Christ-like character, and have raised up an impotent figurine of Christ, made in their own religiously preferred image.

Many mistakenly assume that if a Christian has a wonderful personality, a "clean life", and they know how to *"win friends and influence people"*, they're being like Christ. The Christ of scripture is radically different from many of the likable people who've become icons in the modern Western church. Natural goodness is not the same as spiritual Christlikeness.

"Our Lord never "patches up" our natural virtues, that is, our natural traits, qualities, or characteristics. He completely remakes a person on the inside – "…put on the new man…" (Ephesians 4:24). In other words, see that your natural human life is putting on all that is in keeping with the new life. **The life God places within us develops its own new virtues, not the virtues of the seed of Adam, but of Jesus Christ. Once God has begun the process of sanctification in your life, watch and see how God causes your confidence in your own natural virtues and power to wither away.** *He will continue until you learn to draw your life from the reservoir of the resurrection life of Jesus.* **Thank God if you are going through this drying-up experience!**

The sign that God is at work in us is that He is destroying our confidence in the natural virtues, because **they are not promises of what we are going to be, but only a wasted reminder of what God created man to be. We want to cling to our natural virtues, while all the time God is trying to get us in contact with the life of Jesus Christ** *— a life that can never be described in terms of natural virtues. It is the saddest thing to see people who are trying to serve God depending on that which the grace of God never gave them. They are depending solely on what they have by virtue of heredity. God does not take our natural virtues and transform them, because our natural virtues could never even come close to what Jesus Christ wants. No natural love, no natural patience, no natural purity can ever come up to His demands. But as we bring every part of our natural bodily life into harmony with the new life God has placed within us, He will exhibit in us the virtues that were characteristic of the Lord Jesus."* — Oswald Chambers[41]

The person who follows Christ progressively becomes more like Christ. This is because they're being transformed by the Holy Spirit who is one with the *"Spirit of Christ"* (Romans 8: 9). When Christ says *"follow Me"*, He means follow His words, His character, His example, His mind, His heart, His ways, and His Truth. He literally calls to walk in His Spirit so that, once again, Christ is revealed in human flesh. Consider the following scriptures:

"For even hereunto were ye called: because Christ also suffered for us, **leaving us an example, that ye should follow His steps***, who committed no sin, nor was deceit found in His mouth"* (1 Peter 2: 21-22).

"Imitate me, just as I also imitate Christ" (1 Corinthians 11: 1).

"He who says he abides in Him ought himself also to walk **just as** *He walked"* (1 John 2: 6).

"A disciple is not above his teacher, but everyone who is perfectly trained will be like his teacher" (Luke 6: 40).

"Therefore be imitators of God as dear children" (Ephesians 5: 1).

These are just a few of the scriptures that teach that Christ is our example. Never forget this, because looking at Christ will *keep you spiritually balanced* as you seek to follow Him. Immerse yourself in the Word (for He speaks through the entire Word, and the entire Word speaks of Him) and you will see His glory. Muse on Him as he walks through the gospels, and take hold of Him as He is revealed in the lives and writings of His Spirit-filled Apostles. As you do this you will discover how uniquely other-worldly, yet down to earth Christ is. You'll see the infinite character of God walking in the finitude of human flesh—a divine paradox that the Holy One longs to replicate in every earthen vessel that He inhabits.

Some may assume that it's impossible to grow in Christlikeness; they'd be right. The Christian life is not about learning doctrine and then trying to live it out to the best of our ability. The Christian life is not about discipline, good morals, "clean livin", and church activity. It's about complete trust in the Father, wholehearted love for Christ, and absolute surrender to the Holy Spirit. This bears repeating: *It's about complete trust in the Father, wholehearted love for Christ, and absolute surrender to the Holy Spirit.* If you're not ready to follow Christ in such a manner, it will indeed be impossible for you to grow like Him. The *most* you'll amount to is a clean, disciplined, church-going, self-ruled, worldly, professed Christian, devoid of fruit and power.

The Christian is called to live their life *"looking unto Jesus"* and surrendered to the gentle guidance of the Holy Spirit. As we do this, *"we all, with unveiled face, beholding as in a mirror the glory of the Lord (Jesus), are being* **transformed into the same image** *from glory to glory, just as* **by the Spirit of the Lord"** (2 Corinthians 3: 18). If we resolve to uphold Christ as our chief example, it gives us a marvelously clear perspective of God's will for us in every facet of our Christian walk. However, it's not that we try to imitate Christ *in our own strength*; rather, that we fix our eyes Him, yield to Him, and He performs the work within us.

Though we'll never arrive, this should be the Christian's foremost pursuit in life. This was the *"one thing"* that Paul pressed for. Paul passionately pressed toward the mark of being like Christ in every respect. After explaining his passionate pursuit in Philippians 3: 7-17, he concluded by saying, *"Brethren, join in following my* **example**, *and note those who so walk, as you have us for a* **pattern.**"

Afterward, Paul expressed his deep grief and tears over those who were filled with selfishness and worldliness. He described them as those *"whose* **God is their belly** [self], *and whose glory is in their shame, who* **mind earthly things"** (Philippians 3: 19). These were the opposite of Paul's example; these are the opposite of Christ. Identifying with Christ in every way was the central theme of Paul's life, and he passionately challenges us to follow his *"example."*

Thus far, we've considered the importance of *literally* following Christ — not simply claiming to follow Christ, yet living according to one's own wonderful personality traits and religious affinities. Dear reader, set Christ as the focal point of your faith; again, this will keep you spiritually balanced and on course.

In the next section we're going to learn *how* to follow Christ. What does it mean to *look unto Jesus*? Time, Truth, brutal experience, and the wisdom of the *spiritually* aged has taught me (and is still teaching me) how this is accomplished. What I've discovered is that there are four primary elements to following Christ:

1. We are enabled to follow Christ according to the power of the **Holy Spirit.**
2. This Spirit-empowered walk is attained and sustained by **faith**
3. This faith must be founded in the *Person* and *Truth* of the **Word of God.**

4. Finally, this faith is *vitalized* and *empowered* through a <u>**surrendered love**</u> for the *Person* and *Truth* of the Word of God.

These four principles enable us to follow Christ. Let's consider the first one; the role of the Holy Spirit.

Christ In You, the Holy Spirit

"Nevertheless I tell you the truth. **It is to your advantage that I go away***; for if I do not go away, the Helper will not come to you; but if I depart, I will send Him to you… I still have many things to say to you, but you cannot bear them now.* ¹³ *However, when He, the Spirit of truth, has come,* **He will guide you into all truth***; for He will not speak on His own authority, but whatever He hears He will speak; and He will tell you things to come.* ¹⁴ **He will glorify Me, for He will take of what is Mine and declare it to you.** ¹⁵ *All things that the Father has are Mine. Therefore I said that He will take of Mine and declare it to you"* (John 16: 7-9, 12-15).

"And I will pray the Father, and He will give you another Helper, that He may abide with you forever – ¹⁷ *the Spirit of truth, whom the world cannot receive, because it neither sees Him nor knows Him; but you know Him, for He dwells with you and will be in you.* ¹⁸ *I will not leave you orphans;* <u>**I will come to you**</u>*"* (John 14: 16-18).

When Christ was physically on earth, His disciples followed the example of His every step and command. However, as the crucifixion drew near, Christ started explaining to His disciples that they would soon have to follow Him in a different manner. As a matter of fact, He told them that this new arrangement would be better than having Him physically there with them.

During that period, Christ was confined to one location at a time. He labored trying to teach spiritual truths to the natural minds of His disciples. On various occasions He gave them *temporal* power to minister to the people. And throughout His life He vigilantly stood guard to keep His disciples from the schemes of the enemy. But the time would soon come when Christ would be *in* them in the person of the Holy Spirit. The Holy Spirit would indwell all of them at the same time, open up their capacity to discern spiritual truth, give them overflowing power for ministry, and enable them to overcome the schemes of the Devil and walk in the likeness of Christ.

The moment a Christian is born-again, they are immediately indwelt by the Holy Spirit and baptized [literally: *"immersed"*] into the Body of Christ. They are a completely *"new creature"* in their inner, spiritual nature. However, at this stage they're still filled with the influence of the fleshly self and the ways of this world. As long as they are filled with self and this world, they cannot be consistently filled with the Holy Spirit. Being "filled" with the Holy Spirit does not mean that a person has more of the Holy Spirit; it means that the Holy Spirit has more of the person. Unfortunately, denying self and being crucified to the world does not come easy to us. That's why this is one of the first things the Holy Spirit enables the *surrendered* saint to do. Consider this quote from A B Simpson:

> *"This is the greatest crisis that comes to a Christian: when into the spirit that was renewed in conversion, God Himself comes to dwell, to make it His abiding place, and to hold it by His mighty power in holiness and righteousness. After this occurs, one would suppose that we would be lifted up into a much more hopeful and exuberant spirit, but the prophet gives a very different picture. He says when this comes to pass we shall loathe ourselves in our own eyes. The revelation of God conveys a profound sense of our own nothingness and worthlessness and lays us on our face in the dust in self-denial.* **The incoming of the Holy Spirit displaces self and disgraces self forever. The highest holiness is to walk in self-renunciation.***"*[42]

The Holy Spirit starts here. Why? Because that's where Christ started – *"Deny yourself."* The Holy Spirit must get our *self* out of the way so that He can fill us with Him*self*. If self is not being humbled within us, it is because we are not surrendered – we are resisting the Holy Spirit; or worse yet, still spiritually dead. But as we surrender to Him, the Holy Spirit fills us and begins to break down the self-nature.

> *"A* **surrendered will** *and life is the great key to receiving the Holy Spirit.* **Everything hinges on this***. We may plead with God for the filling of the Holy Spirit, but* **unless we are yielded to Him to the very center of our being***, nothing is likely to come of it"* – R. A. Torrey.[43]

The Holy Spirit doesn't bend our arm and force His infilling on us; we can *"grieve"* Him and *"quench"* Him. Being filled with the Spirit is not something that we work up in the emotional atmosphere of a church service; it's something that we soberly and submissively surrender to. Being filled with the Spirit does not make a person fanatical, erratic, and boisterous – it makes them like Christ. This bears repeating: *Being filled with the Spirit does not make a person fanatical, erratic, and boisterous – it makes them like Christ.* Christ was the only man ever who was perpetually filled with the Holy Spirit, yet calm sobriety, holiness, love, and wisdom marked His character.

Tozer wrote:

"…(Christ) maintained a certain quiet poise and freedom from strain throughout His earthly sojourn…Our Lord was able to work with a minimum of weariness because He was a man completely possessed by the Holy Spirit… Peter explained that Christ "went around doing good and healing all who were under the power of the devil," after **God had "anointed [Him] with the Holy Spirit and power" (Acts 10:38)."**[44] – [It's important to note here that the anointing that Christ received at John's baptism was for power to fulfill His ministry. Hence, His first miracle (John 2) was after this baptism. However, Christ was always filled with the Holy Spirit. But I digress.]

God's will is that we fully surrender to the same Holy Spirit so that the life of Christ can be manifest in our character and behavior. R. A. Torrey wrote the following in his book, *"God's Power in Your Life"*:

"The Holy Spirit brings forth Christ-like graces of character in the believer…But when we give the indwelling Spirit *full control*, realizing the evilness of the flesh, and giving up ever attaining anything good in its power – when we come to the end of self – then [and only then] **these holy graces of character become His fruit in us.**"[45]

Simply put, in order to follow Christ, we must completely yield to the Holy Spirit so that Christ can live through us.

The Holy Spirit Empowers Us to Overcome Sin

One of the main *holy graces* of Christ's character that the Holy Spirit produces within us is victory over sin. The chief attribute of the ***Holy*** Spirit is holiness—separation from sin unto Christ. The Holy Spirit must break us down before He can build us up. To be more precise, as He is breaking down and emptying our old self, He is simultaneously building up and filling our new spiritual nature. But we must surrender to Him continually in order for Him to perform this work within us. It's not enough to simply have the Holy Spirit within us; we must *"walk"* in Him. As we learn the Spirit-filled *walk*, we gain continuous victory over every sin.

*"Walk in the Spirit, and you **shall not** fulfill the lust of the flesh"* (Galatians 5: 16).

And again,

*"If you live according to the flesh you will die; **but if by the Spirit you put to death the deeds of the body**, you will live. ¹⁴ For as many as are **led by** the Spirit of God, these are sons of God"* (Romans 8: 13-14).

    This is the crux of the whole matter. This is what everything funnels down to. This is the primary goal of this book—to teach us how to consistently *"walk in the Spirit."* Walking in the Spirit enables us to overcome *all bondage to all sin, in God's way and by God's power*. Many assume that victory over sin occurs in one dynamic experience of deliverance, and the Christian never feels tempted toward certain sins any more. This is not true; not even Christ ceased being tempted! Victory is a walk, not a one-time event. This bears repeating: *Victory is a walk, not a one-time event.* If we stop walking *"in the Spirit"*, then our flesh will begin to regain its strength, and we'll become weak again. Only the Spirit of God can give us power over sin.

    God did not leave it to us to formulate ideas and methodologies to conquer sin—sin is a spiritual issue. A person can no sooner save themselves from the penalty of sin than they can save themselves from the power of sin. It is impossible for us to live the Christian life in the power of our flesh. This was the foolish thinking of the Galatians.

    *"This only I want to learn from you: Did you receive the Spirit by the works of the law, or by the hearing of faith? ³ Are you so foolish? **Having begun in the Spirit, are you now being made perfect by the flesh**"* (Galatians 3: 2-3).

    The Galatians were reverting back to the works of the Jewish law in order to perfect themselves in the faith; however, they were supposed to *"walk in the Spirit"* (Galatians 5: 16-18) so that God could perfect them. Any attempt at perfecting ourselves other than walking in the Holy Spirit's power—Christianized psychology, recovery programs, will power, self-discipline—is a *"foolish"* work of the flesh. It doesn't matter if we look good in our own eyes; God calls us to follow the example of His Son. When we attempt to perfect ourselves within the strength of the flesh we only create a rollercoaster of perpetual failure and unbalanced, preferential morals.

Walking in the Spirit is not an optional extra; a kind of luxury package addition to our Christian life. It is a normative, necessary imperative for every single Christian! Nor is walking in the Spirit an effortless, unconscious reality in every Christian—this has become one of the biggest lies that many self-satisfied Christians have told themselves. A common misunderstanding among many Christians is that when we receive the Holy Spirit at salvation, we are automatically filled with the Holy Spirit from that point on, whether we're seeking it or not. This is simply not true! Instead, walking in the Spirit is an essential requirement for growth that must be consciously surrendered to.

R. A. Torrey put it the following way: "*God floods the heart of the believer, who **surrenders absolutely** to Him with light and joy, and **fills his life with power**. **Absolute surrender** to God is the **secret of blessedness and power**.*"[46]

This is one of the most essential truths that we need to understand concerning what it means to follow Christ—the Holy Spirit empowers and enables us to be conformed into the image of Christ. This means that He empowers us to overcome bondage to *all patterns* sin, for Christ did no sin. It also means He empowers us to live righteously, overflowing with the fruit of the Spirit, which is the character of Christ. Remember, overcoming sin is not the goal; growing into the likeness of Christ is the goal. As we fix our eyes on *this* goal, the Lord Himself makes us free from sin. Consider the following scripture.

"*For you were once darkness, but now you are light in the Lord. Walk as children of light* ⁹ (**for** *the fruit of the Spirit* is in all goodness, righteousness, and truth)" (Ephesians 5: 8-9).

There's a profound insight contained within this scripture that drives home the whole point of the matter. First, this scripture teaches us that *walking in the light* is synonymous with *walking in the Spirit*. Paul's use of the conjunction word *"for"* reveals that *"the fruit of the Spirit"* is a description of what it means to *"Walk as children of Light"*. As a matter of fact, God has several different angles of walking in the Spirit (*"Walk in the Light", "Abide in me", "Walk in love", "Walk by faith", "Be imitators of God", "Follow Me", "abide in my word", "Walk in the Truth", "Be holy, for I AM holy"*, etc. These are several different angles of the same truth. We cannot **genuinely** do any one of these without the others. Walking in the Spirit encompasses all of these.). However, the analogy of light and darkness is significant for how it relates to overcoming sin by walking in the Spirit (See entire context; Ephesians 5: 1-19).

What do we know about darkness and light? First, darkness is literally nothing—i.e., *no thing*. It is the absence of light. Light is something. When light is introduced into a dark room, the darkness automatically, effortlessly, and swiftly flees away. No one has ever turned on a light, and afterward had to get a fan or a broom to shoo the darkness out of the room. I've yet to see someone using a putty knife to scrape the darkness out of the corners of a room after they turned the light on. No. When the light is turned on, the darkness flees. The only darkness that remains is the darkness that is hiding beneath and behind the furniture and other objects in the room.

Sin, like darkness, is the absence of God, who is Light. *"This is the message which we have heard from Him and declare to you, that God is light and in Him is **no darkness at all**.* ⁶ *If we say that we have fellowship with Him, and walk in darkness, **we lie** and do not practice the truth"* (1 John 1: 5-6). Therefore, as long as we walk in the Spirit of God, we are walking in the Light of God—we can't do one without the other. When we thus walk in the Light, God literally drives away our sin like light drives away darkness. It's not a matter of wrestling with our sin or using some psycho-religious strategy; rather, it's about walking in the Spirit, Who is the Light.

The scripture does not say, "Walk in the Spirit, and you'll be able to strategically master a few pet peeve vices." No! It says *"you **shall not** fulfill the lust of the flesh."* Shortly after this verse, Paul gives a *partial list* of the sins *"of the flesh"*—I say *partial* because he ends the list with the words, *"and the like"* (Galatians 5: 19-21). Jesus didn't say that *"the Truth"* will help you to wrestle your way out of bondage to certain sins. He said that *"the Truth will **make** you free"*, for the Truth is the Son who, by His Holy Spirit, makes us *"free indeed!"* And, in the context, Christ is speaking of freedom from the slavery (bondage and patterns) of sin. And this is only accomplished as we walk in the light.

But, the light will only drive the darkness from the areas of the room that are open. As long as the furniture and appliances of worldly distractions are crowding the room of our heart, we'll remain in darkness in those areas. And festering within those dark corners, like black mold, are sinful spores that we unwittingly breathe in day after day, wondering why our soul is constantly plagued with sinful maladies. Make an inventory of your life. Scrap some of that worldly clutter that you've been *covetously* holding on to. Open up the room of your heart to the light of God, and allow Him to drive away the darkness of sin out of your life.

This is what it all boils down to: opening ourselves up completely to God, and walking in the Light of His Spirit. As we do this, He not only drives away our sin, but He fills us with the very character and righteousness of Christ Himself. Next, we're going to consider *how* we enter into and walk in the Spirit.

Faith and Love: The Two Pillars of Spiritual Fruitfulness and Power

Read this section closely and carefully; learning *how to walk* in the Spirit will be the difference between your success or failure. Thus far we've established that following Christ is accomplished by walking in the Spirit—it's literally Christ living through us. It's through walking in the Spirit that we are enabled to overcome our sinful strongholds. However, although many of us know that we are taught to *"walk in the Spirit"*, few of us know *how* this is accomplished. In order to walk in the Spirit, we must walk in *love* by *faith*.

Do not allow this seemingly simplistic answer to fool you—the ramifications of *genuine*, biblical faith and love are broad and far reaching. These two graces are the two pillars of the entire Christian walk, for it is through these two graces that we are enabled to walk in oneness with the Spirit of God Himself. These are the two core attributes that the Apostles always looked for in new believers. When these two pillars were in place, the Apostles knew that the believers were ready to advance to higher levels of spiritual discernment, fruitfulness, and power. Consider the following scriptures:

*"Therefore I also, **after I heard** of **your faith** in the Lord Jesus and **your love** for all the saints, ¹⁶ do not cease to give thanks for you, making mention of you in my prayers: ¹⁷ that the God of our Lord Jesus Christ, the Father of glory, may give to you the **spirit of wisdom and revelation in the knowledge of Him**, ¹⁸ the eyes of your understanding being enlightened; that you may know what is the hope of His calling, what are the riches of the glory of His inheritance in the saints, ¹⁹ and what is the exceeding greatness of **His power** toward us who believe, according to the working of His mighty power"* (Ephesians 1: 15-19).

And again,

"We give thanks to the God and Father of our Lord Jesus Christ, praying always for you, ⁴ **since we heard** of **your faith** in Christ Jesus and of **your love** for all the saints;…as you also learned from Epaphras, our dear fellow servant, who is a faithful minister of Christ on your behalf, ⁸ **who also declared to us your love in the Spirit**.⁹ For this reason we also, **since the day we heard it**, do not cease to pray for you, and to ask that you may be filled with the knowledge of His will in all wisdom and spiritual understanding; ¹⁰ that you may walk worthy of the Lord, fully pleasing Him, being fruitful in every good work and increasing in the knowledge of God; ¹¹ strengthened with all might, according to His glorious power" (Colossians 1: 3-10).

After describing the love of the Philippians who supported Paul's ministry while he was in prison, Paul wrote the following scripture:

"And this I pray, **that your love may abound still more and more** in knowledge and all discernment, ¹⁰ that you may approve the things that are excellent, that you may be sincere and without offense till the day of Christ, ¹¹ being filled with the fruits of righteousness which are by Jesus Christ, to the glory and praise of God" (Philippians 1: 9-11).

And again,

"We are bound to thank God always for you, brethren, as it is fitting, because **your faith** grows exceedingly, and **the love of every one of you** all abounds toward each other" (2 Thessalonians 1: 3).

When Paul was fearful that the Thessalonians might fall away because they were going through tribulation, He sent Timothy to check on them:

"For this reason, when I could no longer endure it, I sent to know your faith, lest by some means the tempter had tempted you, and our labor might be in vain.

⁶ But now that Timothy has come to us from you, and brought us good news of your **faith and love**, and that you always have good remembrance of us, greatly desiring to see us, as we also to see you – ⁷ therefore, brethren, in all our affliction and distress we were comforted concerning you by your faith.⁸ For now we live, if you stand fast in the Lord." (1 Thessalonians 3: 5-8).

I hope you're getting the picture—I could go on. *(Allow me to make a critical point before I move on. The "faith" that Paul is speaking of is not merely the initial faith that a person exercises when they first believe on Christ. Paul is speaking of a faith that is consciously devoted to Christ.)* Faith and love are the two pillars of the entire Christian life. When these two pillars are settled firmly in place, they make it possible for every other aspect of the Christian life to fall into place.

After Paul *"heard"* of the Christian's faith and love, he realized that they were ready to advance spiritually. These spiritual advances included growth in *"spirit of wisdom and revelation* **in the knowledge of Him***"*, *"the exceeding greatness of His power toward us who believe"*, *"the knowledge of His will in all wisdom and spiritual understanding"*, the ability to *"walk worthy of the Lord, fully pleasing Him"*, and the capacity to be *"strengthened with all might, according to His glorious power."* All of this is made possible *after* faith and love are firmly settled and growing within the Christian. But, not every church received these commendations from Paul.

The Corinthians received no commendation for their faith and love because they were severely failing in the area of love. Instead, Paul pleaded with them to get along with one another, reprimanded them for their divisions and conflicts, and he also wrote an entire chapter teaching them what love looks like (1 Corinthians 13). The Galatians also received no commendation for their faith and love because they were severely failing in the area of faith. The Hebrew Christians, though they had the fruit of love (Hebrews 6: 9-12, 10: 32-34), their faith was failing. Therefore, they were constantly admonished to continue in the faith, and they were given an entire chapter dedicated to what *genuine* faith looked like (Hebrews 11). None of these churches were ready to advance in their spiritual growth.

Paul told the Corinthians, *"And I, brethren, could not speak to you as to spiritual people but as to carnal, as to babes in Christ.* ² *I fed you with milk and not with solid food; for until now you were not able to receive it, and* **even now you are still not able***;* ³ *for you are still carnal. For where there are envy, strife, and divisions among you, are you not carnal and behaving like mere men?"* (1 Corinthians 3: 1-3).

He told the Galatians, *"I am afraid for you, lest I have labored for you in vain…*¹⁹ *My little children, for whom I labor in birth* **again until Christ is formed in you***,* ²⁰ *I would like to be present with you now and to change my tone; for I have doubts about you"* (Galatians 4: 10-20).

The Hebrew Christians received the following rebuke: *"For though by this time you ought to be teachers, you need someone to teach you again the first principles of the oracles of God; and you have come to need milk and not solid food.* ¹³ *For everyone who partakes only of milk is unskilled in the word of righteousness, for he is a babe.* ¹⁴ *But* solid food belongs to those who are of full age, that is, those who by reason of use have their senses exercised to discern both good and evil" (Hebrews 5: 12-14).

Compare these comments with the comments made to churches that *were* growing in faith and love. The difference is stark and noteworthy. Faith and love — with them, the Christian is enabled to flourish in every other aspect of the Christian life; without them, the Christian is completely crippled.

"Though I speak with the tongues of men and of angels, but have not love, I have become sounding brass or a clanging cymbal. ² And though I have the gift of prophecy, and understand all mysteries and all knowledge, and though I have all faith, so that I could remove mountains, but have not love, **I am nothing**. ³ And though I bestow all my goods to feed the poor, and though I give my body to be burned, but have not love, **it profits me nothing**" (1 **Corinthians** 13: 1-3).

And,

"Without faith it is **impossible** to please Him" (**Hebrews** 11: 6).

This is where many Christians fail and why most Christians are struggling — we lack *genuine, biblical* faith, and *genuine, biblical* love. We can study the Bible until we're blue in the face, and serve in every office of the church, but if these two pillars are not truly in us, we'll never attain the discernment, fruitfulness, and power that God promises us.

The reason why these two pillars are so critical is because they enable us to enter into the subtle, yet powerful influences of the Holy Spirit. When we're walking in the Spirit, He brings every other aspect of our Christian life into alignment with Himself, thus giving discernment, balance, power, and Christ-like authenticity to our walk. Let's take a slow walk through this section as we explore how faith and love enable us to walk in the Spirit.

How Does Faith and Love Enable Us To Walk in the Spirit?

The situation with the Galatian church provides us with a good starting point for this subject. The Galatian Christians were beginning to turn back to the Jewish law under the flawed assumption that doing so would enable them to improve their salvation and grow in sanctification. As a result, they began living in the strength and understanding of their flesh. When they began living in the strength of the flesh, they ceased from living in the power of the Spirit. Paul condemned this behavior in Galatians 3: 2-3 & 5:

> "This only I want to learn from you: Did you receive **the Spirit** by the works of the law, **or by the hearing of faith**? ³ Are you so foolish? **Having begun in the Spirit**, are you now being made perfect by the flesh?...⁵Therefore He who supplies the Spirit to you and works miracles among you, does He do it by the works of the law, or **by the hearing of faith**?"

Pause and take critical note of Paul's words. When the Galatians were saved *by faith* they received the Spirit. However, they were then expected to *"walk by faith"* in order to continue in the Holy Spirit's power. They had *"begun"* in the Spirit *by faith*; therefore, they were supposed to *continue* in the Spirit *by faith*. This is reinforced in verse 5. Paul, here, is talking about the *walk* of the Christian. As the Christian walks by faith, the Lord continually *"supplies"* them with the Holy Spirit's discernment, power, and fruitfulness. It's not enough simply to be saved by faith. In order to *walk* in the Holy Spirit's influence and power, the Christian must *"walk by faith"* — it's faith through and through.

However, faith is only one wing to this bird. The Christian must not only walk **by** faith, he must also walk **in** love. Don't let me lose you; stay with me. Look at the two parallel verses that Paul wrote to the Galatians:

> "For in Christ Jesus neither circumcision nor uncircumcision avails anything, but **faith working through love**" (Galatians 5: 6).

> "For in Christ Jesus neither circumcision nor uncircumcision avails anything, but **a new creation** [or "new creature"]. And as many as <u>walk</u> according to this rule, peace and mercy be upon them" (Galatians 6: 15).

Do you see it? It's the same verse; however, one verse is telling us that we're supposed to *"walk"* according to our new, spiritual nature, and the other verse is telling us <u>how we're enabled to walk</u> in the new nature — *"faith working through love."* This is the crux of the whole Christian walk. ***Genuine, biblical*** faith and love are the *spiritual* attributes of the *"new creature"* — this is why the apostles always looked for these two essential spiritual graces within new converts. They are the eyes, hands, feet, logic, conscience, and heartbeat of the new nature. It is *impossible* for us to walk in *genuine* faith and love according the natural understanding of our fleshly, self-nature.

Our spiritual nature was ***created*** to be one spirit with Jesus Christ; *"he who is joined to the Lord is one spirit with Him"* (1 Corinthians 6: 17). But, being a *"new creature"* in Christ, and living in *"one spirit"* with the Lord does not automatically transform us. This very same verse in 1 Corinthians tells us that we can drag the Spirit of Christ into a promiscuous relationship (1 Corinthians 6: 15)!

Being one with Christ is one thing, but *walking* in oneness with the Spirit of Christ is something entirely different. Even though we're *"new creatures"* in Christ, we still, by nature, are prone to walk according to our old self. It is the nature of all things to take the path of least resistance. Walking according to self comes natural to us, but walking in the Spirit takes understanding, alertness, intentionality, and surrendered effort. This bears repeating: *"Walking according to self comes natural to us, but walking in the Spirit takes understanding, alertness, intentionality, and surrendered effort."*

Our old selfish nature is not going to lay down and allow our new nature to have his way. The Scriptures tell us to *"****put off…the old man*** *which grows corrupt according to the deceitful lusts,* [23] *and be renewed in the spirit of your mind,* [24] *and that you* ***put on the new man which was created*** *according to God, in* ***true righteousness and holiness****"* (Ephesians 4: 22-24). *"True righteousness and holiness"* can only be produced in the *"new man"*, for only the new man is made after the image of Christ. As it is written in Colossians 3: 10, *"put on the new man, which is renewed in knowledge* ***after <u>the image</u>*** *of him that created him.<u>"</u>* On the contrary, **"false** righteousness and holiness" is produced by the preferential, fleshly morality of man. If a person's standard of *"righteousness and holiness"* is not like Christ, it's false, Pharisaical, and corrupted.

So, how do we put off the old man and put on the new? This command takes effort and understanding; it doesn't happen automatically. We've already considered many aspects of what it means to *"put off"* the old man (self) along with his *"deceitful lusts"* (the world) in previous chapters. So, how do we *"put on"* and walk according to our *"new man"* in *"****true*** *righteousness and holiness"*? The answer is simple yet far reaching: *"faith working through love"* – this is how the *"new creation"* within us functions.

A life that is filled with faith and fueled by love will engender the Holy Spirit's power to overcome sin (among many other things). Faith and love are the two means through which this Spirit-empowered walk is accomplished. Furthermore, faith and love are not merely optional suggestions given by God. They are the two foundational commands given by the Lord to all who claim to be His.

"*²³And this is His **commandment**: that we should **believe** on the name of His Son Jesus Christ and **love** one another, as He gave us **commandment**. ²⁴ Now **he who keeps His commandments** [faith and love] abides in Him, and He [the Holy Spirit abides] in him. And by this we know that He abides in us, **by the Spirit whom He has given us**"* (1 John 3: 23-24).

And again,

"*If we **love** one another, **God** [the Holy Spirit] **abides in us**, and His love has been perfected in us. ¹³ **By this we know that we abide in Him, and He** [the Holy Spirit] **in us, because He has given us of His Spirit**…Whoever confesses that Jesus is the Son of God [faith], God abides in him, and he in God. ¹⁶ And we have known and believed the love that God has for us. **God is love, and he who abides in love abides in God, and God** [the Holy Spirit] **in him**"* (1 John 12-16).

Before we move on, it's imperative that we again recognize that the faith that John is speaking of in these scriptures is not merely the initial faith of salvation; rather, a continuous, abiding faith in Christ. Remember what John told his readers: "*These things I have written to you **who believe** in the name of the Son of God* [i.e., they were already Christians]*, that you may know that you have eternal life, and **that you may continue to believe** in the name of the Son of God*" (1 John 5: 13).

This is the kind of faith that the book of Hebrews spoke of. The great chapter of faith, Hebrews 11, described many saints who *lived by* faith. In the very next chapter, we're told that we're supposed to press on with the same kind of faith, "*looking unto Jesus, the author **and finisher** of our faith*" (Hebrews 12: 2) — not just the *"author"*, but the *"author **and** finisher."* This is the *conscious, deliberate, abiding* faith in Christ that John is speaking of in the above verses.

These are the two foundational *commands* of the Christian life—faith and love; through them the Christian is enabled to *"abide"* (continue, dwell) in Christ, and the Holy Spirit influentially and effectually *"abides"* in the Christian. This is what John is describing in the above verses. Furthermore, the Apostle John is building on what Christ taught us about the Vine and the branches in John 15 (John is the best commentator on his own gospel).

*"Abide in Me, and I in you. As the branch cannot bear fruit of itself, unless it abides in the vine, neither can you, unless you abide in Me. ⁵ "I am the vine, you are the branches. He who abides in Me, and I in him, **bears much fruit**"* (John 15: 4-5).

Jesus commands us to abide in Him in order to bear fruit; John explains to us *how* to abide in Him. According to John, it is through *faith and love* that we abide in Him and His Holy Spirit abides in us; hence, we bear the fruit of the Holy Spirit. This should remind you of the earlier verses that showed how the apostles recognized faith and love as the forerunners of fruitfulness, discernment, and power.

Faith and love, according to John, enable us to abide in Christ and He in us. When we enter into this oneness with Christ, the fruit and power of His Spirit fills us and overflows out of us. No longer are we psychologically striving to live clean lives according to our own preferential morals. Instead, the Spirit of God enables our new nature to both discern and walk in "<u>**true righteousness and holiness.**</u>"

When we walk by faith, motivated by love, we spiritually enter into oneness with the Spirit of Christ. It's a mysterious, paradoxical union between the Spirit of God and the spirit of man. He abides in us, influencing and enabling our faith and love, and we abide in Him, walking by faith and loving everything that God loves. However, if we do not abide in Him, He will not abide in us, and in such a state we *"can do nothing"* — this includes overcoming sin. Therefore, it is imperative that we learn to walk by *"faith working through love"* if we desire to be graced with the Spirit's presence and power.

Oh, I could say so much more about this vital truth! There are many more scriptures that bear out this essential principle of spiritual living, but for the sake of brevity, we'll conclude this section. Glory be to God for the all sufficient grace that He bestows on us for *"all things that pertain to life and godliness"* through the power of His Holy Spirit.

"For this reason I bow my knees to the Father of our Lord Jesus Christ, ¹⁵ from whom the whole family in heaven and earth is named, ¹⁶ that He would grant you, according to the riches of His glory, **<u>to be strengthened with might through His Spirit in the inner man</u>**, *¹⁷ that* **Christ may dwell in your hearts through <u>faith</u>** [i.e.,

Christ abiding in us]; ***that you, being rooted and grounded in <u>love</u>***, ¹⁸ *may be able to comprehend with all the saints what is the width and length and depth and height –* ¹⁹ *to know the love of Christ which passes knowledge;* ***that you may be <u>filled with</u> all the <u>fullness of God.</u>"*** (Ephesians 3: 14-19).

Are you getting the picture? Again, the Holy Spirit gives us power in our *"inner man"* to overcome sin and live the Christian life. But this power is rooted in a life of faith and love. Furthermore, Paul is talking to Christians; therefore, his prayer that *"Christ may dwell in* [their] *hearts through faith"* is not the initial faith of salvation, but the faith that continuously abides in Christ that John speaks of. It is only through these two graces—faith and love—that we can be *"filled with all the fullness of God"*, and therefore enabled to *"walk in the Spirit."*

"But to have Jesus ever near, the heart must be full of him, welling up with his love, even to overrunning; ***hence the apostle prays "that Christ may dwell in your hearts."*** *See how near he would have Jesus to be!...Observe the words-that he may dwell in your heart, that best room of the house of manhood; not in your thoughts alone, but in your affections; not merely in the mind's meditations, but in the heart's emotions. We should pant after love to Christ of a most abiding character, not a love that flames up and then dies out into the darkness of a few embers, but a constant flame, fed by sacred fuel, like the fire upon the altar which never went out.* ***This cannot be accomplished except by <u>faith</u>. Faith must be strong, or <u>love</u> will not be fervent***; *the root of the flower must be healthy, or we cannot expect the bloom to be sweet.* ***<u>Faith</u> is the lily's root, and <u>love</u> is the lily's bloom. Now, reader, Jesus cannot be in your heart's <u>love</u> except you have a firm hold of him by your heart's <u>faith;</u>*** *and, therefore, pray that you may always <u>trust</u> Christ in order that you may always <u>love</u> him."* –Spurgeon[47]

You may say, *"Well, that's simple enough. I can walk by faith and love. This is gonna be easier than I thought!"* Not so fast! The Deceiver is a master at misconstruing vital truths! The concepts of faith and love have been profoundly distorted within much of the modern church. What is love? What is faith? It's not enough to take the words "faith" and "love", and then according to our own understanding of the terms, try to live the Christian life. God didn't merely tell us to exercise faith and love; *He went through great lengths in the Word of God to describe how these two essential graces are exercised and what they look like.* We cannot come to God with just *any* faith and love and expect the Holy Spirit to abide in us, empower us, and bear fruit through us.

Now that we've firmly established that we are enabled to *"walk in the Spirit"* by *faith and love*, the question now is, what does biblical faith and biblical love look like? How are they nurtured and established within us? How are they exercised? This is what we'll be exploring in the next two chapters.

CHAPTER 7

"FOLLOW ME" IN THE SPIRIT BY FAITH

When considering what it means to walk in the Spirit by faith, it's important that we do not get too mystical and mysterious in our thinking. Many of us hope for some influx of spiritual inspiration to come rushing over us, sweeping us off our feet and stepping us through the Spirit-filled walk like a marionette. It doesn't work like that. Demons possess and control people; not the Spirit of God—He's so gentle that He allows Himself to be quenched if we resist Him. God only fills and empowers *surrendered* vessels. So, how do we walk in the *Spirit* by *faith*? Let's demystify it.

When God calls us to live by faith, He doesn't leave it to us to conjure up just any semblance of faith that feels comfortable to us. James says that *"even the demons believe"* (James 2: 19)! The faith that God accepts and honors is distinctly portrayed and defined within the scripture. There are three different key aspects of biblical faith that I want to highlight: **1. Biblical faith is single minded and wholehearted. 2. Biblical faith is grounded in and established by the Word of God. 3. Biblical faith is authenticated by trusting surrender.** Let's consider these key attributes of Biblical faith.

Biblical Faith is Single-Minded and Wholehearted

There are two scriptures that I believe best describe the single-minded, whole-hearted faith that God calls us to embrace as Christians.

*"Trust in the Lord with **all your heart**, and lean not on **your own understanding**; In all your ways acknowledge Him, And He shall direct your **paths**"* (Proverbs 3: 5).

And,

*"If any of you lacks wisdom, let him ask of God, who gives to all liberally and without reproach, and it will be given to him. ⁶ But let him ask in faith, with no doubting, for **he who doubts is like a wave of the sea driven and tossed by the wind**. ⁷ For let not that man suppose that he will receive anything from the Lord; ⁸ **he is a double-minded man, unstable in all his ways**"* (James 1: 5-8).

Before we move on, let's get a little clarification. The immediate context of the previous scripture is about praying for wisdom. However, it quickly broadens to *"all"* the *"ways"* of a person, not just their prayer life; the *"double-minded man, unstable in __all__ his ways."* This person is not merely double-minded in prayer; he's double-minded altogether — his prayer life is simply one of many casualties of his doubtfulness. Now let's move on.

Our *"own understanding"* and our *"doubts"* are two sides of the same coin. We *"doubt"* God's Truth when we begin to believe our *"own understanding."* We never stop believing; we simply redirect belief. When we whole-heartedly trust in God's Truth, we'll inevitably doubt our own understanding. When we place our trust in our own understanding, we'll inevitably doubt God's Truth. When we try to do both, we become a vacillating, double-minded, unstable, unbalanced, selectively biblical professed Christian.

The scripture says that *"we walk by faith, **not** by sight"* (2 Corinthians 5: 7); it doesn't say, "we walk by faith **and** by sight." *"Sight"* is merely a euphemism for our *"own understanding."* We cannot do both and expect to consistently *"walk in the Spirit";* for *"sight"* is natural and *"faith"* is spiritual. A few verses earlier, the Apostle Paul said, *"we **do not look** at the things which are seen, but at the things which are not seen. For the things which are seen are temporary, but the things which are not seen are eternal."* (2 Corinthians 4: 18).

Again, there's a clear line of separation between looking at natural things with the sight of our own understanding, and looking at spiritual things with the sight of faith. Now, this doesn't mean that we walk with our head in the clouds. The Christian still has to live in the everyday realities of life. However, the sight of faith enables them to both see and approach all things from an eternal perspective and in the light of Truth.

"It is purely a matter of faith. **Faith and sight always differ***. To your senses [your own understanding] it does not seem to be so, but your faith must still reckon it so. This is a very difficult attitude to hold, and only as we* **thoroughly** *believe God can we thus reckon upon His Word and His working. But as we do so, faith will convert it into fact, and it will become reality. These two words "yield" and "reckon" are passwords into the resurrection life."* — A. B. Simpson[48]

Since God's truths are completely antithetical and unreasonable to our natural, earthbound mind, when we *unreservedly* trust in God's truth, we are exercising faith. You get it? Wholehearted belief in the *entire* word of God, *as it is written*, is an exercise of faith. As long as a person is minimizing, modifying, or attempting to explain away Truth, he is functioning in the understanding of his natural mind — *"the natural man does not receive the things of the Spirit of God, for they are* **foolishness to him***; nor can he know them, because they are spiritually discerned"* (1 Corinthians 2: 14).

The clearest and surest evidence that a person is walking in their natural, *"own understanding"* is they refuse to fully trust *clear truth* for what it says. The clearest and surest evidence that a person is walking by faith is they fully trust clear truth for what it says. This isn't complicated; let's not over-spiritualize it. In the great chapter of faith, Hebrews 11, every person highlighted in this chapter simply resolved to fully trust in the revealed Truth of God, in spite of how ridiculous it sounded to the natural mind. God highlighted these flawed people, who determined to fully trust Him, as models of genuine faith.

The psychology and worldly philosophies that have permeated much of the modern church have done extraordinary damage in this area. They have managed to make the word of God largely rational, practical, regimented, logical, and understandable *to the natural mind*. Spiritual discernment is no longer needed. We've diluted and explained away many truths that take too much faith, too much sacrifice, and that infringe too greatly on our comfort zone. The fullness of God's word is often diminished and modified in order to fit into the limited container of our natural mind. What's left are "truths" that are manageable to the natural man — neither faith nor the enabling of the Holy Spirit are much needed.

The natural mind does not go deep enough to grasp the ways of the Spirit. Psycho-religious instructions for practical living are not the same as Spiritual enabling for powerful life! The religious, natural mind may enable us to *act* out an incomplete caricature of Christ, but a surrendered spirit fills us with the very nature of Christ.

Wholehearted faith is the only path to truly rested faith. If our faith is leaning on anything other than the Word of God alone, then our faith is not fully rested — we're still propping it up with our own understanding. However, the path to truly rested faith is not easy. It doesn't come overnight. It's often a humiliatingly frightening process of God wrenching every crutch out of our hands, and training us to fully rest our soul's well-being in His hands. But He will not force us down this path; he'll guide us down it — it's up to us to follow.

*"God will have to bring us down very low. A sense of emptiness and despair and nothingness will have to come upon us. It is when we sink down in utter helplessness that the everlasting God will reveal Himself in His power. Then our hearts will learn to trust God **alone**…The great hindrance to trust is self-effort.* **So long as you have got your own wisdom and thoughts and strength, you cannot fully trust God. But when God breaks you down, when everything begins to grow dim before your eyes and you see that you understand nothing, then God is coming near.** *If you will bow down in nothingness and wait on God, He will become all.*

As long as we are something, God cannot be all. His omnipotence cannot do its full work. That is the beginning of faith — utter despair of self, a ceasing from man (self) *and everything on earth* (world) *and finding our hope in God alone.*

And then, next, we must understand that faith is rest. In the beginning of the faith-life, faith is struggling. But as long as faith is struggling, faith has not attained its strength. But when faith in its struggling gets to the end of itself, and throws itself upon God and rests on Him, then joy and **victory** *come."* — Andrew Murray[49]

So, the Holy Spirit responds to whole-hearted, single-minded faith; God has clearly shown that He has great contempt for double-minded "faith". Now, God is gracious and patient with immature faith and weak faith. But double-minded faith is rooted in our *refusal* to take God plainly at His word, choosing rather to modify His truth with our own understanding in order to make it comfortable for our uncrucified self-nature. This will always be manifest in an unstable, unbalanced, selectively biblical life. God will not negotiate or debate His truth with the finite understanding of puny, selfish, corrupted man! Instead,

God only honors faith that is *wholeheartedly* and *single-mindedly* exercised in accordance with His *uncompromised, unabridged, undiluted, revealed truth*; this alone is the basis for true, spiritual faith.

This brings us to the next section — the basis for true faith.

Biblical Faith Must Be Grounded In and Established By the Word of God

Faith needs an object in order to be valid. It's become common for people to say, *"You just have to believe"*, or *"Just have faith"* — faith in what? To put it kindly, these are simply uneducated statements. Faith needs an object — the more immutable the object, the more certain the faith.

Anything that is rooted in man or this fallen creation is subject to change and corruption; therefore, to rest our faith in such would be folly. It doesn't matter how educated, scholarly, Christianized, reasonable, or "scientific" the information sounds; if it contradicts the Truth, it is untrustworthy. Even if it's 95% true, the Deceiver has an uncanny way of making the most out of that deceptive 5%, just like a drop of cyanide in purified water. Anything less than the undiluted, uncompromised Truth of the Word cannot be *fully* trusted. We can trust man to a degree, but we must trust God beyond degree.

> *"All flesh is as grass,*
> *And all the glory of man as the flower of the grass.*
> *The grass withers,*
> *And its flower falls away,*
> ^{25} *But the word of the LORD endures forever."* (1Peter 1: 24).

> *"So then* **faith comes** *by hearing, and hearing by* **the word of God**" (Romans 10: 17).

We are called to *"trust in the Lord with all* [our] *heart."* But, we cannot truly trust someone who we do not know. Nor would we know *how* to trust someone if we do not know what they're capable of, or what their views are, or what they promise to do, or what they will not do, or what they love, or what they hate, or what they want from us, or if they have any conditions that we must meet, or what makes them happy, or what grieves them, or what they give priority to, or what they consider to be trivial, and a host of other intimate details that enable us to truly know another person. This is the stuff that trust is made out of. The means through which we are to gain an accurate and intimate knowledge of Christ is through the Word.

*"And beginning at Moses and all the Prophets, He expounded to them in all the Scriptures the things **concerning Himself**."* (Luke 24: 27).

Therefore, in order to *justifiably* have a confident faith that truly knows the Lord and His will, our faith must be grounded in the Word of God from cover to cover. But, the goal is not to merely learn doctrines about Christ. Many Christians are very skilled at reciting the fundamental doctrines about Christ's nature and attributes. The Lord wants us to get beyond the theology of Christ; He calls us into a surrendered identification with the real Person of the Living Lord Jesus Christ.

This is why He tells us that if we *"continue **in His <u>word</u>**"* we prove ourselves to be *"disciples indeed"* who truly *"**know…the Son**"*. A disciple is not merely an academic student who sits in a class under a teacher, but a protégé, an apprentice, a devotee, a follower. A student merely learns academic facts, but is neither devoted to the facts nor the teacher. A disciple is someone who not only devotes himself to the instructions of their teacher, but entirely to the teacher. Many Christians are admitted "students of the Bible"; God calls for disciples. Such a walk enables the disciple to not only come to *"know the truth* [teachings]*"*, but *"the Son* [the teacher]*."* And the basis for this relationship is faith that is grounded in the Word.

There seems to be many students of the Bible, but very few disciples of the Living Word of God. The *"disciple indeed"* surrenders his *faith* to the Word of God *"as it is written"*. He never exalts the understanding of his natural mind, presumptuously and selectively modifying the Word *of God* as he sees fit. Instead, he *trusts* that God said what He meant, and meant what He said; therefore, God honors his *faith* with light, discernment, and reality.

The Word of God gives substance and direction to our faith. Many people *trust* God for things that He's never promised, or they *believe* things about God that contradict what God says about Himself, or they claim to trust God but have little regard for God's teaching and direction. This is what makes so many Christians *"double-minded"* and *"unstable in all their ways"* — their "faith" is saturated with their own understanding. This is not faith; it's religious presumption. God has revealed Himself to us within His word, not our religious intuition, our presumptuous feelings, our goosebumps, or — dare I say it — the pervasive philosophies of man that have been preferentially Christianized within the modern western church.

However, knowing that we are called to *"abide in* [His] *Word"* is one thing; doing it is an entirely different issue. One of the greatest obstacles that many Christians face is *making* (not *"finding"*) the time to read and listen to the Word. The two greatest obstacles to our spending time in the Word are *self* and the *world* — *self* doesn't feel like it, and there are too many things in this *world* that are more appealing to us than the Word of God. Let's be frank about this. This is one of the most common problems that I run into when counseling people — Christians simply do not want to spend quality time in the Bible. They don't feel like it — self! They're too busy — world! And at some point they've convinced themselves that this is ok. Therefore, one of the first things that we must do is to follow the instructions of the two previous chapters — deny yourself and take up your cross.

Not only must we consistently set aside time for the Word, but we must begin making a conscious effort to take God's word more seriously. We've looked at several scriptures throughout this book (and I've barely scratched the surface). However, any *honest* Christian must admit that many of the *New Testament* Truths that we've looked at are largely (and often completely) ignored within the average church. Either God is blowing out a lot of optional hot air, or He actually means what He says. We've become so accustomed to dismissing God's authority in the name of grace and love, that many of us have learned to tune His Word out like an ungrateful teen does to the instructions of a loving parent. This is because many of us do not truly *believe* that God Himself is speaking to us through His word.

Consider how most of us would respond to receiving a letter from a cherished friend or an individual who we deeply admire and esteem. Our hearts would leap with excitement, and we'd feel a deep appreciation that they considered us enough to write to us. We'd forgo some of our trivial activities, and sit down with a giddy anticipation of what the letter had to say. There are two reasons for this response. One, we truly *believe* that the letter was written by our friend. Two, we truly have a high esteem for our friend.

The Bible is inspired by God—the God who created all things, who knows us on the deepest, most intimate level and still loves us with an everlasting love, Who has every single solitary answer that we'll ever seek in life, who has all the solutions to all our problems, who has charted out a unique plan and purpose for our life, and to Whom we'll ultimately give an account of ourselves one day. This is the Word of God that many of us just can't seem to find the time to read—between the sports game, the gym, the TV shows, the recreational activities, and Candy Crush! The fact of the matter is that many of us do not truly *believe* that our Creator inspired the Bible. We can very earnestly recite the dogma that *"all scripture is inspired by God"*, but this creed has not translated into *reality* for many of us. When we determine to completely trust the Truth, it's like laying the transparent answer sheet atop the questions of our life, and the spiritual makes sense of the natural.

*"He who comes to God must **believe** that He is, and that He is a rewarder of those who diligently seek Him"* (Hebrews 11: 6). Before a person will *"diligently seek"* the Lord in the Word, he must first actually *"believe"* that the Lord is, and that He has spoken. When we actually believe this, there is nothing in heaven or hell that will keep us from scouring through the word of God in order to hear the voice of God and see the face of God.

This is the most fundamental basis for faith. Faith believes that the Word is of God; therefore, faith seeks the Truth of God in the Word. The person who can't seem to muster up an interest in reading the Word, *does not believe* that God inspired it. Deny yourself, crucify the world, and start exercising the faith of your new nature by feeding on *"every word that proceeds out of the Mouth of God."* As your new nature is nourished and built up in the Truth, the sight of your faith will become clearer and clearer. Eventually, like Paul, you'll be able to say,

"We do not look at the things which are seen, but at the things which are not seen. For the things which are seen are temporary, but the things which are not seen are eternal… For we walk by faith, not by sight" (2 Corinthians 4: 18 & 5: 7).

Faith Must Be Grounded in the Lord of the Word, Not Merely the Word

Most of us already know that we're supposed to read the Bible, but few of us understand how to approach the Bible. Many Christians spend little to no time in the Bible at all. However, many Christians dutifully attempt to read the Bible on the regular basis. There are some, though fewer in number, who diligently study the Bible. Unfortunately, in spite of this, many of us are still missing something.

For many years I studied the Bible with the best of them, but in the back of my mind I still realized that something was missing – but I couldn't put my finger on it. My period of chastening *(literally : "training")* completely transformed *how* I approach the Word of God. I experienced more spiritual growth in two years of properly approaching the Word, than I had in nearly two decades of improperly approaching it. What did I do differently? Let's first consider some insights from A. W. Tozer in an open letter that he wrote to John MacArthur.

"Fundamentalism has stood aloof from the liberal in self-conscious superiority and has on its own part fallen into error, the error of textualism, which is simply orthodoxy without the Holy Ghost. **Everywhere among conservatives we find persons who are Bible-taught but not Spirit-taught.** *They conceive truth to be something which they can grasp with the mind.*

If a man holds to the fundamentals of the Christian **faith**, *he is thought to possess divine truth. But it does not follow. There is no truth apart from the Spirit.* **The most brilliant intellect may be imbecilic when confronted with the mysteries of God.** *For a man to understand revealed truth requires an act of God equal to the original act which inspired the text. ... "Now we have received, not the Spirit of the world, but the Spirit which is of God; that we might know the things which are freely given us of God."*

For the **textualism** *of our times is based upon the same premise as the old line rationalism, that is, the belief that the human mind is the supreme authority in the judgment of truth. Or otherwise stated, it is confidence in the ability of the human mind to do that which the Bible declares it was never created to do and consequently is wholly incapable of doing. Philosophical rationalism is honest enough to reject the Bible flatly. Theological rationalism rejects it while pretending to accept it and in so doing puts out its own eyes.* – Tozer[50]

Charles Spurgeon gave a sermon on November 5, 1858 titled, "The Work of the Holy Spirit." In it he recounted this same problem of dead textualism back in his day:

"Now I am astonished to find those persons that thus come before me so well instructed in the doctrines of grace and so sound in all the truths of the covenant, insomuch that I may think it my boast and glory, in the name of Jesus, that I know not that we have any members, whom we have received into the church, who do not give their

full assent and consent unto all the doctrines of the Christian religion… Those which men are wont to laugh at as being high doctrinal points, are those which they most readily receive, believe, and rejoice in. I find, however, that the **greatest deficiency** *lies in this point, forgetfulness of the work of the Holy Spirit."*[51]

The late Leonard Ravenhill, a true prophet to the Church, made the following quotes:

"We've wrapped the Holy Ghost in our theological terminology till he has no freedom!"

"We've imprisoned the Holy Spirit within our creeds!"

The South African pastor, writer, and spiritual sage, Andrew Murray, addressed the mistaken assumption that many textualists have about the Holy Spirit.:

"If it is our belief that God is going to have mercy on His Church in these last ages, it will be because the doctrine and the truth about the Holy Spirit ***will not only be studied, but sought after with a whole heart.*** *It is not only because that truth will be sought after, but because ministers and congregations will be found bowing before God in deep abasement with one cry: 'we have grieved God's Spirit. We have tried to be Christian churches with as little as possible of God's Spirit. We have not sought to be churches filled with the Holy Spirit.'"*[52]

D. L. Moody was a servant of God who was undeniably filled with the Holy Spirit. During his time this humble evangelist led tens of thousands to Christ. However, this farm boy, whose formal education ended at the 5th grade, made the mistake of using the wrong biblical terminology concerning the filling of the Holy Spirit. The biblically surgical Plymouth Brethren nit-picked this minor inaccuracy, and missed the whole picture. Moody recounted this event:

"Oh, why will they split hairs? Why don't they see that this is just the one thing that they themselves need? They are good teachers, they are wonderful teachers, and I am so glad to have them here, but why will they not see that the baptism of the Holy Ghost is just the one touch that they themselves need?"[53]

Dr. Houghton, in response to Moody's words, further said, "*The tragedy is that so many are technically correct and spiritually powerless.*"[54] —and frankly, I would even argue against much of what is considered *"technically correct."* It's one thing to *"technically"* know that Christ is Lord; it's something entirely different to *spiritually **know*** Christ ***as*** Lord. So, the question again is, "how, exactly, do we approach the Word of God" so that we might *"know the Truth?"*

Textualism has become one of the most subtle, yet pervasive issues within modern evangelicalism. The textualist gets so focused on the text of scripture that they lose sight of the Truth of Scripture. They've confused following creeds with following Christ. Then they reproduce. They convince others to become "Bible students", but they shy away from fully embracing God's call for them to be whole-hearted disciples of Jesus Christ. Many young Christians are having their fire snuffed out under such teachers

"Right here is where the wrong kind of Bible teacher can do his damage. The first thing he does is to destroy the new Christian's simplicity. He introduces something between the Christian and Christ. He makes him Biblo-centric [a textualist] *instead of Christo-centric* [a follower of Christ]. *(And there is a difference, let no one deceive you.) The Spirit-anointed Bible teacher will so teach the Word as to keep it transparent, so as to allow it to be what it always should be, a kind of burning bush which God indwells and out of which He shines in awesome splendor. The beholder sees the bush, it is true, but the object of his interest is the Presence, not the bush. The wrong kind of teacher gets so technical about the bush that the fire dims down and the light ceases to fall on the Christian's face."* — Tozer[55]

The appeal of textualism is simple. It enables the Christian to wear a very convincing veneer of Christianity without compelling them to go through the sacrifice and surrender that biblical discipleship calls for. *"Knowledge puffs up, but **love** edifies"* (1 Corinthians 8: 1). Being a Bible student appeals to the pride of man; however, it takes sacrificial love to be a surrendered follower of Christ (we'll cover the subject of love a little later).

However, do not assume for a moment that the follower of Christ is less committed to the scriptures than the Bible student. On the contrary, they're more committed! The follower of Christ, by definition, *follows Christ* — not selectively, but entirely. It is possible to be Biblo-centric without being Christo-centric; however, it is impossible to be Christo-centric without being Biblo-centric. Christ made it clear; we are to seek ***Him*** in the Word, not merely doctrines ***about*** Him.

The whole of Scripture is about Christ. Seek His face, His mind, His character, His ways, His priorities, His heartbeat, His balance, His passion, His grace, His austerity, His will, His love, His lordship, His perspectives, His holiness, His desires. Seek Him with all your heart, for the Lord has promised, *"You will seek **Me and find Me**, when you search for **Me** with **all your heart**"* (Jeremiah 29: 13). This doesn't mean that we should avoid the other truths and doctrines; instead, that they should all be seen in the Light of Christ.

Pastor Zac Poonen of India has a common quote that I've embraced as my own: *"Christ is the dictionary for the Bible."* What does this mean? When the Bible tells us to love, we shouldn't use our religious imagination to figure out love — we should look at how Christ loved. When the Bible tells us to be forgiving, we should look at how Christ forgave. Everything that the Bible tells us to do is directly or indirectly illustrated in the life of Christ and His Christ-filled Apostles. Christ gives substance, balance, authenticity and life to every truth of scripture. Therefore, every truth should be approached in the light of how Christ would view, understand, prioritize, and practice that truth. Christ is *"the Word of God"*; therefore, all of God's Word must be discerned in the Light of Him. This is how we come to *"know the Truth"*, who is *"the Son"*, who makes us *"free"*.

As time goes by, you'll be amazed at how your reasoning, your logic, your priorities, your desires, your perspectives, and your passions begin to balance and align with God's Word. What He feels, you feel; what He hates, you hate; what He loves, you love. No longer will you be religiously selective with your theology and morality; your thoughts will be brought into alignment with God's thoughts. You'll become the *"spiritual"* Christian of 1 Corinthians 2 who has *"the mind of Christ"* (1 Corinthians 2: 11-16; 3: 1-4). Growth, fruitfulness, transformation, and power will be the inevitable result.

*"If you **abide in My word**, you are My disciples indeed. ³² And you shall **know the truth**, and the truth shall make you free… Therefore if **the Son** makes you free, you shall be free indeed!"*

So, we still haven't fully answered the question? *How* do we *"abide"* in the *"Word"* of God in order to develop a *faith* that truly knows the Lord? How do we approach the scripture in such a manner that we become *"disciples indeed"*, trusting in the Living Christ, and walking in complete freedom over the bondage of sin? Do we study harder? Do we read more? The scripture gives two primary manners in which we are to approach the Word *in order to affect spiritual transformation within our lives*. These two means of approaching the Word directly and deliberately affect our thoughts and our actions. Let's consider them.

Learning to Live By the Rivers of Living Water

When the scripture teaches us how to approach the Word it tells us to meditate on it; ponder it. Study is important, but study without meditation only serves to build the intellect—it does little to nourish up the spiritual inner man. Study is good for learning doctrines and biblical information. Meditation so transforms the mind, that our thoughts, our rationale, our motives, our logic, our wisdom, our ideas, and our very conscious are all progressively aligned with the Truth. Psalm 1: 1-3 gives us the definitive, God-ordained manner in which we are to approach the Word, not for academic understanding (which is important), but, *for spiritual growth and fruitfulness.*

"Blessed is the man
Who walks not in the counsel of the ungodly,
Nor stands in the path of sinners,
Nor sits in the seat of the scornful;

*But his **delight** is in the law of the* LORD,
*And **in His law he meditates day and night.***
³ *He **shall be** like a tree*
*Planted by the **rivers of water**,*
*That **brings forth its fruit in its season**,*
Whose leaf also shall not wither;
And whatever he does shall prosper."

This is God's immutable promise for fruitfulness, spiritual vibrancy, and God-glorifying success in all that we do. This promise and the conditions for this promise are very clear—turn from worldly influences and meditate on God's word *"day and night."* Such meditation is like being *"planted"* (settled, abiding) by *"rivers of water."* This sounds familiar.

Christ taught us that if we trust in Him, the Holy Spirit would flow out of our innermost being *"like rivers of living water"* (John 7: 38). What does Christ mean by this? In Ezekiel 47: 1-12, the prophet writes about a vision he saw of the temple of God. In this vision he saw a river of water flowing out from the temple, growing larger and larger, and bringing life and healing wherever it went. The scripture teaches that we are the *"temple of the Holy Spirit"* (1 Corinthians 6: 19). God desires for every Christian to be, not only filled with the Holy Spirit, but overflowing with the Holy Spirit. Unfortunately, we can *"grieve"* and *"quench"* the Holy Spirit and stop up the flow. So, how does a Christian experience the life where *"rivers of Living Water"* are flowing out of them, and bringing life and healing to others?

We need to drink in the Spirit-inspired Word in order for the Holy Spirit to flow more fully. If all we know is John 3:16, then that's all that will flow. When the Lord gave the woman at the well the living waters of truth, she ran into the city and overflowed with what He gave her (John 4: 1-42). The Holy Spirit is not going to inspire us with new scripture—we're not Apostles! We need to read and meditate on what's already been inspired.

Psalms 1 shows us that when we meditate on the Word, we drink in the *"rivers of water"* and bring forth the *"fruit"* of the Spirit, which is the overflow of His *"Living Waters."* This is partially what Christ meant when He said *"if you abide in my Word, you are **My disciples** indeed"* (John 8: 31); and later, *"if my Words abide in you… you bear much fruit; so you will be **My disciples** [indeed]"* (John 15: 7-8). The more that we abide in the Word, the more the Word abides in us, and the more that the Word abides in us, the more influence the Holy Spirit has over our thoughts and actions. Again, simply put, when we're filled with the Word (*"rivers of water"*), we bear the fruit of the Spirit (*"rivers of Living Water"*), and thus prove ourselves to be *"disciples indeed"*.

This same correlation is found in the sister epistles, Ephesians and Colossians.

*"And do not be drunk with wine, in which is dissipation; but **be filled with the Spirit**, ¹⁹ speaking to one another in psalms and hymns and spiritual songs, singing and making melody in your heart to the Lord"* (Ephesians 5: 18-19).

*"**Let the word of Christ dwell in you richly** in all wisdom, teaching and admonishing one another in psalms and hymns and spiritual songs, singing with grace in your hearts to the Lord"* (Colossians 3: 16).

Again, the more we are filled with the *"word of Christ"* [*"rivers of water"*], the more the *"Rivers of Living Water"* of the Holy Spirit will *"fill"* us and overflow out of us in fruitfulness and power. However, notice how Paul instructed us to be filled—through song. This is why our *"psalms, hymns, and spiritual songs"* should be biblically rich and accurate. Not simply quasi-religious songs that are sentimental and uplifting, but indistinguishable from the world's music.

The book of Psalms is the song book of the Bible. Music is a mnemonic device—it helps us to remember. This is why the Holy Spirit led David to start the very first Psalm by teaching us to meditate. As a matter of fact, the word *"meditate"* is found more times in the book of psalms than in every other book of the Bible combined! The Jews often meditated on God's word through song. Even in the early church, many New Testament truths were put to song.

When we continuously sing a song, we are rehearsing and internalizing the message of that song within our minds and consciences. This is why Satan has invested so much in the music industry. Unfortunately, many Christian artists have concluded that if they water down the Truth in their lyrics they'll have cross-over appeal—trying to win the world without the Word. Contrast this with God's musical priorities; the longest chapter in the Bible is a song dedicated to the Word of God—Psalm 119. The 16th century French Christian philosopher, physicist, and writer, Blaise Pascal, made the following insightful statement: *"It's not those who write the laws that have the greatest impact on society. It's those who write the songs."* Even so, God calls us to drink in biblically-rich music in order to foster the infilling of His Holy Spirit.

However, we should not merely rely on songs in order to meditate; there are a host of scriptures that have not been put to music. Instead, we must learn the discipline of being quiet and still in the presence of God, musing upon His word.

Let's consider more closely the role that meditation had among early Christians. Do you realize that for the first 1500 years of Christianity, most Christians did not have their own Bible? It wasn't until around 1450 AD that the Gutenberg printing press was invented. Until then, the only people who had *handwritten* Bibles were predominately the clergy and the rich. Yet, no one can deny that from the time of the Apostles down to the invention of the printing press, the Church exhibited great power and fruitfulness, changing nations and spreading across the world. No one can deny that the irresistible *"Rivers of Living Water"* overflowed in torrents across the nations bringing life and healing every place it went. How did the church flourish and impact the world for nearly a millennium and a half without a Bible readily at their fingertips?

Part of the answer is through meditation on the word of God *(there were obviously other factors as well, but the focus of this section is how to approach the Word of God)*. Not just memorization—meditation! What's the difference? Memorization merely remembers *words*, and then it tucks those words away in the back of the mind where they have no further influence on the *thought life* of the Christian. Someone may say, *"Well, God will remind you of those words when just the right situation arises in the future."* This is sometimes the case, but the Lord calls us to live biblically and spiritually-minded *right now!*—not some unknown, potential time in the future. We are not called to be special occasion Christians, but moment by moment followers of Christ. So, memorization *alone* merely remembers words, but those words have very little impact on the thought life *if they're not pondered*.

Meditation, on the other hand, deeply considers the meaning, the truth, the purpose, the wisdom, the direction, and all the mind of God contained within those words. Meditation on the word allows us to sit at the feet of our Heavenly Father so that He can instill His spiritual wisdom within our hearts. Meditation escorts the Christian down into the depths of God's Word where the Holy Spirit unveils the manifold nature of Christ in every passage of scripture. It compels us to consciously remain in the presence of the Lord, communing with Him about His Word.

I believe that this is why God allowed nearly a thousand and a half years to pass before He granted man the knowledge of how to build a printing press. Not having Bibles readily at their fingertips *compelled* the early Christians to internalize the Word and think more often on it. *(This is why the god of this world has saturated it with an incessant, endless array of intriguing things to do – he keeps our minds **perpetually** occupied!)*. It also caused the early Christians to value it more, and not to take it for granted. They didn't have ten different Bible translations gathering dust on the book shelf. Just let the government try to confiscate our Bibles, and multitudes of ungrateful Christians will suddenly fall in love with this book! God wanted His people to treasure His Word, and He wanted His people to learn this discipline at an early age.

"And these words which I command you today shall be in your heart. ⁷ You shall teach them diligently to your children, and shall talk of them when you sit in your house, when you walk by the way, when you lie down, and when you rise up. ⁸ You shall bind them as a sign on your hand, and they shall be as frontlets between your eyes. ⁹ You shall write them on the doorposts of your house and on your gates" (Deuteronomy 6: 6-9).

In the present day, we have countless Bible translations and Bible study helps, and are none the better for it. Why do I say this? I fear that easy access to the scriptures has done to the church what the calculator has done to the world of mathematics. Thank God for calculators; nevertheless, once upon a time people regularly solved complex arithmetic with raw brain power. Now the calculator does much of the work for us. We appear to be more intelligent than our ancestral counterparts, but in reality, most of us aren't! Standing on the shoulders of another doesn't make you taller than them.

A similar thing has happened to us now that we're surrounded by Bibles. Having Bibles at our fingertips has taken away the incentive of many Christians to treasure up the words of Truth within their hearts and minds. The scriptures are easily accessible to us at any given moment. Why treasure the word in my heart, and muse on it in my mind, when I can just crack open my Bible, or click on a smart phone app and have immediate scriptures?

Having ready access to Bibles has drawn many of us away from living in the Spirit of the word, and confined us to brief rendezvous with the letter of the word – thus, many of us have become powerless textualists. And this is referring to those who actually take the time to regularly study their Bibles; most Christians don't! Add to this the western mentality that says we must be busy, connected, active, and involved in every trendy fad and *happening* thing in order to feel like we *have a life*, and you have a cocktail for spiritual disaster! Most of our lives are consumed with the world, sporadically interrupted by a daily devotional, a verse for the day, or a dash through three or four Bible chapters in order to keep the *"read-the-Bible-in-a-year"* deadline! Pastor Zac Poonen of India said it best; *"I'd rather have the Bible go through me once, than to read through the Bible a hundred times!"*

     Learn to slow down! Be still. Prioritize. You don't need to be involved in *everything*. Solomon immersed himself in every worldly engagement that he could imagine, but in the end, he concluded that *"all was vanity* [emptiness] *and grasping for the wind"* (Ecclesiastics 2: 1-11). We'll constantly need more: bigger, better, more bells and whistles, more thrills…it'll *never* end! Man will *never* be satisfied with worldly pursuits. Cut out the excess stuff that is wedged between you and the Lord. Get serious about your faith. Determine to turn from your natural, fleshly understanding, and regularly drink in the Word of God. *"It is the Spirit who gives life; the flesh profits nothing.* **The <u>words</u> that I speak to you are <u>spirit</u>**, *and they* **are** *[rivers of]* <u>*life*</u>*"* (John 6: 63). Even so, we must abide in His Word *"day and night"* through meditation in order to experience and enjoy the fullness and the overflow of His Spirit.

     "Day and night" may seem scary to some of us. Here are some practical insights on when and how to meditate on the Word. First, we should immediately ponder God's truths after a period of reading or studying the Bible—assuming that you already have a set time for devotion; this should be a given! It is crucial to ponder God's truths while they are fresh in your mind. Furthermore, you don't have to become a "Bible student", dissecting every Greek and Hebrew word, and researching ancient cultures. That's what gifted Bible teachers are for (Ephesians 4: 11-16). However, a little study would be prudent. Read slowly and thoughtfully—this is important. Afterward, simply muse upon whatever scripture the Holy Spirit puts on your heart. Every time you read the scripture, certain truths should leap off the page and grab your heart. Draw close to the Father with this truth; the Holy Spirit may have a lesson for you.

     I've found that times that do not require much mental focus are good times to ponder truths—driving, for instance. Do not be too swift to fill your free time with frivolous worldly stuff. Instead of four hours of TV, give some of that time to the Lord. We should meditate on God's word by listening to biblically-rich music. We should also meditate on God's truth in the silent, waning hours of the night.

     There are no specific times and methods for meditation, only that we should do it. Learn to incorporate it into your daily life. Keep it simple and free; don't get formal and religious about it. Neither allow it to be nothing more than a mental exercise; make it a time of earnestly seeking the mind and face of the Lord. If the word *"meditate"* intimidates you, then use another word: muse, ponder, consider, contemplate, reflect, etc. It's all about learning to commune with your Heavenly Father about His Word *"when you sit in your house, when you walk by the way, when you lie down, and when you rise up."* It's all about learning to think spiritually. It's all about renewing the mind. It's all about replacing your natural conscience with a Truth-filled conscience. It's all about learning the *"mind of Christ."*

This is how we learn to discern our Father's voice from the confusion of every other deceptive "voice" in this world. This is how we weave our roots ever deeper into the pure *"rivers of water"*, absorbing gracious truths into the deep recesses of our conscience, purifying our deepest motives toward God and man. This is the most fundamental principle of renewing our mind; not trying to manipulate our surface thoughts through some psycho-religious rigmarole, but allowing God to purify our innermost motives and desires. This alone will produce genuine, sustained transformation in our life, for we are *"**transformed** by the renewing of* [our] *mind."* In such a state, we are no longer trying to force our old nature to act religious; rather, we are freeing our new nature to be righteous.

I'll close this section by giving you another sister verse:

*"Blessed is the man who **trusts** in the* LORD,
*And whose **hope** is the* LORD.
⁸ *For he shall be like a tree planted by the waters,*
Which spreads out its roots by the river,
And will not fear when heat comes;
But its leaf will be green,
And will not be anxious in the year of drought,
Nor will cease from yielding fruit" (Jeremiah 17: 7-8).

This scripture conjoins with Psalm 1: 2-3. Notice that *"meditation"* and *"trust"* [faith] are used interchangeably to affect the same result. Meditating on the Word means *nothing* if we don't have whole-hearted *"trust"* [faith] in the Word; and faith means nothing if it is not grounded in the Word. And the most effectual way to ground ourselves within the word is through meditation. The Word of God is represented by the *"rivers of water."* Faith is represented by the unseen roots that drink in the water. Meditation is the *abiding* by the *"rivers of water"*, constantly drinking in the truth. This, and this alone, enables us to experience the unwithering vibrancy, and overflowing fruitfulness of the Spirit-filled walk. *"If you **abide in my word"**,* Jesus said, you shall *"know the Truth…the Son"*, and He shall make you *"Free indeed."*

*"We cannot obtain or maintain **power in our own lives** or in our work for others unless there is **deep and frequent meditation on the Word of God**. If our leaf is not to wither and whatever we do is to prosper, our delight must be in the law of the Lord, and we must meditate on it day and night."* —R. A. Torrey[57]

Again,

*"We should be better Christians if we were more alone, waiting upon God, and gathering through meditation on his Word spiritual strength for labour in his service. We ought to muse upon the things of God, because we thus get the real nutrition out of them…**Why is it that some Christians, although they hear many sermons, make but slow advances in the divine life? Because they neglect their closets, and do not thoughtfully meditate on God's Word.** They love the wheat, but they do not grind it; they would have the corn, but they will not go forth into the fields to gather it; the fruit hangs upon the tree, but they will not pluck it; the water flows at their feet, but they will not stoop to drink it. From such folly deliver us, O Lord, and be this our resolve this morning, "I will meditate in thy precepts."* —Spurgeon[57]

And again,

*"**I was growing** in the faith and knowledge of Jesus, **but** I still preferred reading religious books instead of the Scriptures. I read tracts, missionary newsletters, sermons, and biographies of Christian people. God is the author of the Bible, and only the truth it contains will lead people to true happiness. **A Christian should read this precious Book every day with earnest prayer and meditation.** But like many believers, I preferred to read the works of uninspired men rather than the oracles of the Living God. **Consequently, I remained a spiritual baby both in knowledge and grace.**"* —George Muller[58]

In the same way, the Lord, for a season, led me away from the writings and teachings of man, and drew me back to the pure basics of the Word. The Lord taught me to seek Him with all my heart through prayer, reading, study, and above all, meditation. One of the primary contributing factors to spiritual immaturity and barrenness is a refusal to meditate on the Word. And this is largely because we have given our minds over to the preoccupation of so many other things—and we wonder why we're not growing.

However, meditating on the word is not enough. What good is meditating on the truth if we have no intention of yielding to it, or if we only intend to yield to parts of it? When the Lord tells us to *"abide"* in His word, this doesn't only mean to think on it, it also means to surrender to it. Let's consider the next vital component of how to approach the word of God.

Biblical Faith is Authenticated by Trusting Surrender

We're still very much on the subject of faith. First, faith must be single-minded and whole-hearted; God will not regard double-minded faith that is compromised by our own understanding. Second, authentic faith must be grounded in the immutable Person and Truth of the Word of God. We've just considered how to approach the word in order for our faith to be properly grounded and nurtured. However, authentic faith must also be exercised.

Biblical faith is not only passive; it's active. In the great chapter of faith, Hebrews 11, virtually every example of faith was active – *"By faith Abel **offered**"*, *"By faith Noah…**prepared**"*, *"by faith Abraham **obeyed…went…dwelt…offered**"*, *"By faith Moses…**was hidden…refused…forsook**"*, etc. The Apostle James, known as *"the apostle of faith"*, said it plainly and bluntly, *"Faith without works is dead"* – it's a dead, empty, impotent faith. It's a faith that is no better than that of a demon (James 2: 14-20)! Therefore, genuine faith must be authenticated by surrendered obedience.

Meditating on God's Word fills us with the Truth. However, in order to *"**walk** in the Spirit"* we must embrace this truth by faith, and surrender to it. ***An honest and earnest pursuit of surrendered obedience** is the second principle that we must embrace in how we approach the Word*. God brought these principles of meditation and obedience together when He was admonishing Joshua.

*"This Book of the Law shall not depart from your mouth, but **you shall meditate in it day and night, that you may observe to <u>do</u> according to <u>all</u> that is written in it**. For then you will make your way prosperous, and then you will have good success"* (Joshua 1: 8).

Before we move on, allow me to make a critical point in regards to this scripture. Many Christians have made the mistake of connecting obedience with law or legalism. An honest, simplistic, surface reading of the New Testament reveals that this correlation is utterly misguided. The teachings of Christ and the

Apostles are filled with spiritual truths that the Christian is *commanded* to obey. The refusal to acknowledge this fact is rooted in the *"threshold Christian"* mentality which always considers whether or not something is necessary for salvation. If it's not, the *"Threshold Christian"* will typically down play the importance of the scripture, explain it away, minimize it, or modify it in the name of grace. But remember, *"Grace is not given to us to avoid the responsibilities of the Christian life; it's given to us to fulfill the responsibilities of the Christian life."*

When we get beyond the threshold of faith, we realize that surrendered obedience is absolutely *essential for spiritual growth.* The Children of Israel symbolically experience salvation when the blood of the Passover lamb saved the first born from death. God saw the blood, and allowed His judgment to *"pass over"* them. However, under Joshua, they had to conquer all of the strongholds of Canaan in order to enjoy the *fruitfulness and rest* of the Promised Land. They didn't accomplish this by hiding under the shelter of the blood, but by obeying every word of the Lord.

Meditating on and obeying God's Word is not the best military strategy, whether we're fighting against strongholds of men or strongholds of sin. We prefer to formulate sensible schemes, strategies, and methodologies in order to gain victory. God tells us to march around a wall seven times blowing trumpets! Imagine if Joshua decided to consult some of the highly intelligent pagans around him in order to get their scholarly ideas. Then he could've mingled their brilliance with Gods Truth and started a twelve step program on how to break down walls. That would have been the height of foolishness! Joshua resolved to *obey every single word* of the Lord—in spite of how ridiculous it sounded—and he trusted God to somehow give the victory; and thus, God gets all the glory. It's the same with us; one of the most vital components to overcoming our strongholds is the whole-hearted obedience of genuine faith.

"God's own people may sell themselves into captivity by sin. A very bitter fruit is this, of an exceeding bitter root. What a bondage it is when the child of God is sold under sin, held in chains by Satan, deprived of his liberty, robbed of his power in prayer and his delight in the Lord! Let us watch that we come not into such bondage; but if this has already happened to us, let us by no means despair.

But we cannot be held in slavery forever. The Lord Jesus has paid too high a price for our redemption to leave us in the enemy's hand. The way to freedom is, "Return unto the Lord thy God." Where we first found salvation we shall find it again. At the foot of Christ's cross, confessing sin, we shall find pardon and deliverance. Moreover, the

Lord will have us obey His voice according to all that He has commanded us, and we must do this with all our heart and all our soul, and then our captivity [bondage] *shall end."* —Spurgeon[59]

Throughout the scripture, the way to victory and deliverance was always through turning back to the first basic principles of obedience. This is recorded many times in the Old Testament. However, this admonition is also seen throughout the New Testament to the Church. When the Ephesian church got off track, Christ Himself had to warn them through the Apostle John; *"Remember therefore **from where you have fallen**; repent and do the **first works**, or else I will come to you quickly and remove your lampstand from its place – unless you repent"* (Revelation 2: 5). God always calls His people back to the basics – not to be saved all over again – but to get back on track in our spiritual walk, and to gain victory over the things that have been tripping us up.

This is why man's methods are not only futile, but foolish! For they don't call us *back to the Truth*, but they lead us ever *further from the Truth*. They're replete with new ideas, new methodologies, and new concepts, but littered with just enough scriptures to deceive the simple. Nevertheless, God always calls us **back** to the basic, *"first works"* of obedience, and this obedience must be the product of wholehearted faith.

If our faith in a truth is genuine, then obedience will naturally follow. Conversely, every honest act of obedience is an act of genuine faith. If we refuse to surrender to the truth, it is because we do not fully trust it. We're still trusting our own understanding in that area. It's imperative that this connection is understood. It's not so much about obedience as it is about faith. The lack of obedience is the evidence of a lack of faith.

Faith responds to Truth. The "Truth" *concerning salvation* tells us that we don't have to perform good works in order to be saved. Faith embraces this truth, and therefore, it refrains from attempting good works when seeking salvation.

Again, *"faith responds to Truth."* The "Truth" *concerning sanctification* tells us that we must *"do"* certain things in order to overcome sin and grow like Christ. Faith embraces these truths, and therefore, earnestly seeks to yield to them as they are written. Whatever Truth says, faith responds accordingly, thus proving its authenticity. When Noah *was told* to build an ark, he didn't rest on his laurels and trust God to do it; he got up and started building, thus his faith was authenticated. When Abraham *was told* that he would be the father of many nations, He didn't simply trust that it would happen; he began flirting with Sarai! Faith responds to whatever Truth says; this is the case with everyone in the chapter of faith, Hebrews 11.

    Any pursuit of victory must be rooted in faith. This means that we must *trust* everything that God says we must *do* in order to obtain victory. Renounce the foolish idea that says, *"My sin is too difficult to overcome. God knows it's too strong for me. I'll just trust Him to take it away."* This is wishful thinking, not truthful thinking; it's no place found in scripture. The Word of God clearly lays out Truths that God expects us to *obey* in order to obtain victory. If God reveals a truth to us and we resist it, it's because we don't trust Him — it's that simple.

    Two sections ago, I explained that our faith must be in the Lord of the word, not merely the word. This is critical for obedience. Allow me to give you this simple illustration.

    A sister tells her brother, *"Go clean your room."* The response of the brother is both inevitable and obvious; *"Go take a walk!"* So, let's try this again. Now, the sister tells her brother, *"Daddy said, 'Go clean your room.'"* What's the response? The son either gets up to clean his room, or he goes to verify this information with his father, then he goes to clean his room. The command is exactly the same in both illustrations. What changed? I'll tell you what changed; the authority behind the command was recognized.

    Bible student or not, the average Christian is a textualist. This means that the average Christian, though able to quote a text, is often disconnected from the Authority behind the text. Therefore, they tend to cherry-pick, modify, and manipulate the word of God according to the preferences of their own understanding. *They* are the authority over the word because they've deified their preferential, self-understanding above the authority of the Lord.

    Let's consider this illustration again, and apply it to a common mistake that many diligent textualists often make. *"Go clean your room."* The textualist son diligently considers his father's words and begins to study them. *"'Go.' This is a deep word. In the original Greek and Hebrew, it means to 'proceed' or 'advance'. Let me study how many times 'Go' is mentioned in the Bible. 'Clean'. Ooohh. I won't even be able to scratch the surface of this word! It implies that the thing to be cleaned is 'dirty', or 'filthy', or 'unclean'. 'Your'. This word speaks of ownership. It teaches us that Daddy has entrusted something to us. Imagine that! Daddy has given us something that belongs to us! 'Room'. In the original Greek and Hebrew, this word can be applied in many ways; bedroom, bathroom, living room, and laundry room. But in some cases, even though the word 'room' is not specified, the original languages seem to teach that it also apples to the kitchen and the den. Now, let's study the nature of Daddy. This is a deep subject!'"*

The textualist son gets so immersed into the study of his father's words, that he never gets around to the simplicity of obeying them – *"Go clean your room!"* It's like a person who takes apart a complex device, but doesn't know how to put it back together so that it can be functional.

The obedient son doesn't over-complicate his father's words. After he has adequate clarity and understanding, he simply obeys — even if he'd rather be playing video games. And as he consistently obeys from day to day, the rationale, wisdom, and discipline of his father is instilled within his own character. When he matures into an adult himself, his father's will makes perfect sense, and like many children, he becomes just like his parent. Now, don't misunderstand me. Study is important, but study without whole-hearted obedience is impotent.

Don't allow these things to discourage you beloved reader. All of this talk about obedience can be really disheartening. However, the Lord is very gracious and patient with the humble soul who is willing to trust and obey Him. Moreover, like a father who patiently helps his son learn to walk, our Heavenly Father patiently assists and enables us in all of our faith-filled efforts to follow Him. God doesn't expect perfection, but He does expect submission. For God's enabling grace is only given to those who submit their will to His.

"Every time I obey, absolute Deity is on my side, so that the grace of God and natural obedience coincide." —Chambers

Absolute Surrender Does Not Mean Perfection, but It Does Mean No More Excuses

Surrendered obedience is not to be confused with *perfect execution* of that obedience. A young child may be absolutely surrendered to their parents with a deep love for them, and yet still make a lot of blunders. God's patient and longsuffering with us. He forgives us 70 X 7 times and beyond! However, He will not tolerate stiff-necked, hard-hearted, selectively compliant rebellion. God calls for whole-hearted trust and absolute surrender, and He commits Himself to help us through the ups and downs that are sure to accompany such a commitment.

Think about a person who needs physical therapy. The therapist never says, *"Alright now, let's get you up and moving! Come on, do what I do. Keep up with me!"* No! The therapist knows that the patient is debilitated and inhibited. They realize the patient needs step-by-step, measured exercises, and a lot of patience. Often times the therapist will have the patient do seemingly trivial exercises that appear to have nothing to do with the main problem. The therapy will likely hurt as we try to move limbs and joints that have been injured. But, whatever the case, the patient is still expected to put forth an honest and earnest effort in their therapy.

God knows that we're broken people. We have all sorts of problems and weaknesses. We need spiritual therapy. But God doesn't demand that we walk like Christ overnight! He patiently works with us from session to session. Sometimes the therapy He prescribes will seem like a trivial waste of time. Sometimes it'll be painful. We only have two things to ask ourselves in these times; *"Does the Word of God tell me to do this?"*, **and** *"Do I trust Him enough to do it?"* If the answer is yes to both of these, then the argument is over. Trust Him and obey.

Before long, you'll begin to see that your *spiritual* limbs and joints are beginning to function properly with more ease and less pain. But, if you refuse to go to your sessions, dismissing them as unnecessary, your spiritual nature will not only remain broken, but your spiritual injuries will become more settled and rigid.

The disciples abandoned *everything* to follow Christ; look at how much they fumbled and screwed up. We often talk about the blunders of the disciples, yet most of us haven't even taken the *first step* of discipleship as they did — surrendering to Christ above everything else. This faith-filled surrender makes all the difference with God. Consider this critical distinction. Christ never forsook His disciples, in spite of their many screw-ups. However, whenever Christ encountered someone who made excuses about following Him, He counted them unworthy to be disciples (Luke 9: 57-62, Luke 14: 15-33).

What's the difference between the two? Were Christ's disciples more righteous than those who made excuses? No. The difference is that Christ's disciples resolved to surrender to His Lordship by faith, and the others put self and the world before Christ. There's a world of a difference between a child who earnestly strives to obey his parents, yet fumbles every now and then, and a child who perfectly obeys what they feel like obeying, yet defies their parent's authority in other areas.

The disciples never made any excuses in order to avoid any part of the Lord's will. Whatever the Lord told them to do, they did with reverence and immediacy. Their behavior may not have been the best, but their surrendered faith was strong. This is what matters to the Lord. When Christ discerned that Peter was going to fall, he didn't pray that he would not fall; instead, he prayed that his *"faith should not fail"* (Luke 22:32). Absolute surrender does not mean perfection, but it does mean no more excuses, rationalizations, redefining, or minimizing of God's truths. Surrendered obedience is exercised by determined faith and earnest love for the Lord, and every word that proceeds out of His mouth.

This is very intimidating for many Christians. We've got the doctrines down, and we know the right words. But transforming the rhetoric into reality is where many of us get cold feet. We'll profess our faith in a truth, yet when confronted face-to-face with the reality of actually yielding to the truth, we become better escape artists than the great Houdini! It's exceptionally difficult for us to reject our self-understanding, and daringly surrender to unreasonable, uncomfortable, unearthly truths. However, such is the manifestation of authentic, single-minded, God-approved faith.

Do you trust the Lord when He says *"My yoke is easy and My burden is light"* (Matthew 11: 30)? Do you believe God when He tells us that *"His commandments are not burdensome"* (1 John 5: 3)? I speak from experience; when I dismissed and minimized certain truths under the flawed assumption that it would make the Christian life easier, I found the opposite—following Christ became more difficult! Why? Because I was walking according to my fleshly self-nature. The fleshly self-nature will *always* treat God's word like a selective buffet. The spiritual new nature will *always* treat Gods' word like __God's__ Word, and will thereby be graced with power to obey it.

"As long as we try to serve two masters, ourselves and God, there will be difficulties combined with doubt and confusion. Our attitude must be one of complete

reliance on God. Once we get to that point, there is nothing easier than living the life of a saint. We encounter difficulties when we try to usurp the authority of the Holy Spirit for our own purposes." — Oswald Chambers.

Utterly renounce the spiritually stultifying excuses of your own understanding. Surrender your all to the Lord. Yield to every one of His truths. Press pass every fleshly distortion, every earthly distraction, and every satanic deception. No more excuses! If a truth is clear, don't over think it and don't study it do death; yield to it. God honors such yielding with His power.

Moreover, not only does God give us power as we yield to Him, but He also gives discernment. His truths become our truths. We begin to obey, not merely because God says so, but because His truths have become real and reasonable to us. Like a child who reaches adulthood, the Father's instructions begin to make perfect sense.

Surrendered Obedience to the Truth Enables Discernment of the Truth

We want understanding before obedience. God wants us to surrender to the limited light that He has given us, and then He'll give greater discernment. However, we're often not comfortable with simply yielding to Truths that don't make sense to our natural mind. At its core, this resistance is not due to a misunderstanding, but to a distrust of God Himself. That's why God tells us to come to Him as little children. Little children trustingly surrender to authority, even though they don't have all the answers. God is greatly pleased with this simplistic trust and surrender; therefore, He honors such meekness with Light.

*"In that hour Jesus rejoiced in the Spirit and said, "I thank You, Father, Lord of heaven and earth, that You have hidden these things from the **wise** and **prudent** and **revealed** them to **babes*** (which, according to the context, were His surrendered disciples). *Even so, Father, for so it seemed good in Your sight"* (Luke 10: 21-24).

Spiritual truth cannot be comprehended. God alone holds the prerogative to hide or reveal truth, and the intellectual acumen of the individual is a thoroughly irrelevant factor in God's judgment. *"Where is the wise? Where is the scribe? Where is the disputer of this age? Has not God made foolish the wisdom of this world"* (1 Corinthians 1: 20)? I cannot stress this point enough; spiritual truth is *revealed* to those who humbly surrender; it is not merely studied and ascertained. R. A. Torrey, in his book "How to Obtain Fullness of Power", (Another book I highly recommend on how to walk in the Spirit) put it the following way.

>"**Knowledge of the truth** *comes with the surrender of the will. There is nothing like it to clear one's spiritual vision. "God is light, and in Him is no darkness at all" (1 John 1: 5). Surrender to Him opens our eyes to the light which He Himself is. It brings us at once to harmony with all truth…The greatest truths — eternal truths — cannot be learned by mere investigation and study. They cannot be reasoned out.* **They must be seen. And the only one who can see them is the one whose eye is cleared by absolute surrender to God.**"[60]

One doesn't give precious valuables to those who do not appreciate them, nor does God give treasured truths to those who do not love Him enough to fully yield to them. If Christ commanded us not to cast our pearls before swine, how much more does He not cast the treasures of His truths to indolent rebels? Learn to surrender to the first, rudimentary things of the faith. If you obey in simple obedience, the Holy Spirit will reveal more to you.

>"*A simple statement of Jesus is always a puzzle to us because we will not be simple. How can we maintain the simplicity of Jesus so that we may understand Him? By receiving His Spirit, recognizing and relying on Him* [faith], **and obeying Him as He brings us the truth of His Word, life will become amazingly simple.**"[61]

And again,

>"*The golden rule to follow to obtain* spiritual *understanding is not one of intellectual pursuit, but one of obedience. If a person wants scientific knowledge, then intellectual curiosity must be his guide. But if he desires knowledge and insight into the teachings of Jesus Christ,* **he can only obtain it through obedience.** *If spiritual things seem dark and hidden to me, then I can be sure that there is a point of disobedience somewhere in my life.* **Intellectual darkness is the result of ignorance, but spiritual darkness is the result of something that I do not intend to obey.**
>
>*No one ever receives a word from God without instantly being put to the test regarding it.* **We disobey and then wonder why we are not growing spiritually… Examine the things you tend simply to shrug your shoulders about, and where you have refused to be obedient, and you will know why you are not growing spiritually.**" —Oswald Chambers[62]

As we learn and obey the first, rudimentary truths of following Christ, the Holy Spirit will entrust us with more. A student must learn their lesson both in knowledge and practice before their trainer will bring them to the next level. Paul and the writer to the Hebrews both understood this; they both withheld deeper teaching because their audience was not growing through obedience (1 Corinthians 3: 1-3, Hebrews 5: 12-14). Both the Corinthians and the Hebrews were stunted spiritually because they were not *obeying* the spiritual basics of following Christ; as I said earlier, they were not walking in *faith and love*.

The Corinthians, for instance, had a lot of Bible knowledge; Paul told them that *"you were enriched in everything by Him in all utterance and **all knowledge"*** (1 Corinthians 1: 5). But, he later told them that *"Knowledge puffs up, but love edifies"* (1 Corinthians 8: 1). Paul spent a year and a half in Corinth teaching this church. Furthermore, he didn't only teach on Sundays; he most likely taught every day both *"day and night"* (Acts 20: 31). Imagine sitting under the teaching of Paul for this amount of time. Apollos, who was *"mighty in the Scriptures"* (Acts 18: 24), continued to teach them after Paul left. Even the Apostle Peter taught the Corinthians for a period of time. The Corinthians, no doubt, had a lot of good doctrine...they had the best doctrine! They had better doctrine than most (if not all) Bible *scholars* today! But, even though the Corinthians were filled with accurate Bible knowledge, they were not growing in the Spirit *because they were not walking in obedience*. They were filled with *"envy, strife, and division."*

*And I, brethren, could not speak to you as to **spiritual people but as to carnal, as to babes in Christ**. ² I fed you with milk and not with solid food; for until now you were not able to receive it, and even now you are still not able; ³ for **you are still carnal. For where there are envy, strife, and divisions among you, are you not carnal and behaving like mere men?**"* (1 Corinthians 2: 12-16, 3: 1-3).

Notice how Paul directly connects their level of spiritual maturity, not to their knowledge of the Bible, but their *obedience* to the Bible. The Corinthians were refusing to turn from sin. Two of their sins are listed in Romans 1: 28-32; *"being filled with all unrighteousness...full of **envy**, murder, **strife**...who, knowing the righteous judgment of God, that those who practice such things are deserving of death, not only do the same but also approve of those who practice them."* The Corinthians (like many Christians today) were *shrugging their shoulders* at *"envy, strife, and divisions"* (among other things); therefore, Paul could not speak to them as *"spiritual people but as to carnal, as to babes in Christ."*

It was the same with the Hebrew Christians. The writer to the Hebrews realized that these Christians were not growing spiritually because they were not practicing what they'd been taught. Their lack of obedience stunted their spiritual discernment.

"For though by this time you ought to be teachers, you need someone to teach you again the first principles of the oracles of God; and you have come to need milk and not solid food. ¹³ *For everyone who partakes only of milk is unskilled in the word of righteousness, for he is a babe.* ¹⁴ *But solid food belongs to those who are of full age, that is, those who* **by reason of use** *have their senses exercised to* **discern both good and evil**" (Hebrews 5: 12-14).

When we *"use"*, or practice the truths that we've learned, we mature our ability to discern spiritual Truth, because it exercises the spiritual *"senses"* of our new nature. But, notice closely how this obedience transforms our discernment. At the fall, man developed his own *"knowledge of good and evil."* I've already explained how this puts man in the place of God, filling him with the delusion that he can decide what's *"good and evil"* according to the judgment of his own corrupted mind. God wants to bring the discernment of our *"knowledge of good and evil"* back into alignment with His Truth. And the means through which this is accomplished is through, not merely only our learning the Truth, but through our yielding to the Truth. This and this alone exercises our new nature.

Every child has milestones of growth; it's the same with every child of God. The Corinthians and Hebrews had not reached their spiritual milestones of growth; therefore, they were carnal, still living in spiritual infanthood. What are some of the primary attributes of babies? Babies and toddlers are very prone to soiling themselves and stumbling. It's the same with spiritual babies. However, the apostle John gives us the next three stages of spiritual growth; little children, young men, and fathers. Consider for a moment the characteristics of a spiritual young adult. *The primary attributes of spiritual young adults is that they're strong in the Lord, the word of God is treasured up within them, and they have power over the influence of the Wicked One.* Therefore, the Wicked One is unable to bring them into bondage to any habitual sin, i.e., they no longer uncontrollably soil themselves and stumble.

"I have written to you, young men, Because you are **strong**, *and the* **word of God abides in you**, *And you* **have overcome the wicked one**" (1 John 2: 14).

Every Christian should earnestly aim for this goal and beyond. This is the stage in which the Christian truly begins to learn how to walk in the discernment and power of the Holy Spirit.

Discernment is not obtained by digging into the Greek and Hebrew, the cultural context, the etymology of words, and following the correct hermeneutical structure in order to properly exegete the text. Neither is discernment piecing together interesting connections in the Bible. Both of these are very profitable and important, but they do not give discernment. Any naturalistic theologian can do these things. An agnostic can comprehend the exact same biblical facts as a textualist. Discernment is the God given privilege to actually *see* the truth *as God sees it*; albeit, not to the same omniscient extent. The Christian who truly begins to discern the truth is given the same *balance* and *heartbeat* of God *for* the truth.

Whenever you come across a truth that is unsettling to you, you haven't discerned that truth yet. You may have comprehended the surface meaning of it, but you haven't discerned it within your heart yet. The fleshly self-nature is burdened by the truth; the spiritual new nature exuberantly loves the truth. If you're burdened by a truth, it's because your self-nature is still dominant in that area. Deny yourself, flex the muscles of your spiritual nature, and obey the truth into reality. Eventually you'll *see* it, and you'll wonder why you resisted God for so long. This is discernment, when we actually begin to *see* and *think* like Christ. Discernment is when a truth comes down from the proverbial head to the heart—it's when a truth becomes real to us.

"But **he who is spiritual** judges [literally: "discerns"] *all things, yet he himself is rightly* [discerned] *by no one.* 16 For "*who has known the mind of the* LORD *that he may instruct Him?" But we* [spiritual Christians] **have the mind of Christ**. *And I, brethren, could not speak to* **you** [the Corinthians] *as to spiritual people* **but as to carnal, as to babes in Christ**" (1 Corinthians 2: 15-16 & 3: 1).

The Corinthians were not walking in the Spirit; therefore, they weren't *"spiritual"* and they weren't overcoming sin. It's impossible to be truly *"spiritual"* without walking in the Spirit of Him who makes you spiritual. Please, don't confuse Paul's use of the word *"spiritual"* with how this word is commonly used in our present time. Paul is not referring to someone who wears beads, speaks softly, and dabbles in various religions and mystical practices! The spiritual Christian is one who walks in the Spirit.

The Christian is called to *"walk in the Spirit."* We *"walk in the Spirit"* by faith. This faith must be single-minded and wholehearted; not double-minded with our own understanding, and half-hearted in our devotion. This faith must be grounded, nurtured, and matured by the word of God through meditation and surrender (among other things). This kind of faith is graced with discernment; a heart, a mind, and a will that is in sync with the Living Truth. Finally, this Spirit-filled faith is graced with the power to do what it has a heart, mind, and will to do, *"for it is God who works in you both to will and to do for His good pleasure"* (Philippians 2: 13).

O GOD,

Thou hast taught me
  that Christ has all fullness and
 so all plenitude of the Spirit,
that all fullness I lack in myself is in him,
 for his people, not for himself alone,
he having perfect knowledge, grace,
    righteousness,
  to make me see,
  to make me righteous,
  to give me fullness;
that it is my duty, out of a sense of emptiness,
  to go to Christ, possess, enjoy his fullness
    as mine,
  as if I had it in myself, because it is
    for me in him;
that when I do this I am full of the Spirit,
  as a fish that has got from the shore to the sea
  and has all fullness of waters to move in,
  for when faith fills me, then I am full;
  that this is the way to be filled with the Spirit,
  like Stephen, first faith, then fullness,
  for this way makes me most empty,
  and so most fit for the Spirit to fill.
Thou hast taught me that the finding of
  this treasure of all grace in the field of Christ
  begets strength, joy, glory,
  and renders all graces alive.
Help me to delight more in what I receive
  from Christ,

more in that fullness which is in him,
   the fountain of all his glory.
Let me not think to receive the Spirit from him
   as a 'thing'
  apart from finding, drinking, being filled
   with him.
To this end, O God,
 do thou establish me in Christ,
 settle me, give me a being there,
 assure me with certainty that all this is mine,
  for this only will fill my heart with joy
    *and peace."*__The Valley of Vision, "Fullness of Christ"

CHAPTER 8

"FOLLOW ME" IN THE SPIRIT OF LOVE

The Apostle John teaches us that love is the essential, core evidence of a true Christian. However, John takes it even further. As I mentioned earlier, we are either following Christ or following the Devil. There are no gray areas with God — God hates the double-minded middle! Consider what the Apostle John wrote in 1 John 3: 10-11. The decisive factor that differentiates between whether we are following Christ or the Devil is *love*.

*"In this the **children of God** and the **children of the Devil** are manifest: Whoever does not practice righteousness is not of God, nor is he who does not **love** his brother.* [11] *For this is the message that you heard from the beginning, that **we should love one another**."*

Although this verse teaches that *"righteousness"* and *"love"* are the determining factors, it is out of *love* for the Lord that we live *righteously* before Him. True righteousness is impossible without Love, for *"love is the fulfillment of the law"* (Romans 13: 10). The Pharisees had law, but they had no love. We are called to have love, and therein we will walk in the righteousness of the law. Therefore, love (or the lack thereof) is the primary evidence that *"manifests"* whether a person is following Christ or following the Devil.

Remember when Peter was unwittingly used by Satan? Satan is very subtle. He has many perversions of love that appear to be of God, but at the core are filled with *self*-interests, *worldly* influences, and *devilish* deceptions. For instance, I believe that Peter had selfish *inner motives* for rebuking Christ;

however, I also believe that his *surface feelings* were loving toward Him. Why do I say this?

In Matthew 19: 27-28, *"Peter answered and said to Him, "See, we have left all and followed You.* **Therefore what shall we have?** *"²⁸ So Jesus said to them, "Assuredly I say to you, that in the regeneration, when the Son of Man sits on the throne of His glory, you who have followed Me will also sit on twelve thrones, judging the twelve tribes of Israel."* This verse clearly indicates that Peter was expecting some form of reward for following Christ. *(Don't be too hard on him for this; most spiritually mature Christians hope for a reward when they stand before Christ. But Peter expected a reward in his lifetime.)* When Peter heard Christ speaking of His death, it threatened Peter's expectation of some earthly reward. When Jesus rebuked Peter, He told him, *"you are not **mindful** of the things of God, but **the things of men**"* (Matthew 16: 23). Peter didn't have the discernment to understand the spiritual big picture. His thinking was earthbound and selfish, and that's why Satan could manipulate him.

There was another occasion when Peter's thinking was self-oriented, thus making him vulnerable to Satan yet again. Jesus told Peter, *"Simon, Simon! Indeed, Satan has asked for you, that he may sift you as wheat"* (Luke 22: 31). Shortly after, Peter, in an attempt to preserve *himself*, denied Jesus three times!

Remember Satan's favorite tools: the self-nature and the world. When we're walking according to the self-nature and following the ways of this world, we, like Peter, are highly susceptible to the sway of the Devil. The reason is because *these two inclinations directly compromise our ability to walk in the love of Christ*; they quench the Holy Spirit's influence over us. Self only thinks about itself, and the love of the world extinguishes the *"love of the Father"* within a person (1 John 2: 15-17). Satan is the father of selfishness (five times he declared *"I will"* Isaiah 14: 12-15), and he is the *"god of this world"*. Therefore, to walk according to self and the world is to walk in his nature and on his turf. These are the opposite of the Spirit of Christ. So, let's take a closer look at how faith and love work together to enable us to walk in the Spirit.

Faith Must Function Through Love

So far we've looked at faith; however, the Apostle Paul tells us that we are to live by *"faith working **through love**."* What does this mean? Faith enables us to both see and trust the revealed truth of God; love motivates us to follow it with the right heart motive. This bears repeating: *"Faith enables us to both see and trust the revealed truth of God; love motivates us to follow it with the right heart motive."* As we've seen in the previous section, biblical faith surrenders to the Truth; however, it is love *for* the truth that motivates this surrender. Our faith must work *"through love"*; otherwise, our response to the Truth will be compromised.

Without love, our response to the truth will be selective, obligatory, reluctantly forced, self-oriented, and swaying to and fro with the ebb and flow of our double-minded understanding. The truths that we prefer, we'll follow religiously. The truths that are uncomfortable or insignificant to our self-nature, we'll half-heartedly dabble with, or explain away altogether. Such is the consequence of having faith in the truth, absent of genuine, Christ-like love *for* the Truth. Therefore, it's imperative that our faith works—operates, functions—through love.

The Holy Spirit responds to genuine faith and genuine love by giving it light, power, and effectiveness. Faith and love are our part; divine enabling is God's part. However, even the faith and love that we exercise is awakened within us by the Holy Spirit; albeit, not forced. God will give us the tools, but He won't force us to use them. If we quench His influence, we'll remain in darkness. If we yield to His prompting, He gives light to our faith and power to our love. Together, these two spiritual graces enable us to *"walk in the Spirit"* in every area of the Christian life.

However, just like faith, the concept of love is also a term that has been diluted and compromised. On one extreme, love is viewed as an emotion—an internal feeling. However, the Apostle John tells us, *"let us not love in word or in tongue, but in deed and in truth"* (1 John 3: 18). Orpah had a deep, emotional love for Naomi, but Ruth *"clung to her"* (Ruth 1: 6-18). Orpah's emotional love—though filled with tears and kisses—was compromised by a love of self and the world. Therefore, she went *"back to her people and to her gods."*

On the other extreme, love is viewed as any charitable deed—an external action. However, charitable deeds do not constitute biblical love; we can do good without love. *"Though I bestow all my goods to feed the poor, and though I give my body to be burned, but have not love, it profits me nothing"* (1 Corinthians 13: 3). The

Pharisees did a lot of charitable deeds without an ounce of love. The term love has been mangled and contorted in order to accommodate a thousand opinions, political agendas, and emotional affinities. Part of the confusion is due to the fact that we use one, all-encompassing word for love, but the ancient Greeks used four words that related to four different kinds of love.

First, there was *"storge"*, which is an affectionate or familiar love. This is the love that a person has for a loved one or a pet. Secondly, there is *"phileo"*, which relays the idea of friendship or fondness. This is the love that a person has for their friends. Such love can also be "fond" of food and things. Thirdly, there is *"eros"*, from where we get the word erotic. This love obviously relates to sensual love. Finally, there is *"agape"*. This is selfless, sacrificial love. This love goes beyond the first two in that it selflessly loves those who are outside of the family, and it also loves its enemies, not just its friends. Furthermore, it doesn't only embrace the things that it's naturally *"fond of"*. Instead, agape love *"sacrificially"* embraces the things that it knows to be true, right, and good, because deep within this love is a passionate longing for the things of God, and it is willing to forgo self and the world in order to pursue them.

This is the love of Christ. The natural man is utterly incapable of walking in it. Christ-like love can only be instilled within our new, spiritual nature through the working of the Holy Spirit. Don't forget the point that was made in a previous chapter.

"For in Christ Jesus neither circumcision nor uncircumcision avails anything, **but faith working through love"** (Galatians 5: 6).

"For in Christ Jesus neither circumcision nor uncircumcision avails anything, **but a new creation** [i.e., new creature]*"* (Galatians 6: 15).

Our fleshly old nature functions according to our own understanding. Our spiritual new nature functions according to *"faith working through love."* Both of these spiritual graces compel us to relinquish the lordship of our self-nature unto to the Lordship of Christ. Faith is the complete *dependence* of our new nature on the Truth, in spite of the objections of our own understanding. Love is the sacrificial *surrender* of our new nature to the Truth, in spite of the resistance of our stubborn flesh. The utter dependence of faith and the absolute surrender of love are the two feet of the new nature. When we are thus submitted to the Lord, the Holy Spirit fills and overflows our inadequacy with His all-sufficiency. Thus, the new nature is enabled to *"walk in the Spirit."*

Without Christ-like Love, All of Our Good Works Are Nullified

"Though I speak with the tongues of men and of angels, but have not love, I have become sounding brass or a clanging cymbal. ² And though I have the gift of prophecy, and understand all mysteries and all knowledge, and though I have all faith, so that I could remove mountains, but have not love, **I am nothing**. *³ And though I bestow all my goods to feed the poor, and though I give my body to be burned,[a] but have not love,* **it profits me nothing**" (1 Corinthians 13: 1-3).

Consider what Christ said to the church of Ephesus in the Book of Revelation.

"I know your works, your labor, your patience, and that you cannot bear those who are evil. And you have tested those who say they are apostles and are not, and have found them liars; ³ and you have persevered and have patience, and have labored for My name's sake and have not become weary. ⁴ Nevertheless I have this against you, that **you have left your first love**. *⁵ Remember therefore from where you have fallen; repent and do the first works, or else I will come to you quickly and remove your lampstand from its place — unless you repent"* (Revelation 2: 2-5).

All of these good qualities compromised by one little infraction — *"you have left your first love!"* Seriously? Yes, seriously! But the sin of this church was no small sin. The church of Ephesus, by all practical purposes, was the ideal church. Yet they forgot their first love. This *"first love"* is the simplistic, pure love of Christ — *"We love Him because He first loved us"* is the beginning of the Christian's walk. 1st Corinthians 13 tells us that the best of our good works are rendered null and void if they're not rooted in Christ-like love.

The Ephesian church in Revelation had lost their simplistic, surrendered love for Christ. I believe that these Ephesian Christians had become legalistic textualists. They really took Paul's warnings and instructions seriously (Acts 20: 28-31)! They should have paid more attention to Ephesians 5: 1-2. They became strict on doctrine, scrutinizing of false teachers, and diligent in ministry — which is all great! *But, they lost sight of* **Who** *they were doing it all for.* This was no small matter, for Christ threatened to remove their *"lampstand"* unless they repented. Their light would be snuffed out! Christ will not share the throne of our heart with anything — not even our good deeds!

These truths should compel every one of us to deeply consider whether or not our works are done in the love of Christ, or some other motive. Are our good works performed out of obligation, to get recognition, to feel good about ourselves, to impress others, to feel religious, for position, or some other self-serving motive? If so, we're merely heaping up mounds of wood, hay, and stubble. Worse yet, we run the very real danger of Christ snuffing our light out. I don't fully understand what this means, I just know that I want no part of it! — you shouldn't either!

If our love is real, Spirit-led works will naturally follow. If it is not real, then any good works we perform will be selective, and rooted in some other motive besides love.

How Do We Develop Sacrificial Love Within Ourselves?

So, how exactly do we walk in love? First, let's consider again the nature love. Biblical love is sacrificial love — it is selfless. *"If you love Me, keep **My** commandments"* (John 14:15). In other words, love puts God's will before our self-will.

"***By this we know love*** [In other words, "This is how we know what genuine Christ-like love is.], *because He laid down His life for us. And we also ought to lay down our lives for the brethren"* (1 John 3: 16). In other words, love will put the legitimate needs of others before ourselves.

But, these scriptures still do not answer the question of *how* we're enabled to love *with a true, Christ-like heart*. Remember, a person can keep God's commandments, and do good to others for reasons other than biblical love. And for God, who weighs the motives of the heart, this really matters. So, what is the barrier that hinders us from keeping God's commands and doing good to others out of a genuine, sacrificial, Christ-like love?

The chief barrier to Christ-like love is our inability to discern the love of God for us. Therefore, the basis of genuine, Christ-like love is a spiritual recognition of God's great love for us. When we truly *"see"* the great love that God has for us, then our love for Him will awaken into reality. This is the basis for sacrificial, Christ-like love. *"We love Him **because** He first loved us."* The degree to which our sacrificial love toward God and others is authentic is dependent upon the degree to which we truly recognize His love for us. The more the love of God is revealed *to* me, the more the love of God will be manifested *within and through* me.

Most reasonable people, upon learning that someone has made a great sacrifice on their behalf, are moved with gratitude, and compelled to return the love. No loving sacrifice of man can even come close to sacrifice of Christ. However, even though we may know this doctrinally, few of us actually *see it* realistically.

It's naturally easier for us to discern the natural. I can readily understand the immensity of someone donating a kidney to save my life. Such knowledge will fill me with a **grateful sense of willful indebtedness** to this person for as long as I live. However, it takes faith to truly see what Christ has done for us. The natural mind readily understands natural things, but the spiritual mind can only discern spiritual things by faith. In order for our faith to have a clear vision of the Truth, the dense fog of our own understanding has to be cleared out of the way.

When I *truly see* what the Lord has done for me, there is no sacrifice too great for me to *joyfully* offer up in order to please Him and honor Him. I'll say with the psalmist, *"I love Your commandments more than gold, yes, than fine gold"* (Psalm 119: 127)! Furthermore, when I truly see the awesome sacrifice of Christ for an abominable miscreant such as myself, there is not a soul on planet earth that I could ever allow myself to withhold the offer of full forgiveness and reconciliation—70X7! When I truly see the faithful compassions that God has for me in all my needs, weaknesses, and inadequacies, it only compels me to show the same compassions to the needy, the weak, and the inadequate. All of these have one thing in common; *"when I truly see."* If a person doesn't *"see"* the love of Christ, they won't *know* the love of Christ, and therefore, they won't *show* the love of Christ toward God or man with any authenticity or consistency.

If you're looking for a truth to meditate on, here's a great place to start— the love of Christ as it is revealed in His Person and work. Do not view these truths with an overfamiliar, casual disposition. A lifetime will not allow us to plumb the depths of the love of Christ. The Apostle Paul prayed that we *"may be able to comprehend with all the saints what is the width and length and depth and height —* [19] *to know the love of Christ which passes knowledge; that* [we] *may be filled with all the fullness of God"* (Ephesians 3: 18-19).

Not even eternity will afford us the time to comprehend the love of Christ. Indeed, the love of Christ will be the center of our worship throughout the timeless ages of heaven.

"You are worthy to take the scroll,
And to open its seals;
For You were slain,
And have redeemed us to God by Your blood
Out of every tribe and tongue and people and nation,
10 And have made us kings and priests to our God;
And we shall reign on the earth."

11 Then I looked, and I heard the voice of many angels around the throne, the living creatures, and the elders; and the number of them was ten thousand times ten thousand, and thousands of thousands, 12 saying with a loud voice:

"Worthy is the Lamb who was slain
To receive power and riches and wisdom,
And strength and honor and glory and blessing!" (Revelation 5: 9-12).

When the Apostle Paul meditated on the love of Christ, the conclusion he came to completely transformed his life.

*"For the love of Christ compels us, because **we judge thus** [i.e., he gave it some thought]: that if One died for all, then all died; 15 and He died for all, that those who live **should live no longer for themselves** [deny yourself], **but for Him who died for them and rose again**"* (2 Corinthians 5: 14).

The same thing happened with the repentant prostitute in Luke 7. When she grasped the immeasurable love of Christ for her, she sacrificially lavished her love on Him. Her love for Him was directly linked to her understanding of how much she had been forgiven.

"Therefore I say to you, her sins, which are many, are forgiven, for she loved much. But to whom little is forgiven, the same loves little" (Luke 7: 47).

None of us should be content with "little love", for it reveals that we do not truly know the love of Christ, and it cripples our efforts to love Him as we should. If a person is still putting self before the Lord, they haven't *fully seen* the love of Christ—it's not real to them yet. For many years I had a doctrinal understanding of Christ's love, but it wasn't fully real to me, and I knew it. The love of Christ didn't *"compel"* me to surrender to Him with all my heart, and this fact disturbed me. But I didn't know how to wrap my mind around the reality of Christ's love for me.

Does the *"love of Christ"* compel you to selflessly live for Him? Be honest. If not, it's because you don't *"see"* it yet. You know the doctrines about Christ, but you have yet to come to know Christ. Let's make this our earnest pursuit, for when we truly discern the love of Christ for us, it awakens our love for Him, and enables us to selflessly follow Him with all our heart.

So, how does this relate to our being enabled to overcome our stronghold? Let's take a closer look at how the love of Christ enables us to overcome sin in the power of the Holy Spirit.

How Walking in Love Enables Us to Overcome Sin

As we've already seen, the Holy Spirit gently influences us to walk in love. As we surrender to His influence, embracing the love of Christ as our own, He then enables us to walk in the power of that love. When we have a wholehearted love for Christ, it enables us to walk in the righteousness of Christ out of a true heart.

*"Jesus said to him, "'You shall love the LORD your God with **all your heart**, with **all your soul**, and with **all your mind**.' ³⁸ This is the first and great commandment. ³⁹ And the second is like it: 'You shall love your neighbor as yourself.' ⁴⁰ **On these two commandments hang all the Law and the Prophets**"* (Matthew 22: 37-40).

Love is a command — it is the preeminent, all-encompassing, highest command of God for the Christian. However, in an age where a misunderstanding of grace has turned *"commandment"* into a four-letter word, it's difficult for us to really comprehend the gravity of what it means to be commanded by God. Moreover, our common misconceptions of love have made it difficult for us to grasp how love can even be commanded the first place! Nevertheless, sacrificial love is indeed a bonafide command of God.

The misunderstanding is found in the fact that we tend to automatically associate *reluctant obligation* with commands. A command conveys the idea that a person obeys because they *have to*, not because they *want to*. However, God's command to love is a command for the willing *heart*, not the reluctant *flesh*. The O.T. commands began with *"Thou shall."* God's N.T. command/promise begins with *"I will write my law on their hearts."* Therefore, God not only gives us the command to love, He gives us the heart to love. It's important that we distinguish the reluctance of our flesh from the willful compliance of our new, spiritual nature. Our new nature not only wants to obey the Truth, it *loves* to obey the Truth!

*"For I **delight in the law** of God according to the **inward man**. 23 But I see another law in my members, warring against the law of my [spiritual] mind, and bringing me into captivity to the law of sin which is in my [fleshly] members"* (Romans 7: 22-23).

And again,

*The spirit indeed is **willing**, but the flesh is weak"* (Matthew 26: 41).

Our spiritual, inner man, *by nature,* has a wholehearted love for the Lord; any resistance that we feel is coming from the flesh. Unfortunately, the self-nature within many of us is so dominant that the desires of our new nature are being suffocated and muffled. Add to this the fact that many of us are satisfying the fleshly nature with every titillating thing in this world, and our spiritual inner man doesn't stand a chance!

However, the more that we deny our self-nature, and the more that we're crucified to this world, the fewer blockages there'll be between our spirit and the Spirit of God. The more that we clear the path between ourselves and the Lord, the more we'll see His great love for us. This is the fertile soil out of which the sacrificial love of Christ will be nourished and matured within us. The more that the love *of Christ* grows within us, the more we'll have a surrendered love for Him and all that He loves.

There are essentially two kinds of love represented in God's great command: vertical love toward God and horizontal love toward man. When we love God with *"all"* our being, then we, by nature, will selflessly surrender to His vertical commands. When we sacrificially love others, then we, by nature, will selflessly surrender to His horizontal commands. Consider the following scripture.

*"Owe no one anything except to love one another, for **he who loves another has fulfilled the law**. ⁹ For the commandments, "You shall not commit adultery," "You shall not murder," "You shall not steal," "You shall not bear false witness," "You shall not covet,"* **and if there is <u>any other commandment</u>, are all summed up in this saying, namely, "You shall love your neighbor as yourself."** *¹⁰ Love does no harm to a neighbor; therefore love is the fulfillment of the law"* (Romans 13: 8-10)

At first glance, this scripture only seems to address God's horizontal commands toward our fellow man. However, the phrase *"any other commandment"* immediately tells us that God includes the vertical commands as well. *"You shall have no other gods before Me. You shall not make for yourself a carved image… you shall not bow down to them nor serve them…You shall not take the name of the* LORD *your God in vain… Remember the Sabbath day, to keep it holy."* All of these commands are embodied and actualized in the singular, all-encompassing command to love.

[Allow me to make a brief note on the Sabbath day command. This command was symbolic of our resting in the work of Christ alone for salvation. Even the O.T. teaches that the Sabbath was merely a symbolic *"sign"* that revealed that God is the One who does all the work of making us holy: *"Surely My Sabbaths you shall keep,* **for it is a <u>sign</u>** *between Me and you throughout your generations, that you may know that I am the Lord who sanctifies you"* (Exodus 31: 13). Signs are merely shadows of the true substance.

Hebrews 4: 1-10 explains the substance of this sign. *"**For we who have believed do enter that rest**…For He has spoken in a certain place of the seventh day in this way: "And God rested on the seventh day from all His works… For he who has entered His rest has himself also ceased from his works as God did from His."* This scripture clearly states that it's through resting our faith in the finished work of Christ—not our own works—that we enter into His Sabbath rest. This is a rest that we must also consciously abide in. Remember, the Galatians and the Hebrews were turning away from the grace of resting in Christ alone for salvation, back to the legalistic works of the flesh in order to obtain justification. Therefore, the manner in which Christians "keep the Sabbath" is to *"gird up the loins of* [our] *mind, be sober, and <u>**rest**</u>* [our] *hope <u>fully</u> upon the grace that is to be brought to* [us] *at the revelation of Jesus Christ"* (1 Peter 1: 13). Now, let's get back to the subject at hand.]

The entire moral law—the Ten Commandments—is fulfilled in one word--love. It's important to emphasize what Paul is clearly teaching in this verse—***that love enables us to overcome sin!*** Furthermore, there are a host of other sins that branch off of these Ten Commandments: maliciousness, envy, strife, gossip, back-biting, pride, boasting, indifference, unforgiveness, mercilessness, hatred, wrath, selfishness, drunkenness, unthankfulness, slander, haughtiness, lust, lovers of pleasure more than lovers of God, and the like. If a person took the time, they'd be able to relate every sin in the Bible to one of the Ten Commandments.

The 10 commandments are to sin as the primary colors — red, yellow, and blue — are to the color spectrum. Therefore, when we walk in love, not only are we enabled to keep the surface show of the Ten Commandments, but we are also enabled to keep the deeper, spiritual manifestations of these sins as well. The externally righteous Pharisees could do the former, but only the Spirit filled Christian can do the latter. This is because love goes beneath the surface commandments; it goes to the heart of the commandments — a place the Pharisees could never reach. Christ made this truth very clear in the Sermon on the Mount.

"For I say to you, that unless your righteousness exceeds the righteousness of the scribes and Pharisees, you will by no means enter the kingdom of heaven. You have heard that it was said to those of old, 'You shall not murder, and whoever murders will be in danger of the judgment.' 22 But I say to you that whoever is angry with his brother without a cause shall be in danger of the judgment. And whoever says to his brother, 'Raca!' shall be in danger of the council. But whoever says, 'You fool!' shall be in danger of hell fire…"You have heard that it was said to those of old, 'You shall not commit adultery.' 28 But I say to you that whoever looks at a woman to lust for her has already committed adultery with her in his heart" (Matthew 5: 20-28).

Any self-righteous Pharisee can keep a surface show of the letter of the Law. Only a follower of Christ, walking in the Spirit of love, can keep the spirit of God's commands. This is because the Spirit of God Himself will fill the heart of the Christian who seeks to obey Him out of genuine love.

"He who has My commandments and keeps them, **it is he who loves Me***. And he who loves Me will be loved by My Father, and* **I will love him and manifest Myself to him***…If anyone loves Me,* **he will** *keep My word; and My Father will love him, and* **We will come to him and make Our home with him***. 24 He who does not love Me* **does not keep** *My words"* (John 14: 21-24)

This scripture is obviously not talking about when God initially indwells us when we're first saved. The Holy Spirit initially indwells the believer the moment that they're born again through faith in Jesus Christ. This scripture is talking about a deeper, more intimate abiding that is only possible to those who earnestly seek to enter into a love relationship with Christ—a relationship whereby we sacrificially surrender to His Lordship over our lives. The promised response to such love is the indwelling presence of the Spirit of God, who gives discernment and power to our love. Such love is literally endowed with power to overcome sin.

Walking In *Love* Enables Us to Walk In The *Light* of the *Spirit* of God

Walking in love also has another vital component that enables us to overcome sin. Love enables us to *"walk in the light."* The Christian who walks in the light overcomes sin. Listen to how the Apostle John explains this.

"This is the message which we have heard from Him and declare to you, that God is light and in Him is no darkness at all. ⁶ *If we say that we have fellowship with Him, and walk in darkness, we lie and do not practice the truth.* ⁷ *But if we walk in the light as He is in the light, we have fellowship with one another, and the blood of Jesus Christ His Son cleanses us from all sin"* (1 John 1: 5-7).

God has no middle ground – *"In Him is no darkness **at all**!"* We're either walking in the light, or walking in darkness. However, what does it meant to walk in the light? How exactly are we enabled to walk in the light? The Apostle John answers this very question in the next chapter.

"He who says he is in the light, and hates his brother, is in darkness until now. ¹⁰ **He who loves his brother abides in the light**, *and* <u>there is no cause for stumbling in him</u>. ¹¹ *But he who hates his brother is in darkness and walks in darkness, and does not know where he is going, because the darkness has blinded his eyes"* (1 John 2: 9-11).

This scripture clearly teaches that when we walk in love, we are walking in the light, and this light keeps us from *"stumbling"* into sin. This word, *"stumbling"*, is the Greek word *"skandalon"*, from which we get the word "scandal." Before the eyes of God, every sin is a scandal. However, both Paul and John agree, when we walk in love, we are given the ability to overcome *bondage* to every sin (Remember Romans 13, love gives us the power to overcome the sins associated with the Ten Commandments). So, how exactly does love relate to light, and how does this light enable us to overcome sin? Remember what we read earlier.

"*For you were once darkness, but now you are light in the Lord.* **Walk as children of light** ⁹ (**for the fruit of the Spirit** *is in all goodness, righteousness, and truth*)" (Ephesians 5: 8-9).

When we walk in the light we're walking in the Spirit, and when we "*walk in the Spirit*" we "*shall not fulfill the lust of the flesh.*" We cannot walk in the light apart from the Spirit of God, and if we're walking in the Spirit, we will invariably have light. The simple illustration of the lampstand bears witness to this truth. The Holy Spirit in the scripture is represented by oil; hence, the "anointing". Every ancient Hebrew lamp needed oil in order to burn the flame and give light. It's the same with us. However, John gives us the pivotal key to this promise — it is *walking in love* that enables us to "*walk in the Spirit*", Who in turn causes us to "*walk in the light.*"

These are three angles of the same truth; we cannot do one without the others. How do they relate to one another? Walking in sacrificial love is our part — **this is our surrender**. God both influences and responds to this surrendered love by filling what we've emptied. The Lord won't force Himself on us, nor will He take possession of us. God only takes free-will offerings given out of love, not grudgingly or out of obligation. Wherever self is yielded and the world is crucified, God fills with Himself — **this is God's response to our surrender**. "*God is Light, and in Him is no darkness at all*"; therefore, wherever God is, there will be Light — **this is the inevitable result of the first two**. In short, surrendered *love* is our part, the filling of the *Spirit* is God's part, and the inevitable result is spiritual *light*.

On the contrary, wherever we're holding on to self and the world, we'll remain in darkness. This is because the Holy Spirit will not share lordship with self, nor will He vie with the world for our worship. The love of self and the love of the world shows Him that He is not welcome. It literally makes us the "*enemy of God*" (James 4: 4). He is not welcome to run our life, nor is He welcome to be the object of our devotion. Therefore, we'll be left to our own understanding and our own desires. The inevitable result will be *darkness*.

Darkness simply means that a person is living in the fallen, natural understanding of the self-nature. They refuse to surrender to the Lord in *sacrificial love*, which means they're resisting the ***Spirit of God*** *who is Love*, which means they'll remain alienated from ***the light*** that is only found in God who *"is light"* — thus, they remain in darkness. According to Paul and John, a person walks in darkness when they continue in sin (Ephesians 5: 3-14, John 3: 16-20). This is because the person doesn't *see* where they're going, so they stumble.

"Are there not twelve hours in the day? If anyone walks in the day, he does not stumble, because he sees the light of this world. ¹⁰ But if one walks in the night, he stumbles, because the light is not in him." (John 11: 9-10).

And again,

"The way of the wicked is like darkness; they do not know what makes them stumble" (Proverbs 4: 19).

Remember, the most crucial character trait of Christ-like love is that it's *selfless*. When a person is filled with self, they're not filled with Christ; and vice versa. If a person is filled with self, they're filled with what self wants. Self has an insatiable appetite for sin. All of the sins that we lust after are somehow related to this world. As long as we are looking through the eyes of our corrupted self-nature at the things of this world, we will remain in darkness concerning the spiritual things of God. But, when we *"walk by faith and not by sight"*, and we offer ourselves up to the Lord in order to love Him with all our heart, He will accept our surrender, and fill us with Himself. Thus, He enables us to see as He sees and walk in His light.

This light is progressive; we don't' get it all at once. It grows as we grow — not as we physically age, but as we spiritually grow. Our growth at every stage is determined by our love, not our doctrinal prowess. As our love grows stronger, our light grows brighter; for stronger love simply means that Christ is filling more and more of our vision, and self and the world are fading into the shadows. As our vision of Him increases, our Light increases, and as our Light increases, we are progressively given the Spirit's enabling to walk in both the *"discernment"* and *"righteousness"* of that light.

*"The path of the just is like the shining sun,
That shines **ever brighter** unto the perfect day.
¹⁹ The way of the wicked is like darkness;
They do not know what makes them stumble"* (Proverbs 4: 18-19).

What is the Evidence That We're "Walking in the Spirit" Through Love, and Not Simply Straining in the Flesh?

How do we measure whether or not we're truly walking in love by the power of the Spirit, versus trying to follow truth in the strength of the flesh?

"*By this we know that we love the children of God, when we love God and keep His commandments. ³ For this is the love of God, that we keep His commandments. And* **His commandments are not burdensome**" (1 John 5: 2-3).

This how we know that we're walking in the love of Christ by the enabling of the Holy Spirit – "*His commandments are not burdensome.*" Is it a burden to you to obey God in certain areas? Do you find yourself following Christ in certain areas out of grudging obligation? Do you neglect and avoid certain truths because they're too difficult, or they take too much sacrifice? Do you selectively choose to follow certain truths, yet explain away other truths that make you uncomfortable? Do you rationalize self-serving motives that make it comfortable for you to externally "obey" God? What are your heart-motives for "obeying" certain truths? For the eyes of others? Because you have to? If so, you're love for Christ is either weak or non-existent.

If there is any fleshly resistance when we're confronted with the Truth, it's a clear indicator that the will of our flesh is more dominant than the love of our inner man. This shouldn't make us feel condemned. It should motivate us to seek the Lord more earnestly. It should compel us to examine ourselves, exposing which aspect of our self-nature is resisting the truth, and how we're being influenced by the world. Slow down and draw closer to the Lord. Like David, ask Him to, "*search me, O God, and* **know my heart**; *Try me, and know my anxieties;* ²⁴ *And see if there is any wicked way in me, And lead me in the way everlasting*" (Psalm 139: 23-24).

One of the primary themes of John's epistle is teaching us the essential importance of walking in love—hence, his well-known title, *"The Apostle of love."* If we truly love God with a love that is empowered by His Holy Spirit, none of His commands will be *"burdensome"* to us. This is John's point. This is the evidence that our love has been perfected. *"But **whoever keeps His word**, truly the love of God **is** [not "will be"—"**is**"] **perfected in him**. By this we know that we are in Him"* (1 John 2: 5). It is a joy for the Christian to wholeheartedly follow the Lord *if the Spirit of the Lord* is filling that Christian with a love for God's truth. If there's any part of God's truth that is a burden to you, it's because that particular truth is conflicting with your self-nature and your love for this world. It's critical that you recognize this point.

The words of Christ are the words of every Christian; *"The spirit indeed is willing, but the flesh is weak"* (Matthew 26: 41). The spiritual nature longs for Christ; the fleshly self hates Him! If it's a strain for you to follow Christ, it's because you're forcing or manipulating the fleshly self-nature to do something that it's utterly incapable of doing. You're using some Christianized psychological ploy or religious willpower to follow Christ. You're not walking in the Spirit, and that's why you're not liberated to love the things that God loves.

God does not contradict Himself. He doesn't modify, minimize, or explain away His own Word! He's not schizophrenic, nor does He have multiple personality disorder—God says He means and means what He says. He doesn't make mistakes, He doesn't give us unnecessary drivel, and He doesn't give us optional suggestions. God's Word is absolute and immutable, and He is in perfect oneness with His own Word – *"In the beginning was the Word, and the Word was with God, and the Word was God"* (John 1: 1).

Therefore, the evidence that my spirit is walking in union with His Spirit, is that I have the same heartbeat and love toward every word that proceeds out of His mouth. He doesn't minimize or explain away His word, and if I'm walking in oneness with His Spirit, I won't minimize or explain away His word. But If I'm resistant (not struggling to obey, but refusing to obey) to any part of God's Word, it is firm evidence that my "natural" self-nature and the world are suffocating my spiritual nature in that area—or worse yet, I'm still spiritually dead.

Again, the surest evidence that our love is mature and being influenced by the Holy Spirit, is that the Lord's commands will not be a burden to us. We won't be compelled to explain them away or minimize them in the name of

grace. Rather, when we see God's truth, we'll say with our Lord, *"Behold, I come;… **I delight to do Your will, O my God, and Your law is within my heart."***
(Psalm 40: 7-8).

Decisively Resolve to Follow Christ

Begin the process. Wherever there's any resistance within you to the truth, persistently bring that area of yourself before the Lord. Find out where the spiritual blockage is. Never embrace the dismissive attitude that says, *"God knows I'm not perfect. He understands. Besides, I'm under grace."* Mercilessly crucify such thinking! Either you want stumbling mediocrity or overcoming victory—make up your mind! If you truly want to grow in Christ and overcome your stronghold, you have to resolve to take every Word of God seriously. Remember, *"Examine the things you tend simply to shrug your shoulders about, and where you have refused to be obedient, and you will know why you are not growing spiritually."*

Do want to grow spiritually? Do you want to overcome your strongholds? Do you want to walk in the fruitfulness and power of the Holy Spirit? Then begin exploring and learning what it means to love the Lord with all your heart, and how to love others with the love of Christ. The continual casualty of this pursuit will be your self-nature along with its attachments to this world. It won't be easy nor will it be pleasant. But, eventually you'll reach a tipping point—your new nature will have gained spiritual leverage and momentum.

That old nature, starved and neglected, will begin to stagger and lose ground. The farther he falls behind, the more faint his selfish cries will become. As his voice is silenced, you'll begin to hear more clearly a Voice that has been there all along—a *"still, small voice."* *"Your ears shall hear a word behind you, saying, "This is the way, walk in it," Whenever you turn to the right hand or whenever you turn to the left"* (Isaiah 30: 21). It is the Voice of the Word that you've been abiding in—the Word that comes naturally to the conscious of a renewed mind. It is the Voice of the Good Shepherd.

*"He brings out his own sheep, he goes before them; and **the sheep follow Him, for they know his voice…My sheep hear My voice, and I know them, and they follow Me**"* (John 10: 4 & 27).

Even so beloved Christian, earnestly resolve to follow the Voice of the Lord as it is written in the Word and illuminated by the Spirit. The Wind of His Spirit will be at your back. The smile of your Father is at the goal. So purify your heart and set it solely on Christ, and run after Him with everything you've got! You'll discover that the Lord will be a debtor to no man, for you'll find the words of His promise to be true.

"If you abide in My word, you are My disciples indeed. [32] And you shall know the truth, and the truth shall make you free…Therefore if the Son makes you free, you shall be free indeed."

So, *"Walk in the Spirit, and you shall not fulfill the lust of the flesh."*

The Conclusion of Following Christ

This is by no means an exhaustive explanation of everything a Christian needs to follow in order to grow in spiritual fruitfulness and power. It's vital that we also maintain a healthy prayer life, and that we regularly fellowship and worship with other Christians *who are seeking to follow Christ*. Please do not assume that since I have not elaborated on these essential practices that they are not important. They are indispensable—you *will not* overcome without prayer, praise and worship, and fellowship! However, for the sake of brevity, I'll forgo elaborating on these absolutely essential tenants of our faith. The truths contained within these chapters on following Christ present the *foundation* for every other aspect of the Christ-centered life. If one surrenders to these, everything else will come together.

To conclude these essential chapters on what it means to "follow Christ", allow me to bring these principles together into a nutshell. To follow Christ means to walk in His Spirit. We walk in His Spirit by faith working through love. Biblical faith is undiluted with our own understanding, grounded in the word, and authenticated by surrendered obedience. Biblical love is the all-encompassing, highest command for the Christian. It is cultivated by looking unto Jesus and allowing the Holy Spirit to fill us with His love, which in turn enables us to walk in the light of His truth and righteousness.

These are the two essential, spiritual pillars of the Spirit-filled walk. With them, all that we do is accepted and empowered by God. Without them, *"it is impossible to please Him."* These are the two pillars that enable us to continue in His word as *"disciples indeed"*. This is what it means to obey the command of our Lord – *"Follow Me"*. And this is how we obtain the power of the Holy Spirit to trounce every single sinful stronghold within our life.

CHAPTER 9

BRINGING IT ALL TOGETHER

Under Command – In Command!

It had been forty long years — forty wasted years. They were years that incessantly haunted the mind of the young general with the merciless thoughts of what could have been. He never forgot the sweet taste of the succulent grapes that they'd retrieved in their original reconnaissance mission to Eshcol. Nor did he ever forget the bitter taste of having a promised paradise stripped from his hands due to the selfish cowardice of his ten comrades who demanded a return to Egypt's world. They refused the promise, so God refused them the promise, and the wilderness not only consumed them, but their entire generation — besides two: Joshua and Caleb.

This time, Joshua would not be denied. The Jordan lay behind him, and the impregnable *Stronghold* of Jericho before him. Moses, his spiritual leader, mentor, and friend, was dead. Now, the whole weight of the mission lay on his shoulders. He would not allow the Children of Israel to stray from the prime directive as before. He was determined to follow every minute detail of God's direction for entering the Promised Land.

Joshua had methodically observed every direction the Lord gave him for crossing the Jordan. God miraculously stopped the flow of the great river, the priests held the Ark of the Covenant in the center of it, the entire company crossed over, and they erected 12 memorial stones, in and out of the river, to commemorate the event. Then he had all the men circumcised according to the ordinance given to Abraham. Everything was progressing smoothly according to God's will. Joshua's confidence began to grow. He knew that God was with him. He was ready to take on the world! He set his sights on Jericho, and emboldened his resolve to lead the army of Israel to certain victory. But, little did he know that victory was not certain—not yet.

In his path stood a Soldier. The Soldier's armor wasn't familiar to Joshua; it was magnificent and glorious to behold. The Soldier's sword was drawn. Joshua, undaunted by the awesome appearance of the stranger, faced him down and demanded that he make an account of his allegiance. *"Are You for us or for our adversaries?"* When the stranger spoke, the voice was familiar, though he'd never heard it spoken through the vocal cords of a man. He'd heard it in the terrible rumbles of thunder on the mountain, and he'd heard it in the whispers of the Holy Cloud that communed with Moses in the door of his tent…but he'd never heard it like this.

"'No, but as Commander of the army of the Lord I have now come.' And Joshua fell on his face to the earth and worshiped, and said to Him, 'What does my Lord say to His servant?' 15 Then the Commander of the Lord's army said to Joshua, 'Take your sandal off your foot, for the place where you stand is holy.' And Joshua did so" (Joshua 5: 13-15).

Joshua immediately relinquished his command, and in doing so, he gained full command over all the battles ahead.

"The Battle Is the Lord's!" —Laying Hold of Our Promised Victory

The name Joshua is the Old Testament is the same name as Jesus in the New Testament. There's a picture here. Moses, who represented the Law, could not bring the people into their promised rest. Only Jesus Christ can lead us into the Promised Land of victory, fruitfulness, and rest. Along with Joshua was this mysterious Commander. This Commander would be the invisible power that would both lead Joshua's army, and rout every foe they faced. However, the help of the Commander was dependent upon the faith and obedience of Joshua and the people—if they didn't trust, obey, and fight, He wouldn't fight for them. It was a joint venture: surrendered trust and enabling grace.

This Commander was no doubt the preincarnate Christ—He spoke as God and Joshua worshipped Him. However, He is also a lot like the Holy Spirit. He was the *invisible* power that led them to every victory. The people followed the lead of the *visible* Joshua, and walked in the power of the *invisible* Commander. We are not called to follow the Holy Spirit; we're called to follow Jesus, and in doing so, we walk *in* the Spirit. We cannot follow the divine, omnipotent, omniscient, omnipresent, transcended, Spirit of God; we follow the Man Jesus Christ who identified with us and gave us a human example. The children of Israel followed the visible man Joshua/Jesus, and they walked in the power of the invisible, divine Commander.

The leadership of Joshua/Jesus, and the presence of the Commander completely transformed the Children of Israel in the Promised Land. Consider these three fundamental changes that occurred among the Jews as they followed Joshua.

One, in the wilderness, the Children of Israel were full of selfishness. They constantly murmured against God's heavenly bread, and lusted after flesh. They were always complaining against Moses and challenging God's truth with their own understanding. Instead of fighting for the Promised Land under Moses, they chose rather to protect themselves and reject the land that God promised them. They refused God's promise of victory, fruitfulness, and rest because it seemed too difficult—many Christians do so as well. However, under Joshua, the people stopped rebelling, were no longer selfish, and completely relinquished their own understanding. Jericho was won, not by the strategic understanding of man, buy by complete trust and surrender to God's exact instructions.

Two, throughout their wanderings in the wilderness, the people constantly looked back to Egypt with longing eyes and cries. They despised the Bread from Heaven, and longed for the food of Egypt. As a matter of fact, when they refused to go into the Promised Land the first time, they joined together against Moses and a made a resolute decision to return to Egypt (Numbers 14: 1-10)! However, under Joshua, the people *never again* even mentioned Egypt! They were utterly crucified to it. After the people were circumcised, God said, *"This day I have rolled away the reproach of Egypt from you"* (Joshua 5: 9). No longer did they look back at Egypt, but they looked forward to the Promised Land.

The armies of Joshua had victory over all their enemies, except one—Ai. They ultimately defeated Ai; however, their initial attempt to defeat them was completely thwarted. Why? There was one man who was filled self and the world — Achan. When Jericho was defeated, God commanded the people not to take any of the plunder for themselves. Achan, filled with selfish desires, looked at some of the treasures of Jericho (the world), and was likely tempted by Satan to take it. This man's selfish worldliness caused the Children of Israel to be *utterly defeated* by an otherwise, inferior enemy. Joshua searched him out and stoned him to death, thus he utterly removed this self-centered, worldly member of his army. From this point on, they defeated Ai, and every other foe they faced.

Finally, number *three*, the people complained and murmured against Moses constantly in the wilderness. A few times they were ready to stone Him! Moses (the Law) simply could not control such a large company sinners! On one occasion, their rebellion frustrated him so much that it drove him to disobey God and sin. This sin was so serious that it caused him to forfeit his right to enter into the Promised Land. However, the people followed Joshua with complete trust and absolute surrender. Under Moses the people were constantly rebelling, sinning, murmuring, and lusting after Egypt as they wandered in circles in the wilderness. However, "*Israel served the LORD all the days of Joshua, and all the days of the elders who outlived Joshua, who had known all the works of the LORD which He had done for Israel*" (Joshua 24: 31).

This is the difference between trying to clean ourselves up in our own strength, and following Christ by walking in His Spirit. Under Moses, the people were filled with selfishness, lust for the things of Egypt, and a doubleminded, rebellious attitude towards Moses's leadership. Under Joshua, the people denied their own will, renounced Egypt, and fully surrendered to his leadership. Just as the Children of Israel followed Joshua to victory, fruitfulness, and rest, we are called to follow our Heavenly Joshua in the same way. So, let us leave the wilderness of wandering and struggling in our own efforts to be moral, and let us follow Christ into the spiritual life of victory, fruitfulness, and rest that He has *promised* us.

"That I May Know Him" — Pressing Forward

Everything that has been written in this book is for the sole purpose of instructing the reader of how to become an overcoming disciple of Christ. There are no 12 steps or 40 days to this goal. There are no steps to follow, only foundational principles and truths. As we embrace and yield to these, the Holy Spirit wisely leads, refines, and establishes each individual believer accordingly. When Christ calls His disciples, He calls them to a life, not a program. It is only to *"disciples indeed"* that Christ promises total liberation from the bondage of sin—not partial liberation from one or two "major" sins, but complete freedom from all *habitual slavery* to sin. Dear reader, this is not special or unique; it is normal, biblical, healthy Christianity.

Following Christ is not as complicated as it may seem. I know that I've written a lot, but it was important to do so. Most of what I've written has been for the sake of explaining truths that have long been forgotten, and explaining away false ideologies that have permeated much of modern evangelical thought. I guess you could say that much of what I've written was for the sake of biblical renovation. It's a lot easier to build something from the ground up, than it is to renovate a structure that's overrun with religious dry rot. It was important to tear down a host of unbiblical beliefs and traditions of men in order to build solely on the solid foundation of truth.

This book could have been reduced down to one page if all I had to write was, *"Walk in the Spirit, and you shall not fulfill the lust of the flesh."* But, what does this mean? What exactly does it mean to *"walk"* in the Spirit of the Living God? What does it mean to continue in His word as a *"disciple indeed"*? I refused to be satisfied with a textually correct answer; I wanted an answer that was both true to the scripture and real in my life. This is what the Lord drove me to pursue, and by His grace I was given both understanding and experience. The Lord had to bring me back to the basics of scripture in order to deliver me, and I dare not do anything less for the reader.

The University of Michigan has a large stone on their campus. This stone has been painted over with a new message about every month or so for decades. Nevertheless, beneath all of these different artificial, painted messages, the stone still remains, unaltered and unmoved. Man has painted countless artificial, psycho-religious ideologies atop the immutable rock of God's truth. They bear the same shape, but not the same substance. One created by God; the other by man. It was imperative for me to cut through the thick layers of various painted messages in order to get to the solid rock of invariable truth. For therein lies the only sure foundation upon which we can build our lives as *"disciples indeed"*—a journey back to the basics of scripture.

It is the will of God that every child of God be a completely liberated, overcoming, follower of Christ. I've attempted to expand on this truth to the best of my understanding according to the Word of God, my personal experience, as well as the testimony of many trustworthy witnesses. I trust the Holy Spirit has been with me. All that has been written is built on the premise and the promise of John 8: 31-36:

"Then Jesus said to those Jews who believed Him, "If you abide in My word, you are My disciples indeed. ³² And **you shall know the truth, and the truth shall make you free**…*Most assuredly, I say to you, whoever commits sin is a slave of sin.* ³⁵ *And a slave does not abide in the house forever, but a son abides forever.* ³⁶ **Therefore if the Son makes you free, you shall be free indeed."**

I explored some critical questions. What does it mean to *"abide"*, or continue in His word? What does it mean to be a *"disciple indeed"*? What does it mean to come to **"know the Truth"** – *"the Son"* — Who ultimately makes us free from the bondage to sin? What's so important about coming to *"know the Truth"*?

Many Christians do not realize that God *"desires all men to be saved **and** to come to the **knowledge of the Truth**"* (1Timothy 2: 4) — there are two stages here: salvation and sanctification. Unfortunately, multitudes of professed Christians are *"always learning* [like the textualists] *and never able to come to the **knowledge of the Truth**"* (2 Timothy 3: 7). They have a *"form of godliness but denying its power"*; therefore, they turn to man-made solutions. Until a believer comes to *"know the Truth"*, they'll never realize the authentic fullness of the Christ-filled life.

Coming into the *"knowledge of the Truth"* is not simply knowing the doctrines about Christ; it is knowing Christ, *"the Son"*, on a deeper, more intimate, transformative level. This is the foundation of the entire Christian walk; seeking to intimately know Christ, and watching as He transforms you thoroughly from the inside out.

Christ is everything for the Christian; He saves us from sin in every stage of salvation. He saves us from the *penalty* of sin when we're justified, from the *power* of sin as we're sanctified, and from the *presence* of sin when we're glorified. In each stage we look to Christ in a different way. Salvation is a singular look of repentant faith, sanctification is a lifelong gaze of loving faith, and in glorification He says *"watch and be ready"* with expectant faith. Jesus Christ, alone, is the *"Author and Finisher of our faith."* He is our Savior through and through, on every level and at every stage. No philosophy of man can add to, improve upon, or in any way assist His mighty work within our lives.

The late Alan Redpath, former pastor of Moody Church in Chicago, who himself struggled with sin and passed through a death and resurrection experience, put it the following way.

> "Any battle for victory, power, and deliverance - from ourselves and from sin - which is not based constantly upon the gazing and the beholding of the Lord Jesus, with the heart and life lifted up to Him, **is doomed to failure**."

Wholehearted devotion to Christ is everything! If I can get this point through to the conscious of the reader, then I've fulfilled my duty. When we pursue Christ with all our heart, self and worldly influences will begin to die away, He'll become more real to us, and He'll make Himself more real through us. This is what it means to *"know Christ"* — when we identify with Him to such a degree that His Spirit and our spirit are of one mind and one heart. This should be the singular aim and drive of every Christian; such was the aim of Paul.

> *"What things were gain to me, these I have counted loss for Christ. ⁸ Yet indeed I also count all things loss for the* **excellence of the <u>knowledge of Christ Jesus my Lord</u>**, *for whom I have suffered the loss of all things, and count them as rubbish, that I may gain Christ ⁹ and be found in Him, not having my own righteousness, which is from the law, but that which is through faith in Christ, the righteousness which is from God by faith;* ¹⁰ **<u>that I may know Him</u>** *and* **the power of His resurrection**, *and* **the fellowship of His sufferings, being conformed to His death**, ¹¹ *if, by any means, I may attain to the resurrection from the dead."* To which he went on to say, *"Brethren,* **join in following my <u>example</u>, and note those who so walk, as you have us for a <u>pattern</u>**" (Philippians 3: 7-17).

This is the heart and soul of what it means to be a self-denying, crucified, genuine *"disciple indeed"*. Paul's highest aim was to know Christ, not only to be justified, but to fully identify with His crucifixion and resurrection power. However, notice Paul's final instructions; follow *"my example"*, and follow everyone else who follows this *"pattern."* In the very next chapter Paul says, *"The things which you* **learned** *and* **received** *and* **heard** *and* **saw in me**, *these* **<u>DO</u>**" (Philippians 4: 9).

How will you respond to this? *"Well, that's good for you Paul, but we're all at different levels. God doesn't expect perfection. Besides, we're saved by grace, not by works. Don't be so legalistic! And remember, according to Romans 7, Paul struggled with sinful bondage too. Besides, Paul tells us in this very scripture that he hadn't arrived yet."* Lord have mercy on us!

One thing is true; we are all on different levels. Paul addressed this in verse 16. *"Nevertheless, to the degree that we have already attained, let us walk by the same rule, let us be of the same mind.*" In other words, whatever level you're on in your Christian walk, the *"same rule"* still applies.

Paul exemplified the perfect *"pattern"* of the Christian walk, and he, speaking under the inspiration and authority of the Holy Spirit, commands us to embrace the *"same mind."* This isn't Paul's opinion! This isn't Paul's way! This is Paul's God-given, apostolic authority to instruct all Christians concerning how to live the Christian life. Any other approach to the Christian walk is no longer following in the footsteps of Christ. It has veered off the narrow path, and is entangled in the dense wasteland of man's religious understanding. Unfortunately, there are multitudes of professed Christians who are perfectly satisfied with this buffet style Christianity.

One of the greatest tragedies within the church is that so many Christians are self-satisfied. They have their trophy profession of faith, all the correct doctrines, a few selective values, and for them that's enough. They've redefined and minimized a host of sins, allowing them social sanction among their ranks, *"not knowing that there is anything wrong."* They go from Sunday to Sunday in a dead routine of church life, having no drive or aspirations to ascend to the heights of spiritual power and vibrancy. They're largely satisfied with having plateaued at doctrinal orthodoxy and ecclesiastical orthopraxy. Such regimented religion puts all of the power within our hands, and the Holy Spirit is merely there in an advisory role. Paul knew nothing of this stunted, self-satisfied Christianity – he wanted more! He wanted to experientially and intimately know Christ in every way possible.

What things are gain to you? What things give you confidence in the ability of the fleshly *self*? What things in this *world* inhibit your pursuit of this intimate knowledge of the Living Lord? Take up your cross and crucify them! We are in a long distance race; therefore, we are called to lay aside everything that weighs us down and trips us up. We are called to run, unimpeded by self and the world, with our eyes singularly focused on Christ (Hebrews 12: 1-2). And the most descriptive way for us to accomplish this is for us to surrender to Christ's signature call for every disciple – *"Deny yourself, take up your cross daily, and follow Me."*

When we follow Christ on His terms, as *"disciples indeed"*, we'll inevitably gain power over habitual strongholds. For a few, this occurs the moment they come to an end of themselves and turn to Christ for salvation. Victory over a stronghold doesn't need to be a long, drawn-out process; however, following Christ is a lifelong pursuit. Remember, the goal is not victory over a habitual sin; the goal is Christlikeness – victory over habitual sin is one of the many divine byproducts of this pursuit. Nevertheless, while a unique few experience immediate victory, most Christians continue to struggle with habitual sin well into their Christian walk. The reasons for this are varied.

For some, their struggle has not produced a sufficient sense of urgency within them, so their efforts to overcome are lackluster. For others, the self-nature may be so strong and entrenched within them, that the Lord may have to bring them through unique circumstances to bring them to the end of self. The same may apply to some within whom the world is deeply entrenched. Then there are those who are entangled in the confusion of man's solutions. The reason for our continued struggle could be any combination of these, or some other reason not mentioned here. Whatever the case may be, this immutable fact still remains: self, the world, and the Devil have more influence and sway over the person than the Holy Spirit does. Therefore, our resolute and determined goal must be to *"walk in the Spirit, and* [we] *shall not fulfill the lust of the flesh."* This is not an easy goal; nevertheless, it's an essential goal for everyone who is called by the name of Christ.

Bringing It All Together Into Some Final Reminders and Insights

Let's conclude this book by bringing together some of the truths and principles that we've learned. I don't have any *steps* for you to follow; only principles. God directs all of us differently, but by the *same* principles. If you will follow God's truths and principles with all your heart, He will give you the *steps* to follow. Let's bring it all together.

Take firm hold of your assurance in Christ. Make sure your faith is firmly grounded in the person and work of Christ. If it is, make it point to drive out every ounce of doubt and fear. Even after you've fallen again and again, God still forgives again and again — don't take this for granted. If you feel doubt, or fear, or condemnation, always remember that these feelings are inspired by the Wicked One and harbored in a carnal mind. Take hold of the truth, defy every deceitful feeling that contradicts the truth, and press forward in the joy of the Lord. Read the chapter on *"Assurance"* again if you need to be reminded of some of these truths.

Remember the goal of Sanctification. Overcoming a handful of pet-peeve sins and then living according to our own preferred morals is not the goal. Christ has called His church to a higher standard of righteousness. Overcoming all habitual patterns of sin and growing into the likeness of Christ is the goal. Furthermore, it is as we pursue Christ with all our heart that He makes us free from sin. We're not called to fight sin; we're called to follow the Savior of sinners.

He doesn't *"set"* us free; this feeds into the idea of loose grace. He *"makes"* us free—there's a difference. Any master can open their gates and *set* their slave free; however, they're not truly free, they're just loose—still running from the law. However, if the master gives the slave the official documentation that validates their freed status, then they are no longer slaves, but they've been *made* into free men. Christ literally begins to live through those who've surrendered to Him as *"disciples indeed"*. They are *made* into free beings because they are living in surrendered oneness with the One who is eternally free from sin. He doesn't *set* us free apart from Himself; He *makes* us free in union with Himself. It is a freedom that can only be achieved as *let go* of our natural self, and learn to walk in Christ according to our spiritual nature.

"It is only when God has transformed our nature and we have entered into the experience of sanctification that the fight begins. The warfare is not against sin; we can never fight against sin— Jesus Christ conquered that in His redemption of us. **The conflict is waged over turning our natural life into a spiritual life.** *This is never done easily, nor does God intend that it be so."* —Oswald Chambers[63]

How does the natural become spiritual? The body of a lamb is sectioned into pieces, each piece is laid on the altar, and then the offering is set aflame. As it burns, the physical body transforms into a fragrant, smoky essence and ascends into the air. It is the willful offering up of the natural that transforms it into the spiritual. Any part of the offering that we leave off the altar will remain natural. There is a picture in this if you'll receive it.

Deny yourself. The self-oriented nature within us is the greatest hindrance to the nature of Christ being manifest within us. Utterly eradicate from your vocabulary the self-deifying phrase, *"that's just how **I AM**."* If how you are is not how Christ is, you have to deny yourself, not bolster yourself! Determine to walk carefully with your eyes focused on Christ in His word—He'll teach you. Be alert. Consciously avoid walking according to your own, self-oriented, *"knowledge of good and evil."* Whenever your fleshly character or understanding conflicts with the Word, don't deny the word by explaining it away, but deny yourself. In spite of how painful or difficult it may be, keep at it; the Lord will help you

Take up your cross. Taking up our cross means being crucified to this world. Refuse to allow your life to be so filled with the things of the world that Christ is pushed to the fringes of it. Make the sacrifices! Pluck out your proverbial "eye"! Approach your liberties and legitimate worldly pleasures wisely. It's foolish to think that we can render to Christ the scraps of our life and still expect Him to fill us and give us victory!

Crucify yoked relationships with those who hinder your faith. Scrutinize every idea, trend, philosophy, and point of view under the light of scripture. Don't allow yourself to be swept away in the overflowing deluge of worldly thinking. Never mingle the word of God with any philosophy of man — especially not humanistic, naturalistic psychology! Embrace the pure, undiluted word of God as a *"a lamp to* [your] *feet And a light to* [your] *path."*

Follow Christ. Christ is our example; this is the most paramount truth that will keep us balanced and on the road to true sanctification. Like an earnest son continuously looks to his dad as he guides him through a complicated task, let us ever look to Christ so that He can guide us through this complicated life. He guides us as we yield to the Holy Spirit. We yield to the Holy Spirit by a faith that is fueled by love.

Our faith must be grounded solely in the Word of God — both the written and the Living Word. But, we cannot *merely* approach the word through study, nor by trying to read through the Bible in a year. The scripture is clear and consistent; we must meditate on the Word — think on it. The more that we think on the word, the more our thinking will be aligned with the Word. Furthermore, our faith in the word cannot be mingled with our own understanding — the Lord despises double-minded faith.

But, genuine faith is not only grounded in the word, it also surrenders to the word, for *"faith without works is dead."* Genuine faith will obey what it believes to be true. If it doesn't obey, it doesn't truly believe. This obedience is not based merely upon the word, but upon the Lord who spoke the word. If I truly recognize Christ as my Lord, then nothing He says is minor. If someone that you highly regard told you to do a seemingly minor task, you'd do it. Not because the task seems major, but because the person who gave you the task is major in your eyes. When we disobey, it's because our perception of Christ is small — this is the evidence of weak faith.

However, this faith can, and must, be strengthened and fueled by sacrificial love. Christ-like love is not based on our feelings—sacrifice rarely *feels* comfortable. But, the more that we seek the face of Christ, discovering His unsearchable love for us, the more our love for Him will be awakened and energized. Furthermore, our love for Him must also be cultivated by sacrificing our will to His will. As we do this, our old selfish nature will decrease, and the influence of His Holy Spirit within us will increase. Thus, we'll be enabled to *"walk in the Spirit."* And, when we're walking in the enabling of the Spirit, *"His commandments are not burdensome"*, so that we *"shall not fulfill the lusts of the flesh."*

Our main concern should be on building our relationship with Christ. Never forget this paramount truth: Christ is our example. Paul pursued Christ with all of his being, and he implored us to *"join in following* [his] *example"* (Philippians 3: 17). Being a *"new creation in Christ"* is not simply a nice verse to quote; it's our new, God-given nature that should be *nurtured and explored to the fullest*! The old adage, *"the dog that you feed the most wins"* is actually pretty accurate. Let's get beyond merely quoting nifty adages, and decisively resolve to commit them to our lives. Victory is all about strengthening our spiritual nature; we cannot accomplish this if most of our time is spent catering to our fleshly nature. Difficult? Yes. Complicated? No.

The very thought of this seems intimidating I know; however, what within you is resisting this? Is it your new, spiritual nature? Of course not! If you're a child of God, I know this bears witness with your spirit. It's that old fallen self-nature that's holding back with reluctance, excuses, and arguments. It's that old covetous self that's concerned about how such a walk may infringe upon his worldly agenda and comfort zone. Whenever "self" attempts to argue with or steer you from the truth, deny it and press forward. If certain things in this world are crowding Christ out of your life, or distorting your vision of Him, crucify them and press forward. The Christian life is all about pressing hard after Christ, and trampling every obstacle that hinders this goal. Once you get over the hump, it'll all get a lot easier.

Rouse Yourself and Follow Christ With All Your Heart

God loves you, beloved Christian. The call to follow Christ is not to lay a grievous burden on you; it is to liberate you from the strongholds of the world, the flesh, and the Devil into the glorious rest of the Spirit-filled life. Following Christ is liberating, not laborious! The only difficult parts are giving up your right to yourself, and crucifying your detrimental attachments to this world. Go through the strain and the pain; God will help you. He doesn't expect perfection; He expects faithfulness and perseverance without any excuses. It is only the *"outward man* [that] *is perishing, yet the inward man is being renewed day by day"* (2 Corinthians 4: 16). And when the Holy Spirit breaks through with His liberating rest, peace, and joy, you will know beyond a shadow of a doubt that it was all worth it — and you'll want more of Him!

I close with the words of A. B. Simpson:

*"It is **easier** for a consecrated Christian to live a total life for God than to live a mixed life. A soul redeemed and sanctified by Christ is too large for the shoals and sands of a **selfish, worldly**, sinful life…Beloved, your life is too large, too glorious, too divine for the small place in which you are trying to live. Your purpose is too petty. Arise and dwell on high in the **resurrection life of Jesus** and in the inspiring hope of His blessed coming.*

Rise with thy risen Lord,

Ascend with Christ above,

And in the heavenlies walk with Him,

Whom seeing not, you love.

Walk as a heavenly race,

Princes of royal blood;

Walk as the children of the light,

The sons and heirs of God."[64]

Amen.

Notes

1. http://www.expastors.com/how-many-pastors-are-addicted-to-porn-the-stats-are-surprising/
2. http://psychcentral.com/lib/an-overview-of-sex-addiction/
3. Andrew Murray, "Absolute Surrender" (New Kensington: Whitaker House, 1982), 115.
4. https://www.cmalliance.org/devotions/simpson?mmdd=0901
5. http://legacy.biblegateway.com/devotionals/morning-and-evening/1952/02/18
6. https://www.cmalliance.org/devotions/simpson?mmdd=0719
7. A. W. Tozer, "The Pursuit of God" (Camp Hill: Christian Publications, 1993), 16.
8. http://teenchallengeofthesmokies.com/about_us.html
9. http://www.sermonindex.net/modules/mydownloads/singlefile.php?lid=4551&commentView=itemComments
10. http://www.sermonindex.net/modules/mydownloads/singlefile.php?lid=4625&commentView=itemComments
11. http://www.sermonindex.net/modules/mydownloads/singlefile.php?lid=21552&commentView=itemComments
12. R. A. Torrey, "How To Obtain Fullness of Power" (New Kensington: Whitaker House, 1982), 44.
13. http://www.sermonindex.net/modules/articles/index.php?view=article&aid=2039
14. Andrew Murray, "Absolute Surrender" (New Kensington: Whitaker House, 1982), 67.
15. https://www.wordsearchbible.com/products/20732-a-w-tozer-bundle
16. A. W. Tozer, "The Warfare of the Spirit" (Camp Hill: Christian Publications), 142-143.

17. A. B. Simpson, "Days of Heaven Upon Earth" (Nyack: Christian Alliance Publishing Co., 1897), 124.
18. http://www.desiringgod.org/messages/four-essentials-to-finishing-well
19. https://utmost.org/classic/pull-yourself-together-classic/
20. R. A. Torrey, "How To Obtain Fullness of Power" (New Kensington: Whitaker House, 1982), 85.
21. https://utmost.org/the-cost-of-sanctification/
22. https://utmost.org/classic/the-consecration-of-spiritual-energy-classic/
23. https://www.cmalliance.org/devotions/simpson?mmdd=0715
24. Andrew Murray, "Absolute Surrender" (New Kensington: Whitaker House, 1982), 58.
25. https://utmost.org/sanctification-1/
26. R. A. Torrey, "God's Power in Your Life" (New Kensington: Whitaker House,1982)
27. https://www.cmalliance.org/devotions/simpson?mmdd=0719
28. https://utmost.org/the-opposition-of-the-natural/
29. A. W. Tozer, "The Pursuit of God" (Camp Hill: Christian Publications, Inc., 1993), 42-43.
30. https://utmost.org/complete-and-effective-dominion/
31. Corrie Ten Boom, "Each New Day" (Old Tappan: Fleming H. Revell Company, 1977), 70.
32. https://www.cmalliance.org/devotions/simpson?mmdd=0518
33. http://www.faithbiblechurchnh.org/tozer_new_cross.htm
34. Charles Spurgeon, "Mornings and Evenings With Spurgeon" (Green Forest: New Leaf Publishing Group, 2010)
35. http://vancehavner.com/
36. https://utmost.org/the-cost-of-sanctification/
37. https://utmost.org/the-opposition-of-the-natural/

38. J. C. Ryle, "Christian Leaders of the 18th Century"(Carlisle: The Banner of Truth Trust, 1997), 71.
39. https://www.cmalliance.org/devotions/tozer?id=1257
40. http://www.heartlight.org/spurgeon/0406-am.html
41. https://utmost.org/and-every-virtue-we-possess/
42. https://www.cmalliance.org/devotions/simpson?mmdd=0825
43. R. A. Torrey, "God's Power in Your Life" (New Kensington: Whitaker House, 1982)
44. https://www.cmalliance.org/devotions/tozer?id=1012
45. R. A. Torrey, "God's Power in Your Life" (New Kensington: Whitaker House, 1982)
46. R. A. Torrey, "How To Obtain Fullness of Power" (New Kensington: Whitaker House, 1982)
47. http://www.heartlight.org/spurgeon/0823-pm.html
48. https://www.cmalliance.org/devotions/simpson?mmdd=0807
49. Andrew Murray, "Absolute Surrender" (New Kensington: Whitaker House, 1982), 114.
50. http://www.charismanews.com/opinion/41471-an-open-letter-to-john-macarthur-from-a-w-tozer-he-being-dead-yet-speaketh
51. http://www.spurgeon.org/sermons/0178.php
52. Andrew Murray, "Absolute Surrender" (New Kensington: Whitaker House, 1982), 97.
53. http://www.wholesomewords.org/biography/biomoody6.html
54. http://www.desiringrevival.com/critical-topics/29-anointing-of-god-then-and-now
55. https://www.cmalliance.org/devotions/tozer?id=920
56. R. A. Torrey, "How To Obtain Fullness of Power" (New Kensington: Whitaker House, 1982), 20.
57. http://www.heartlight.org/spurgeon/1012-am.html

58. George Muller, "The Autobiography of George Muller" (New Kensington: Whitaker House, 1985), 7.
59. http://www.gospelweb.net/SpurgeonDevotions/Spurgeon0505.htm
60. R. A. Torrey, "How To Obtain Fullness of Power" (New Kensington: Whitaker House, 1982), 86.
61. https://utmost.org/look-again-and-consecrate/
62. https://utmost.org/the-way-to-knowledge/
63. https://utmost.org/classic/do-it-yourself-classic/
64. http://www.gutenberg.org/files/28416/28416-pdf.pdf?session_id=1245f95057908682be621bc5c73fab2c97daf7d5

www.ingramcontent.com/pod-product-compliance
Lightning Source LLC
Chambersburg PA
CBHW071454040426
42444CB00008B/1339